WHAT'S IN AN
ENGLISH PLACE-NAME?

A History of England in its Place-Names

ALSO BY WILLIAM LEWIS

What's in your Surname?

What's in an English Place-Name?

A History of England in its Place-Names

William Lewis

BRAZEN HEAD PUBLISHING

ABINGDON

Published by Brazen Head Publishing 2011
PO Box 584, Abingdon, OX14 9FL, Oxfordshire, United Kingdom
www.brazenheadpublishing.co.uk

First published 2011

Typeset in Minion by Fantod Design
www.fantod-design.com
Cover Design by Fantod Design

ISBN 978-0-9565106-1-7
A CIP catalogue record for this book
is available from the British Library

*This book is dedicated to my grandchildren
Jenny and Matty Gibson with
love and affection.*

Table of Contents

Acknowledgements

I would like to record my grateful thanks to John Day for his constant support of my work on this book and for his expertise and assistance in its presentation.

My thanks also must go to my daughters Maggie and Kate for their advice and encouragement throughout the period of research and writing.

PREFACE

'WHERE DO YOU LIVE?' 'WHERE WERE YOU BORN?' These are questions almost as commonly asked as, 'What is your name?' and ones that we've all been asked many times, whether by a new acquaintance or when we're having to fill in a form. The replies we will give will nearly always mention the name of a city, town or village. It may be that the locality is in a foreign country and we will want to make that clear too: "Alexandria in Minnesota, USA", will pinpoint our home town as clearly as "Bewdley in Worcestershire", as long as we are in Britain when the question is asked. Sometimes we may feel a little awkward if our answer is an unusual place-name, such as **Bearpark**, **Giggleswick**, **Feltwell** or **Pishill**, in which case we will be ready for a 'humourous' remark, which we will have heard many times before. In such cases it is always a good idea to have an historical explanation of the place-name at the ready as a firm 'put-down' to the joker, as well as to show that we know our stuff! Once deflated, our questioner will usually begin to show some interest and may begin to ask us about the name of his or her own home town. The intention of this book is to help with such a challenge and to point the way towards a fascinating and entertaining exploration of the history of English place-names.

I have not covered place-names from Wales, Scotland or Ireland in this book, as I believe they deserve a volume to themselves.

Over the last fifteen hundred years, England has accommodated itself to the long term consequences of a number of invasions from the near-Continent and has come through it all with the results that we see today – a vital, expressive and versatile language and a population which has descended from Britons ('Celts'), Romans, Anglo-Saxons, Angles, Danes, Norsemen, French, as well as some possible combinations of these. The English also have an engaging history to look back on and to explore, if we are so inclined.

Place-names will convey us back in time and will contribute to the formation of a giant jigsaw which describes and reveals so much of our country's history. I hope this book will go some way towards showing how far we can go back by looking at our place-names. I have also tried to link the development of place-names to the evolution of some of our surnames, since the two threads are so much a part of our inheritance.

WILLIAM LEWIS, Oxford, August 2011.

Introduction

OUR ENGLISH PLACE-NAMES IN THE FORM that we know them today, as well as our personal names, have been the result of over two and a half thousand years of evolution. It has not been a smooth or trouble-free process, however, for it has progressed in a series of surges – the result of a succession of mostly aggressive invasions of England, each leading to a long occupation of the country by the respective intruders. Five of these invasions have been successful in imposing foreign rule, each with its attendant culture and language influences. These were the 'Celts' (a label that became widely used only in the 18th century), Romans, Anglo-Saxons, Scandinavians and Norman French – all of whom have left a greater or lesser legacy in our place-names. There have been two serious invasion failures of course – by Spain in 1588 and by Nazi Germany in the early 1940s.

There was to be no 'place-name forming period' in quite the way that there would later be a 'surname forming period' (that is, during the 11th – 14th centuries). Names for places in Britain had already been in use for over 1500 years and more were being created before the gradual emergence of English surnames and of course, personal names of individuals date from the furthest antiquity. However, there is a distinct 'bulge' in the graph of place-name formation from the end of the 5th century AD to end of the 10th century AD, an era that notably encompasses the Anglo-Saxon and Viking periods of the country's history.

Peasants of the 'old millennium', that is pre-AD, would find themselves indicating to each other a local feature in such a descriptive way as would easily become adopted as its local identity – words or phrases meaning the 'green hollow', the 'stag valley', the 'white hill', the 'river bend', the 'high ridge', 'Caradog's ground' – there would have been thousands of such descriptions (in their own ancient language of course) and, amazingly, we can still detect many of them that have come down to us, though in forms much modified by 20 centuries of speech and language evolution.

The naming process continues to this day: children will invent names for spots where they like to play and the names will become their own special toponymy. Four such places come to mind from the days of my own youth. We youngsters named a pleasant nearby meadow, through which gurgled a tree-lined brook, 'The Dingle' and a neighbouring small pointed hill was soon called 'Top point' on account of its pyramid-like shape. A nearby deep pool, with an eerie reputation, was nicknamed 'The Brettle', for no obvious reason that I ever discovered, while a thicket of trees that concealed a patch of boggy ground near the school fence, was called 'The Stinky' – this time for a very obvious reason! I'm sure the reader will be able to add examples from his or her own memories to this list. In addition, we are for ever naming our houses, farms, hospitals, schools and parklands, with sometimes highly fanciful names, as a means of identification. Even features on the surfaces of other planets are quickly named.

A question that must be considered before we get any further, however, is what are we to understand by the word 'place' in the term place-name? It can simply indicate a point on the landscape picking out a local feature – the brook field, the pebble beach, the woody slope, the old tree stumps, or it can be the name of a river, a village name, a town or a shire. It would seem that place-names are very much akin to nicknames – they are descriptions of a particular spot which, in the case of dwelling places, seem to have stuck in the local consciousness and have eventually have become 'proper' names.

In this book I shall concentrate to a great extent on the origins and development of the 'proper names' of settlements – some of them no more than hamlets it's true, or indeed a single farmstead in some cases – for it is within these small units that the greater part of English history is concealed. The larger districts of course (the early tribal territories and later, the shires) will make their contributions too, but the story would be incomplete without including many of the other important features of the countryside – the rivers, lakes, hills, valleys, heaths, moors, fens and so on – whose names are ancient and often, well-known.

℺

> "Neither was there, or is there, any town, village, hamlet or place in England,
> but hath made names unto families."
> William Camden, 'Remains' 1605.

Place-names have a special significance for a great many people, for their surnames are also names of English places: some will have local feature names such as Brook, Hill, Bridge, Wood and Field and some will have names recalling the village, town or district from which a mediæval ancestor originated – **Aldworth** (Berkshire), **Preston** (Lancashire), **Kent** and even the country name **England**, for example. Most of us can probably think of someone we know whose surname is a place-name. However, realising that an occasional slightly unusual surname is really a place-name can elude us. I once knew a person whose surname was Stokoe, but of course at the time, I never realised that it was a mild transformation of the place-name **Stockhow** in Cumbria. The group of surnames based on place-names is a very large one, as can be imagined.

Knowing that your surname is also the name of a village, town or city, however, is potentially only half of the fascination. The other half is that of discovering what the name of the place actually meant to those early inhabitants in whose language it was coined and why it was given the name in the first place. **Preston**, for instance, has its origins in the Old English words '*prēosta-tūn*', that is, 'the living-place of the priest(s)' and **Dudley** turns out to be '*Dudda's lēah*' – 'the woodland clearing of the man *Dudda*'. Many place-names are easy to spot when used as surnames, especially when they have give-away endings like '*-ton*', '*-ley*', '*-ham*', '*-wick*', '*-ford*', '*-thorpe*' and so forth. But some are less easy: few people would realise that **Potto** is both a place-name (in North Yorkshire) and a surname, though a rare one now. **Ince** and **Tarvin** too, lack the appearance of place-names, but these small Cheshire townships have long histories. **Ince** too, is a not an uncommon surname and **Tarvin** is a brave, though rare survivor in the surname register.

Most people think about their surnames sometimes and are interested in their histories but, unless one's town or village is blessed with an unusual name, **Pity Me** (Durham), **Iwerne Shroton** (Dorset), **Piddle** (Worcestershire), **Crackpot** (Yorkshire) and **Yazor** (Herefordshire), all of which are pleasantly unusual I think you'll agree – we tend not to give them much thought. **Wolverhampton**, **Manchester** and **Birmingham** may not seem to offer much at first sight, but 'the high settlement belonging to the woman *Wulfrun*', 'the encampment on a breast-shaped hill' and 'the settlement of *Beornmund's* folk' will surely reveal the delight in finding what often lies hidden in a place-name. So, like our surnames, all place-names have a story to tell and discovering what we can about them will give us a fascinating insight into our country's long and absorbing history.

BC to AD – A Look Around

Modern evidence suggests that near-humans, or our pre-human ancestors, have been living in the land we call Britain for perhaps 900,000 years. Norfolk seems to have been the location of these earliest inhabitants, whose recently unearthed stone tools from near the village of **Happisburgh** are clues to the earliest prehistoric occupation of the land. At this period – amazingly nearly a million years ago – Britain was not yet an island, but was linked to the European mainland by a wide, low-lying swathe of land (recently given the rather unappealing name of Doggerland). This land bridge is thought to have included the whole of the coastlines of Norfolk, Suffolk and Essex from the Wash to the Thames estuary and to have stretched, in a low basin, across what is now the North Sea to the Netherlands, Northern Germany and Denmark.

Such a convenient natural feature would have made access to the peninsula, which was later to become Britain, an easy task for our wandering prehistoric ancestors. Nine thousand centuries later, however, the journey would be very much more difficult, for the land bridge had long disappeared under many fathoms of the North Sea and Britain had become an island. However, such an inconvenience as a few miles of choppy water did not deter inquisitive Greek travellers, in the 3rd century BC, and Romans two hundred and fifty years later, from coming ashore to explore the countryside and eventually to establish a few trade links with the native Britons.

So what was the nature of this island that these travellers had come to investigate? What sights would have met the eyes of these foreign explorers as they disembarked somewhere on the coast of modern-day Kent or Sussex? Would we recognise the England we know today? The answer to this last question is of course – no. Apart from those magnificent white cliffs, visible on a clear day from the French coast, there was very little else that would have resembled our modern 'typical' English landscape. We shall discover in more detail the appearance of the early landscape as we meet the occupiers of the country in the following chapters.

Finally, in this introduction, we must consider how place-names – in this case the settlement names – can be classified. Like surnames, place-names can be arranged into a number of main groups, together with a couple of sub-groups. Here is the way I have chosen to categorise them for the purposes of this study:

Ia   Place-names derived from features of the natural landscape
Ib   Place-names derived from the fauna and flora of a locality
II   Place-names reflecting human activity
IIIa Place-names incorporating a personal name
IIIb Place-names based upon ancient tribal names
IV   Place-names originating in words of uncertain meaning, foreign words or foreign places
V   Place-names of late invention and those having miscellaneous meanings.

It is probably not surprising that the most frequent source of place-names has been provided by the natural landscape, its plants and its wildlife, while the results of human activity – men's occupations, the farms, fields, enclosures, ditches, bridges, roads, churches, forts, and even ancient stone circles, form another common source, having also become absorbed into the landscape.

Personal names, tribal names and sometimes even names of deities feature strongly in English place-names. There is also a small number of place-names which have other origins than those just mentioned, such as foreign words and foreign place-names and they form a small, but interesting, group. Then, in my final group, there are those names which have come into existence much more recently and many of which are obviously fabricated.

In the first chapter though, we will take a look at the people who inhabited the land that is now known as England, in the centuries up to the turn of the first millennium AD.

Chapter 1

THE NATIVE BRITONS BC

AT THE BEGINNING OF THE 1ST CENTURY AD, much of the south of England (Kent, Sussex, Hampshire, Surrey and Dorset), was forest and moorland, crossed here and there by rivers and streams and with only rough tracks to carry the occasional traveller across country – for no fixed routes, as we might imagine them today, existed at that time.

Trekking across high ground, from hilltop to hilltop and following ridges was a sensible, if arduous, means of covering ground and keeping to the right direction. Here and there, where the soil was favourable and usually located close to a river or stream, a farmstead, or even a small settlement would be seen, the latter no more than a handful of simple dwellings, each of circular pattern and built from wood (and stone, if it were available) and having reed or turf-covered roofs.

Forest and scrub clearances around the village would be evident so that fields could be ploughed for crop cultivation and enclosures constructed in which to keep sheep and cattle to sustain the village. Towns, as we tend to think of them, did not exist: only larger clusters of dwellings, accounting perhaps for only a few dozen souls at the most, the men working the surrounding land. Hillforts, defensive structures enclosing habitable quarters and permitting some industry and food storage within their ramparts, could be encountered on some of the prominent high ground and afforded not only protection from the raids of neighbouring tribes, but good lookout positions too. Such were the hillforts at **Danebury**, a few miles west of Stockbridge in Hampshire and **Maiden Castle**, a mile or so south of Dorchester in the county of Dorset. There is some archæological evidence, however, to suggest that by the turn of the 1st century AD many of these refuges had been abandoned in favour of more widespread use of farmsteads and small clusters of family dwellings in the lowland areas.

This was indeed as different a world from that which we know today as is possible to imagine, but this was the landscape and the culture which were to herald the new millennium.

THE SITTING TENANTS

What of the native inhabitants themselves at the beginning of the new millennium AD – who were they? The origins of most of these people are thought to lie with settlers from western Europe who gradually extended their occupation of Ireland and the west of Britain over a period of several centuries from about 550 BC, so that by the beginning of the 1st century AD nearly all of the population of what we now call England and Wales was speaking dialects of a Gaulish language known as Brythonic (much later referred to as 'Celtic').

More modern thinking, however, is that, although there must have been some permanent drifting and infiltration of Europeans during this period, the essential Britishness (or 'Celticness') was the result of a more internal evolution, as the native inhabitants absorbed and developed a host of foreign ideas, all the time evolving their own cultures. The map on page 9 (Figure 1) shows that Britain had become a nation of tribal 'kingdoms' during the five hundred or so years leading up to the turn of that first millennium AD. The Brythons' development and their revolutionary use of iron, which would largely displace the softer alloy bronze for tools and weapons, was a hugely significant and far-reaching gesture at the opening of the new era.

Many of the Brythons (whom I will call the British, or Britons, from now on) were assertive and often readily aggressive and territorial disputes between neighbouring tribes frequently led to fierce battles. The combatants, often steering lightweight horse-drawn chariots, would discharge their spears and flourish their swords to bloody and decisive effect, triumphantly displaying the severed heads of their defeated adversaries on poles as trophies of their campaigns.

Their religious activities and rituals were deep rooted, centred round the veneration of their ancestors and the cycle of the seasons. Water too, played an important part in their beliefs and many personal and valued items were cast into rivers, pools and even bogs, as ritual offerings to the mysterious water deities. **Hardwell** (Oxfordshire), though only the site of a farm now, still includes on its site the remnants of an ancient moat which may have been the historic setting for such oblations. A very early record of AD 856, in which the place is named as *Hordwyllæ*, shows that its meaning was 'treasure-spring'.

Ancient British society was strongly built around spoken traditions and the recording of ideas in written or pictorial form was very rarely practised. Only a few short inscriptions have survived of pre-Roman British texts and most of what was later to be written down would use the Roman alphabet and would be expressed in Latin.

So these then, were the native people of Albion, as the 1st century writers Pliny the Elder and Ptolemy referred to Britain – aggressively territorial, excitable fighters and ritualistic in their mystical venerations, but still farmers and lovers of the earth. Now, if there were ever to be an invasion of their country by a determined foreign aggressor, it would be seriously to underestimate the powerful territorial spirit of the ancient British to imagine that they would resign themselves to fate and quietly hand over their lands, allowing themselves to become absorbed into the invaders' culture, while renouncing all of their historical beliefs, practices and language. No doubt any new occupiers would wish this could be the case, but the reality would almost certainly be that many, if not most, of the British tribes would, without much hesitation, mount a stiff resistance to such an invasion. Were the worst to happen and the newcomers to overrun the lands of the British, they, the new rulers, would have to accept that the two cultures and languages would, to a great extent, have to run parallel, each inevitably having some influence on the other.

We cannot know for certain whether our ancient Britons' rulers felt they had reasonable grounds to consider such possibilities, though the landings on the Kent coast by one Julius Caesar and his army, in 55BC and again in the following year, may have given the Britons some cause to worry.

If the language of the Britons was rarely written down, how are we to identify their legacy and recognise any traces of their words present in our place-names today? The answer to this is two-fold: first, the British language always remained viable amongst the native people and was never displaced, so that names of places and objects remained unchanged and were spoken generation

Figure 1 Britain in about AD 40, showing the large number of native tribes and their territories. The boundaries are very approximate.

after generation. Second, many of these words, or parts of words, would indeed be preserved in writing – not in the script of the Britons, however, but in the writings of a later wave of invaders whose society and scholarship was a great deal further advanced than that of their Brittonic adversaries.

We are fortunate to have a few precious historical texts from which we can glean the meanings of some of the original ancient British words. Without such documentary material, determining the origins and meanings of such words and names would be at best guesswork. However, few things in ancient studies are straightforward. Similar or identical elements in different place-names can have different original meanings and this is where the documentary evidence is vital.

For example, the place-names **Ardington** (Berkshire), **Arden Forest** (Warwickshire), **Ardley** (Oxfordshire) and **Ardsley** (Yorkshire) all begin with the element '*Ard-*', but early documentary evidence shows that each is derived from a different root: **Ardington** is from an Old English personal name and means '*the settlement of Æthelred's people*'; **Arden Forest** contains the British ('Celtic') word '*Ardu*' which meant '*high*', probably meaning '*a hill forest*'; **Ardley** is first recorded in a list dating from the late 10th century and is a reference to another personal name, '*Eardwulf's Hill*' and **Ardsley** is thought to refer to '*Eordes Hill*' – yet again a personal name is recalled. There is also the complication that fragments of a few place-names are thought to have their origins in languages spoken in Britain even before the arrival of the first invaders in about 550BC and would have been assimilated into the newcomers' vocabulary. The word '*abona*', meaning 'a river' (see the following table), may be one such example which pre-dates the original Brythonic language.

Below are some of the early Britons' words which have survived more than twenty centuries' use (though in modified spellings) thanks to their inclusion in place-names. I have not differentiated between pre-Briton and British ('Celtic') words in this chapter:

British element	Original meaning	Place-name example	Meaning
Ardu	high	**Arden Forest** (Warks)	High forest
Abona	river	**Avonmouth** (Som)	River estuary
Cumb	valley	**Ilfracombe** (Devon)	Valley of Ælfred's people
Crūc	hill	**Cricklewood** (Middx)	Wooded hill
Dunu	stronghold	**Dunterton** (Devon)	Village by the castle
Iska	water	**Exmouth** (Devon)	Estuary of the River Exe

Lann	church	**Landulph** (Cornwall)	Church of St Dilph or Dilic
Lindo	pool	**Lincoln** (Lincs)	Settlement by the lake
Pen	hill, head	**Pennard** (Somerset)	High hill
Tor	rocky hill, peak	**Brentor** (Devon)	Steep hill
Tre	dwelling, village	**Tremaine** (Cornwall)	Village at the stone

The reader may have noticed that the majority of these places are to be found in the West Country. This is no accident, for the influence of the Britons (or 'Celts', as they much later came to be called) and their language remained strongest in the South-West, being furthest from the South-East, where any continental invader would establish a natural stronghold and with a naturally greater cultural impact. The West Country – and Cornwall in particular – together with Wales of course, maintained a much stronger tradition of the spoken Brittonic language than anywhere else in these islands.

Having mentioned some of the surviving Brittonic elements traceable in the names of places, we can now investigate some of the other features of ancient British life which have left clues in our modern place-names.

THE NATURAL LANDSCAPES OF ENGLAND, BC

WATER – RIVERS, STREAMS AND LAKES IN PLACE-NAMES

Ancient Britain was almost wholly an agricultural society with the great majority of the population living in villages and hamlets, tilling the land and tending livestock. A few communities lived within the confines and security of scattered hillforts, which were also local centres of trading goods at markets, but wealth was still defined in agricultural terms.

Successful crop harvests required reliable water supplies, so most arable land was located in the lowland districts where the soils were good and rainfall was dependable with effective natural drainage. Cattle-rearing too required a ready water supply from a year-round source. Any large-scale road map will confirm that England is criss-crossed by many hundreds of rivers and streams and local maps will add hundreds more brooks and springs to the country's total natural water supply. For thousands of years human habitations tended to be located near these sources of water and grazing pastures have naturally arisen adjacent to them.

Water was of course, well recognised as an essential life factor and as such its presence gave rise to a mystical aspect in the ancient Britons' minds. For many generations, running water had been believed to possess magical properties by the ancient inhabitants of Britain. Spirits and deities were thought to reside in streams, springs and wells, which, to our ancestors' minds, seemed to rise from a dark and mysterious realm beneath the earth.

Water was also seen as a natural boundary between life and death: above its surface a person could live; beneath the surface he entered the unknown and mysterious regions of death. The ancient Britons therefore venerated sites of natural running water and saw them as the means by which they might approach its deities, to whom they would make pleas for cures for their ills, for good harvests, for retribution for ill-will and into whose waters they might cast personal offerings to pacify and please the water spirits. The many archæological finds, which include personal trinkets, beads, pins, pots, knives and even swords, in the silt at the bottom of country watercourses, pools and bogs have borne testimony to this ancient practice.

There were several female deities associated with water in the minds of the ancient Britons: *Coventina* (particularly associated with wells and springs), *Cuda* (also a goddess of springs and streams, mostly in the Cotswold districts), *Ancasta*, *Dea Latis*, *Sul* (who was later adopted by the Romans at Bath) and *Verbeia*. Female deities were probably thought to be gentler, more motherly, more understanding and more easily approachable than male spirits, who perhaps were feared to be stern and grim.

Of all natural features of the English landscape, the great rivers have always had the profoundest influence on the way humans have organised their lives. Some rivers are tidal, a few exhibiting the surge called a 'bore' and will easily flood their plains – a characteristic of which early farmers would have been very well aware and around which they would have arranged their husbandry calendars.

It is not a surprise then, to find that the names of most of the principal English rivers (as well as a good many of the minor ones) have their origins in the language of those ancient Britons and that each river has its attendant collection of settlement names, often in the simple form of a triplet such as '*A-upon-B*', in which the first name (*A*) usually has its root in the later Saxon ('Old English') language, while the *B* component contains the word derived from the early British.

Working our way clockwise around the coastline of England, beginning in the north-east with the River Tyne, here are ten major rivers whose names originate in that ancient British language:

River	British origin	Nearby Places
Tyne	Possibly from *'ti'* – 'to flow'	**Tynemouth, Newcastle upon Tyne**
Tees	*'tes'* – 'bubbling'	**Stockton on Tees, Hurworth on Tees**
Ouse	Perhaps from *'udso'* –' water'	**Linton-on-Ouse, Newton-on-Ouse**
Trent	*'tri hynt'* – 'trespasser' (i.e. floodable)	**Burton-upon-Trent, Sutton-on-Trent**
Thames	*'tam'* – 'dark'	**Kingston Upon Thames, Thames Ditton**
Medway	*'medu waie'* – 'mead' + an uncertain word	**Tonbridge**
Exe	*'isca'* - water	**Exeter, Up Exe, Nether Exe**
Severn	(*Sabrina*) British, but of uncertain meaning	**Upton upon Severn, Severn Stoke**
Avon	'*abona*' – river	**Stratford-upon-Avon, Bidford-on-Avon**
Ribble	*'ribyll'* – uncertain meaning	**Ribbleton, Ribchester**

Clearly, the establishment of origins and meanings of names, with two thousand year histories and only an oral tradition of communication, is very difficult. The reader may have noticed the ommission of the River Mersey from this list. However, the origin of the name Mersey is shown to be Old English – that is, Anglo-Saxon – and so it must take its place in Chapter Three.

By the turn of the millennium AD, every river and stream and many a lowland brook, spring and rill in England would have been known in its locality by a local British ('Celtic') name, which would nearly always relate to some distinguishing feature of the water itself or to its location.

Having looked at the major rivers, it seems only fair that we should turn our attention briefly to some of the smaller ones, for their names hold interesting meanings too. In the following table I have selected the names of just twelve out of the many dozens of minor rivers, whose names also have their origins in the language of the early Britons. The nearby settlement names will help you to find the locations on a modern road map:

River	Early name	Meaning	Nearby settlements
Axe (Somerset)	*Aesce*	Water	**Axminster, Axmouth**
Calder (Cumbria)	*Kalder*	Rushing water	**Calder, Calder Bridge**
Clyst (Devon)	*Clyst*	Clean water	**Clyst St Mary, Broad Clyst**
Dacre (Cumbria)	*Dacre*	Trickling water	**Dacre, Dalemain**
Glen (Lincs)	*Glenye*	Beautiful stream	**Corby Glen**
Glyme (Oxon)	*Glim*	Shining water	**Glympton**
Isle (Somerset)	*Ile*	Swift spring	**Isle Abbotts, Isle Brewers**
Itchen (Hants)	*Icene*	Of the Iceni tribe	**Itchen Abbas, Itchen Stoke**
Leadon (Glos)	*Ledene*	Broad water	**High Leadon, Upleadon**
Leam (Warwicks)	*Limenan*	River in the elms	**Leamington Spa**
Peover (Cheshire)	*Peuere*	Bright water	**Peover Heath, Lower Peover**
Wylye (Wiltshire)	*Wileo*	Unpredictable	**Wylye, Wilton**

These are only rather small fry in the national river stakes it's true, but they and their families of nearby settlements illustrate the deep rural nature of the England of the Britons' era. A good modern road map will reveal the villages like small pearls cast along the lengths of the rivers – just look up **Savick Brook** near **Preston** in Lancashire, the little **River Noe** near **Bamford** in Derbyshire, or the **River Meon**, a few miles north of **Portsmouth** in Hampshire, to see what I mean.

Another minor water feature is the spring, of which there are thousands across England. The early British word for this was *'funtōn'* – the origin of the modern word 'fountain'. It is fortunate that this old word was adopted by subsequent invaders and we can find it both as a suffix and as a prefix to some hybrid names: **Teffont** (Wiltshire) – 'boundary spring'; **Havant** (Hampshire) – 'spring of a man called *Hāma*'; **Fontmell** (Dorset) – 'spring near the bare hill'. **Fovant** (Wiltshire) is a well-disguised 'spring of the man *Fobba*' and **Urchfont** in Wiltshire tells us something of the early pronunciation of the words, for it means '*Eohrīc's* spring'.

Every locality in the country will have its share of streams and brooks and it makes an interesting holiday project for youngsters to locate and list the names of these minor watercourses within their parish and perhaps plot their courses on a local map and then look into their histories.

Having looked at the river names of England, it would seem appropriate to take a brief glance at those of the lakes too. England has relatively few bodies of natural water and the ones which quickly come to mind of course are in the Lake District of modern-day Cumbria. Apart from this principal collection of lakes, there are scattered smaller ones, called 'tarns' (from an Old Scandinavian word – see Chapter Five) found higher in the hills and of which there are over fifty in Cumbria which incorporate the word 'Tarn' in their names.

Most of the names of the lakes date from periods after the early British era and some of them are associated with a nearby settlement name, for example **Windermere, Buttermere** and **Coniston**, and which I will deal with in a later chapter. Two of the principal Lakes, however, do have names which echo their early British roots: **Derwent Water** recalls the British word for an oak-tree, *'derva'* and tells us that a once oak-lined river, the **Derwent**, flowed into the lake. The other instance is **Crummock Water**, which probably also refers to the stream which fed the lake and comes from the ancient British word *'crumb'*, meaning 'crooked'. A smaller, nearby lake (a 'tarn'), is **Devoke Water** and this name too seems to have a British origin, arising from the word *'dyfoe'*, meaning 'small dark one' and must have referred to the dark appearance of the water's surface.

Before leaving the watery features of the landscape, I'd like briefly to mention a particular stretch of water easily overlooked when dealing with place-names: the **Solent**, separating the **Isle of Wight** from the mainland. Though scholars are certain the word **Solent** is of ancient British origin – its first documented record is by the religious historian Bede in about AD 730, where he writes it as *Soluente* – unfortunately, its meaning has never been established.

HILLS, RISES AND VALLEYS IN PLACE-NAMES

Only a few ancient British syllables, which are known to relate to ridges, up-lands, lowlands and valleys, have survived the wear and tear of the last two thousand years. One of these is the word *'briga'* (a hill) and its abbreviated derivative *'bre'*. The latter is occasionally found, as in **Bredon** (Worcestershire), in which the later, Old English suffix *'-don'* also means 'hill' and in **Brewood** (Stafford-shire), meaning straightforwardly, 'the wood on the hill'. However, most place-names beginning this way do not derive from the old British word *'briga'*, as we shall see later. A more confident survivor of the centuries, however, can be spotted amongst the place-names in the county of Devon, which is noted for its rocky outcrops called *'tors'*. This word survives unchanged from the old British *'tor'* and features in dozens of names given to those craggy towers to be seen on the Devon moors – Fox Tor, Bel Tor and Lynch Tor for instance – as well as in the well-known seaside town names of Torbay and Torquay, each of which speaks for itself.

'Crûc', a British word meaning a small hill or hillock, makes a slightly disguised appearance in a number of English town names: **Crickheath** (Shropshire), 'a wooded hill', **Cricklade** (Wiltshire), 'the crossing at the hill' and **Cricklewood**, mentioned in the first table of the chapter above. **Crick** (Northants) and **Crich** (Derbyshire) mean simply 'hill', while **Crichel** (Dorset), like **Bredon**, has an abbreviated additional Old English suffix, 'hyll', thus giving a curiously duplicated meaning, 'hill-hill'.

Another vestige of the old British language in this context is 'carr'. This fragment seems to have signified a rocky or stone-strewn rise and can be detected in **Carden** (Cheshire), 'a rocky slope', **Carrock Fell** (Cumberland), **Cargo** (Cumberland), 'rocky hill' – combining two elements with similar meaning ('carr' + the later Old Scandinavian 'haugr') – and **Carham** (Northumberland), 'village at the rocks'.

One of the most familiar echoes of the language of those ancient Britons lies in the syllable 'pen'. This small word eventually came to be used to describe places located on higher ground, although its original meaning was probably an enclosure or a pen for animals. Cornwall is England's nucleus of place-names beginning with this element: **Penzance**, **Penryn**, **Penare**, **Penpethy**, **Penpillick**, **Penrose** and many others. Other counties have a small share too: **Pensax** ('hill of the Saxons') in Worcestershire, **Pensnett** ('hilltop woodland') in Staffordshire, **Pentrich** ('hill of the boars') in Derbyshire and even **Pemberton** ('farm by the hill') in Lancashire. Although each of these last four has a later Anglo-Saxon suffix, it shows that 'Pen-' remained a useful element and that there was a broad distribution of this idea. However, 'Pen' has become teasingly transformed into 'Pin-' in **Pinhoe** (Devon – 'pointed hill') and **Pinnock** (Gloucestershire – probably 'little hill').

A surprising and interesting curiosity regarding the prefix 'Pen-', however, arises in the name of England's foremost highland range, the **Pennines**. This famous chain of low mountains, stretching 260 miles up the centre of England, is the most outstanding natural feature of the country and yet there seems to be no ancient name for it, despite the persuasive look of the name we all know: the prefix 'Pen-' certainly presents an old British suggestion of 'hill'. However, it is a clever deception, for the word '**Pennine**' appears to be the invention of an ingenious 18th century author, Charles Julius Bertram, who in 1757, issued a manuscript, '*De Situ Britanniæ*', that he claimed had been written by a mediæval monk and which contained a complete history of Roman Britain and in which England's central highland range is referred to as 'the Pennine Alps'. A century later, however, the document was shown to be entirely spurious, though Bartram's motive for his ingenious fraud has never been explained. The 'manuscript' had by then of course, been accepted for long enough for the word **Pennines** to have become widely adopted by map makers and geographers and thus we have acquired a recent geographical name dressed in ancient clothes and a good story to relate!

Very occasionally we will come across a rare British word with upland associations which has survived by just a thread. Such a word is *'Canto-'* (a rim or edge), which makes its shrouded appearance in the name of the short upland range in northern Somerset, the **Quantock Hills** (whose original British name was *Cantuc*) and in the two delightful villages at the coastal rim of the Hills, **West** and **East Quantoxhead**. The hamlet of **Mindrum** too, on the northernmost edge of the Cheviot Hills in Northumberland, contains a rare pair of ancient British highland elements, *'monith'* and *'trum'* and means 'mountain ridge' and it too, can be pleased with its outstanding British heritage.

Finally, a word about those most picturesque of Worcestershire hills, the **Malverns**. Here too, we have an example of two Brittonic words that have survived the two millennia: *'mẹol'* and *'brinn'*, meaning 'bare hill'.

Where there are hills, there are valleys too and here we must turn our attention to a most successful old British word for a valley – *'cum'* (or *'cumb'*). In its more familiar guise of the suffix *'-combe'*, it has stoutly taken on the challenges of later upstarts such as *'-dale'*, *'-dean'*, *'-dell'*, *'-gill'*, *'-up'* and *'-vale'* and has emerged strong and memorable. It will also be recognised in the Welsh *'cwm'*. There are dozens of *'-combes'*, (occasionally also found as *'-coombes'* and *'-combs'*), especially in the West Country, where the complete place-name itself is usually a hybrid in which the old British suffix is attended by a prefix of a later era. There are many instances of the word in its simplest form: **Combe** (Oxfordshire, Gloucestershire, Somerset and Warwickshire), **Coombe** (Devon, Hampshire,) and as a doublet: **Combe Hay** (Somerset), **Combe Martin** (Devon) and **Castle Combe** (Wiltshire) are only a few. There is also a large number of those hybrid compounds; here are twelve of them:

Place	County	Meaning
Ashcombe	Devon	'ash tree valley'
Bowcombe	Isle of Wight	'valley of the man *Bōfa*'
Creacombe	Devon	'crow valley'

Hascombe	Surrey	'valley of the witches'
Huntercombe	Oxfordshire	'the huntsman's valley'
Iccomb	Gloucestershire	'valley of the man *Ica*'
Milcombe	Oxfordshire	'the middle valley'
Nettlecombe	Dorset	'nettle covered valley'
Pencombe	Herefordshire	'valley with enclosures'
Seacombe	Cheshire	'valley beside the sea'
Stitchcombe	Sussex	'valley infested with gnats'
Witcombe	Somerset	'willow-tree valley'

I have chosen these examples so that there is a reasonable spread across the counties, though the South and South-West will always have the lion's share, while the Midlands and North have very few, a distribution that reflected the enduring geographical strength of the ancient British influence. The first elements of each name in the table, however, date from the later Anglo-Saxon era. **Hascombe** presents an intriguing idea – were there really suspiciously witch-like women roaming that mysterious, ancient Surrey neighbourhood, one wonders? Do the modern residents venture out at midnight?

'*Comb-*' can occasionally do good service as a prefix too, as in **Combwell** (Kent) and **Combrook** (Warwickshire) – each meaning 'the valley with the stream', **Combwich** (Somerset) – 'the dwelling or village in the valley' and, less obviously, **Congreave** (Staffordshire) – 'the grove in the valley'. In these, it is paired with a later Anglo-Saxon element which, as we have seen, is often the case.

It will be appreciated from the twelve examples in the last table the wide versatility of such a suffix as '*-combe*'. One can very easily enjoy creating some fictitious place-names of one's own with the aid of Professor Ekwall's Dictionary of English Place-names: *Ewcombe* would be 'valley where the yew-trees grow', *Excombe* is 'the valley where the cuckoo is heard', *Hancombe* might be 'the rocky valley' and *Lillacombe* 'the valley of the man called *Lylla*'. All of these prefixes and their meanings are genuine and are known from later southern Anglo-Saxon documents, though the places are fictitious of course, since I have just invented them.

Most of the early British elements and words in our place-names have their origins in the landscape and its many natural features. As we have seen, they are most in evidence in the names of rivers, though words for valleys and aspects of uplands also feature. However, we have few other non-archæological links to the pre-first millennium Britons. Other known words or syllables are few:

'lemo' – which seemed to mean either the elm tree or a brook-speedwell flower – is perhaps seen in the place-name **Lemmington** (Northumberland) , *'cuera'* – the ash tree and maybe the first element in **Cuerden** (Lancashire) and *'eclēs'* – a church – and is probably the origin of the name **Eccles** (Lancashire). The words *'scawet'* (an elder thicket) , *'frām'* (lively) and *'colauno'* (a word of uncertain meaning), seem to be ancient British in origin, *'frām'* possibly being the origin of the name **Frome** (a Dorset river) and *'colauno'* a possible root of **Coln** (a Gloucestershire river name).

Fortunately, Old Welsh can probably assist us a little and cast some light on the era since, by virtue of the geographical remoteness of the 1st century inhabitants of far-western Britain, it was able to resist the linguistic changes brought by the Romans and the 5th and 6th century Germanic Anglo-Saxons and flourished even into the times of Norman domination from the mid-11th century. It is very possible that Old Welsh words such as *'lann'* (an enclosure), *'cors'* (marshland), *'moel'* (barren) and *'rhyd'* (a ford) are derived from and are very similar to, the ancient British equivalents.

Flora and fauna in place-names

Plants and animals are an integral, though usually a discrete and unspectacular, part of the seasonal landscape and we shall now see the extent of their role in the formation of ancient British place-names. We have already seen that few genuinely old British place-names have survived into modern times; the majority of the purely British components which have come down to us are usually combined with elements introduced by later occupiers of the country – the Romans and particularly, the Anglo-Saxons.

A careful search will reveal only a very few of the original British words which tell of the Britons' encounters with the plant and animal kingdoms. Taking the flora first, we can logically begin with **Chittoe,** a tiny village a few miles southeast of Chippenham in Wiltshire, which takes its name from an Old British word *'ceto'*, believed to mean simply a wood. This word has also survived in **Chetwode** (Buckinghamshire), producing an odd doublet 'wood-wood', something that we have noticed before. Then, more specifically, we will see that **Cuerden,** a small district on the northern edge of the town of Leyland in Lancashire, derives its name from *'cuera-ddin'*, referring to an ash-tree or rowan-tree and must have recalled a nearby grove of these trees. The alder-tree finds a mention in two place-names, one in Somerset and one in Cheshire: **Wearne** and **Werneth.**

These two words have their origins in an Old British word for the alder, '*verno*'. The first seems to have referred to a stream which ran between the alders and the second may simply have alluded to an alder copse, near to which a dwelling was placed.

It seems likely then, that the ash and alder are the only trees to have made the earliest surviving impression on English place-names, which is a little surprising when the oak and elm are so much associated with the name of England. However, their time will come.

Two other plant-names from the pre-AD British era are known to have clung on to existence in English place-names. Rather surprisingly, these are the words for barley and garlic. **Haydock** (Lancashire), a name reflected in the Welsh '*heiddiog*', tells of a barley farm, while the Old British word for wild garlic (perhaps '*craf*') has given its name to the North Yorkshire district of **Craven**.

So, as I mentioned, there are few members of the plant kingdom from which we have inherited truly British place-names. However, there are even fewer members of the animal realm whose names are detectable in our place-names. It is strange to think that, although there are several hundred examples of place-names originating from the animal kingdom to be found in a good road map of England, probably only the cuckoo and the pig have lent us genuinely Old British animal place-name elements. Probably ninety percent of the rest derive from a later period when the country was under the occupation and crucial linguistic influence of the Anglo-Saxons and which we will examine in detail in Chapter Four.

The trim farming village of **Blencogo**, a few miles south-west of Carlisle in modern-day Cumbria, has the distinction of bearing a wholly British name of an animal. It is derived from the words '*blain*' and '*cogow*' and means 'hillock or crest of the cuckoos', although the village itself appears to be on only gently rising ground. We can just detect our word 'cuckoo' in the ancient British '*cogow*'.

Fourteen miles west of the city of Hereford lies the charming hamlet of **Moccas**. It seems to be the only other place which includes the name of an animal in the ancient British language – '*moch*', meaning 'pigs' and '*rhos*' meaning '*moor*' – hence 'the moorland of the swine'.

That versatile British suffix '-*combe*' again finds itself well employed in fauna place-names, but this time in partnership with later Anglo-Saxon (that is, 'Old English') animal prefixes. In Chapter Four we will see that it presents us with places named after pigs again, eagles, owls, goats, sandpipers and even gnats.

As an appendix to this small, but exclusive section, I might just add that the little **River Ock**, which flows into the Thames at Abingdon in Oxfordshire, owes its distinctive British name to a fish – the salmon (the Old Cornish word *'ehoc'* is the closest we will probably get to the original Old British word).

As we reach the end of our look at which natural features of the Britons' landscape had found their way into the earliest of our surviving place-names, we can perhaps remind ourselves that many English surnames are also those of natural features: Hill, Dale, Wood, Moore, Poole, Brook and Marsh are frequent names in our telephone books. Fauna of various kinds also feature in our English surnames, though less often than inanimate natural features: Fish, Wolf, Hogg, Sparrow, Finch, Wigg and Breese will also be found in our telephone directories. (The last two are words meaning 'beetle' and 'gadfly' – rather puzzling sources of surnames, though clearly originally nicknames). Flora too, have provided well-used surnames: Tree, Ash, Briers, Hedges, Flowers, Rose and Flax are examples.

However, we haven't finished with Brittonic man yet, for it is time now to turn our attention to the man himself, his clans, tribes and his daily activities, to try to discover how much these aspects of his life have influenced our place-names.

THE PEOPLE

TRIBAL AND PERSONAL NAMES IN PLACE-NAMES

It is an entirely natural phenomenon that early settlers in a country should stake out their own tribal territories using natural features as the boundary markers. Rivers were one obvious means of indicating a border between major tribal lands, but hills, rocky outcrops, ridges, woods and so forth were also useful frontier points. Where the more local domains of clans or family units were to be drawn, trees, standing stones, hedges and ditches served as limit markers. Even today, English county borders often follow the natural courses of rivers: Northamptonshire and Leicestershire are divided for much of their length by the **River Welland**, while the **River Stour** separates Essex and Suffolk and modern-day Humberside lies to the east of the **River Derwent** with Yorkshire to the west. The **River Mersey** of course, is the great division between Cheshire and Lancashire. At the other end of the scale, my personal domain is divided from my neighbour's by a fence on one side and a hedge on the other – so nothing has changed in three thousand years!

The map in Figure 1 (page 9) shows how the territorial instinct had evolved by the turn of the new first millennium, with about two dozen major tribal regions, each under the rule of a 'chief'. Within each of these territories were dozens of smaller 'clan' holdings, some covering several hundred acres, similar in area to modern farmsteads and including a number of distinct settlements, each with its own head man.

Settlements

At the beginning of this chapter I mentioned the existence of the hillfort as a characteristic feature of the landscape in early British society. These defensive structures eventually gave way to more permanently agriculturally orientated activities in the lowlands and on the plains where farmsteads and villages could thrive surrounded by their field systems. Settlements were gradually increasing in size, especially in the south and south-east of England, as the advantages of integrating farming, simple industry and domestic activities, together with the use of elementary coinage, were beginning to be understood. This, together with the somewhat less belligerent and more co-operative tribal attitudes, encouraged the notion of what we may regard as small, but embrionic 'townships'.

We have only a few threads of direct evidence which give us clues as to the names these early Britons gave to their settlements, for almost all of their sages and scholars were unversed in the art of writing and all knowledge was passed by strictly oral means. We owe almost all of our earliest information about their society and language to the Romans, a highly literate culture, who came into direct contact (and conflict) with the native Britons during the 1st century AD. The Roman texts, however, nearly always adjust the local place-names into a Latinised form, though often retaining the substance of the native name. As an example of this, the name *Verlamion* was the native name for today's St Albans before it was superseded by the more Romanised version, *Verulamium*. However, with a little persistence, a few distinct Old British place-name survivors can be identified, as opposed to simply abbreviated elements – of which there are a couple of dozen. Here are some surviving complete names, though with spellings that have become modified over the centuries:

Place-name	Location	Meaning
Cardurnock	Cumbria	Fort at a pebbly place
Bossiney	Cornwall	A house, building
Corse	Gloucestershire	Fen or bog
Cumrew	Lancashire	Sloping valley
Dinmore	Herefordshire	Great hill
Dymock	Gloucestershire	Enclosure for pigs

Lamplugh	Cumbria	A barren valley
Mamble	Worcestershire	A breast-shaped hill
Mynde	Herefordshire	Mountain
Reculver	Kent	Sharp-pointed hill
Trunch	Norfolk	Wood on a headland
Wellow	Hampshire	Village near the winding stream
Werneth	Cheshire	Settlement among the alders

Eleven of these twelve places show that natural features of the landscape pro-vided the local settlers with the stimulus for the names and indeed, this is usu-ally the case with the British place-names that have come down to us. **Dymock**, however, is one which makes a rare reference to some sort of human activity – possibly animal husbandry, or else a reference to wild boar. Another feature noticeable from the list is that most of the examples are in districts where the ancient British influence remained strongest, that is in the south west, the coun-ties which border Wales and in the north-western counties of England, though **Wellow**, in Hampshire, **Reculver** in Kent and **Mamble** in Worcestershire are notable exceptions in this respect.

Looking now at the wider picture, some of the modern county names have their roots in the language of the ancient Britons: **Cornwall** and **Devon** are derived from tribal names: Cornovii and Dumnonii – the Roman written versions of the names for the peoples of those districts – while **Berkshire's** first syllable is *'barroc'*, meaning 'hilly', is paired with the later Anglo-Saxon word for a district, *'scīr'*. **Kent's** origin lies in *'canto'* – 'the borderland or coastland'. **Cumberland** and its modern reduction, **Cumbria,** have their roots in the Welsh word for the Welsh people themselves – *Cymry.* The counties of **Gloucester**, **Leicester, Worcester, Cambridgeshire, Lancashire** and **Yorkshire** also contain traces of Old British words buried within their names – sometimes a river name, sometimes a tribal reference or, in the case of **York**, a likely allusion to the yew-tree. **Lindsey**, one of Lincolnshire's three administrative regions, begins with a fragment of a British word we have already met, *'lindo'* (a pool). To this has been added a later, Anglo-Saxon suffix *'-ēg'* (an island), signifying a people – possibly some of the *Iceni* tribe – who may have migrated to the islands of the marshy district which characterised that part of Lincolnshire, long before the drainage of the Fens, which did not begin in earnest until the mid-17th century AD. The same British root, *'lindo-'*, was retained later by the Romans in their own name for **Ilchester** – *'Lindinis'*. The ancient word *'lindo'* is probably also present in **Lindisfarne** (often called **Holy Island**), lying a mile off the North

Sea coast of Northumberland. Two other significant islands whose names go back to Old Brittonic days are **Thanet** and **Wight**. The first of these is no longer an island, but at the time of the Britons, was separated from the mainland of Kent by the Wansum Channel. It may mean 'brightly lit island', perhaps from a beacon of fire customarily lit there as a guide to ancient vessels entering the Thames estuary. The second island, **Wight**, seems to mean 'a place risen from the sea' – a rather fanciful means of describing an impressive island.

As a footnote to this section on settlements and having just mentioned the district of **Lindsey** in Lincolnshire, I might add that another of Lincolnshire's three regions, **Kesteven**, also has a British first element that we have already met, '*cēto-*', a wood – accompanied by a later, Scandinavian suffix, '*stefna*', meaning 'a meeting place'.

We have already seen that two Brittonic tribes, the Dumnonii and the Cornovii, had given their names to two of England's major regions – which were to become the counties of **Devon** and **Cornwall**, while several other counties, mentioned earlier, have traces of British tribal names buried within them. British tribes divided themselves into 'clans' or family groups, each occupying its own territory, as previously mentioned and each village within these smaller units will often have been known by the name of the village leader. Most of the settlements, however, are first recorded only in the *Anglo-Saxon Chronicle* or Bede's *'Ecclesiastical History of the English People'* (completed in about AD 731), or appearing even later than that in Domesday (1086), often with the addition of a two-syllable Anglo-Saxon suffix such as '*-ington*', '*-ingley*', '*-ingham*' or '*-ingfield*', which signifies 'village or land of the people of ....' (see Chapter Four). In spite of their late documentary records, many of these tribes and clans will have histories reaching back many generations to much earlier times.

At this point, it might be interesting to look at the names of some of the tribes that occupied the land we know as England that Roman historians like Ptolemy and Pliny had written about and that the emperor, Julius Caesar, recorded, together with any known place-names that were derived from them.

Tribal name	Location	Earliest record	Place-name
Ancalites	Perhaps S. Oxfordshire	Caesar, 55 BC	No identifiable place
Bibroci	Probably Berkshire	Caesar, 55 BC	No identifiable place
Feppingas	Worcestershire	Bede, 730 AD	**Phepson**

Hæstingas	Sussex	Cartularium Saxonicum[1], 790 AD	**Hastings**
Hicce	Hertfordshire	Cartularium Saxonicum[1], 944 AD	**Hitchin**
Undalas	Northamptonshire	c.715 AD	**Oundle**
Rœgingas	Kent	Cartularium Saxonicum[1], 811 AD	**Rainham**
Hrype	Derbyshire	c.745 AD	**Repton**
Setantii	Lancashire	Ptolemy, 2nd century AD	No identifiable place
Scytlingas	Bedfordshire	c.1060 AD	**Shillington**
Spalde	Lincolnshire	Tribal hidage[2], 7th century AD	**Spalding**
Wixan	Middlesex	Tribal hidage[2], 7th century AD	**Uxbridge**

These tribal names may not sound very much like the words the clansmen will have used to describe themselves, but, by consulting our only sources of information – those contemporary foreign writers who recorded what they heard – they are the nearest we are able to get.

A well-known Old British personal name was *Caradoc* (there are several spellings of this in British history), the meaning of which seemed to be 'good-natured, friendly' and it is from this ancient name that the familiar surname Craddock originates. A tiny place bearing the name **Caradoc** can be found two miles north-west of Ross-on-Wye in Herefordshire. However, in spite of the great number of villages scattered across the British countryside that are known by the names of their later Anglo-Saxon leaders, there are few place-names now that contain any detectable trace of an early Briton's personal name. **Dewsbury** and **Dewchurch** may recall the Welsh personal name Dewi, a form of David, though in each case it is paired with a later Anglo-Saxon suffix ('*-byrig*' and '*-cirice*'). **Tregavethan** (Cornwall) has the Old British prefix '*Tre-*' (a dwelling or village), followed by what must be an unidentified Old British personal name and the same will probably be the case with many other Cornish names of this pattern.

Another line of exploration lies in Cornish place-names beginning with the prefix '*Lan-*', meaning a church, because the second element will often be a personal name, though sometimes an unidentifiable one. The Cornish place-

---

1. Cartularium Saxonicum – a collection of Anglo-Saxon charters, edited by Walter de Gray Birch, Whiting, 1893.
2. Tribal Hidage – a register dating from c. 8th century of regional land holdings measured in 'hides'.

name **Landulph**, mentioned in the first table in this chapter, suggests a probable personal name of *Dilph* or *Dilic*, while **Lanlivery** hints at the personal name *Livri*, though Professor Ekwall[1] prefers to link it to the town of Lanlivry in Brittany. **Lanreath** and **Lansallos** may be pointing to the personal names *Reydhogh* and *Salwys*, but **Laneast**, leaves us guessing as to the personal name concealed therein. One place-name of this type from further afield, is **Landican**, a hamlet near Birkenhead in Cheshire, which almost certainly indicates the Old British personal name *Tecan*, suggesting a meaning of 'the church of *Tecan*'.

Both the Welsh and Cornish languages are of course, related to the original Brittonic tongue spoken in Britain from about 500BC. In England, this original British language (later called 'Celtic') may have continued to be spoken in Westmorland and Cumberland until as late as the beginning of the 11th century.

There are occasional mentions in ancient writings of Britons' personal names of course – though many more instances of those of men than of women are recorded. Some examples of Brittonic women's names are: *Bodicca*, *Genovefa*, *Barita*, *Verica* and *Vectissa*, while *Brice*, *Drest*, *Judoc*, *Tentorigas*, *Vercingetorix* and *Vortigern* are of the men. There seems to be no trace of these in place-names, however. In these days of trends towards novel first names being chosen (or invented) for children, I could imagine that *Verica* and *Vectissa* might have some appeal to modern parents searching for an unusual name for their new-born daughter. *Genovefa* has already become *Genevieve* and *Jennifer*, while *Brice*, together with *Bryce*, is already in occasional use for boys, though the others in my short list are probably lacking in the required modern charm.

HUMAN ACTIVITIES

It would be fascinating to know how the ancient Britons described their farming activities, trading and domestic life and the words they used for common objects and routine tasks, but unfortunately, as we now know, they were not a literate people; even their most learned scholars committed almost nothing to 'writing' and so their language is lost to us, leaving us with only indirect means of learning something of their society and culture. The Welsh language and what remains of Cornish may give suggestions of ancient Brittonic words, but it is largely from the writings of later Roman observers and historians that we have indications of how the Britons lived and organised their society.

The Welsh noun for 'farm' is *'fferm'* and for 'farmer' is *'ffarmwr'*, while in

---

1. Eilert Ekwall – Concise Oxford Dictionary of English Place-names. OUP 1960 ed.

French, the words are *'ferme'* and *'fermier'* and in Old English (derived directly from Anglo-Saxon), a farm is *'feormehám'*. All of these words clearly have a common root and it seems probable that it lies in the ancient Germanic language brought to Britain by those original occupiers from the Continent, who began to drift into Britain from about 550 BC.

We are told that, aside from the frequent inter-tribal conflicts, agriculture, in the forms of arable farming and cattle rearing, was the chief occupation throughout the country. The main crops they grew included wheat, barley, rye and sometimes millet. The common people's diet was supplemented with a type of bean and wild roots, while nuts and berries supplied a seasonal variety and welcome sweetness. Honey, when it could be had, was the usual means of providing sweetening to simple dishes and from it was brewed an alcoholic drink we now call mead. Leafy herbs provided the bulk of the Briton's greenstuff and bread and meat were the staple foods.

In the larger communities, there would be a specialist metal worker, who could produce and repair ironware for ploughs, pots and pans, as well as fashioning and sharpening sword blades, knives and simple tools. He might also have turned his hand to woodwork, when the need arose, though many places would have had a wood craftsman too. However, most tasks around the farms and their dwellings – building walls and fences, digging ditches, cutting wood, ploughing the soil, butchering the meat and so on – would be routinely done by the peasant menfolk.

In places near the East Anglian coast, archæologists have found the remains of large pottery vessels which indicate that salt was obtained on quite a large scale by boiling sea water. In Cheshire too, the remains of earthenware pots show that local brine springs were also a source of this much valued commodity. Thus the nearby Britons were easily able to preserve their butchered meat and fish. Otherwise, hanging the sides of meat high above the open fire within the family house, in order that they could be cured by the smoke, was the only alternative means of preserving meat and fish.

There are few place-names in Domesday (1086) that suggest evidence of ancient salt making. The appropriately named village of **Salt** (Staffordshire) is first mentioned in Domesday, but the district may well have had a centuries' old history of salt production. **Salcombe** (Devon) means 'valley where salt was made', though again it receives only a later mediæval reference. **Saltwood** in Kent has an encouragingly early mention in a 1011 document, pointing to long-standing activity.

England was well furnished with metal ore deposits – tin, copper, lead, silver and of course, iron. By the time of the new 1st millennium, when the so-called 'Iron Age' was at its height, iron smelting was practised in those parts of the country which were close to iron ore deposits. There were several places where the ore could be found and the metal extracted – the Forest of Dean and in the area just south of modern-day Peterborough are two notable locations. However, the centre of this industry was probably in the Sussex Weald, where there was a vast supply of the wood necessary for the smelting process. The ore was probably dug from small pits as well as being lifted from the beds of rivers which ran across the exposed veins of ironstone. Releasing the metal from the rock was a difficult undertaking, for very high temperatures are required – much greater than those in the tin, copper and lead-making processes. The quality of the iron produced would have been very variable and of a rather brittle structure, but nevertheless, sufficiently serviceable for plough tips and knives. How much iron was actually made in this country and how much was brought in from the continent for working into goods is impossible to tell.

Evidence of the iron industry in pre-Roman place-names in these regions is nonexistent, although two places on the present-day edge of Gloucestershire's Forest of Dean may faintly echo such activities, though from several centuries in the future: **Cinderford** (first recorded in 1258), which indicates a river crossing and perhaps even a settlement, whose structural fabric contained slag (*'sinders'*) from the smelters' furnaces and **Coleford** (recorded only in 1534), a nearby village, whose name recalls the charcoal-making industry which always accompanied any iron smelting operations.

On the north-eastern outskirts of Nottingham is a suburb called **Cinderhill**. This too may recall an ancient local iron smelting industry, perhaps using locally dug coal, as well as charcoal, to fuel its kilns.

The Sussex Weald, like the Forest of Dean, may give us a few hints of a continuing iron-working industry in the nearby villages of **Collier's Green** (Kent), **Collier Street** (Kent) and **Coleman's Hatch** (Sussex), each referring to the making of charcoal, though again, only a very late documented mention of **Coleman's Hatch** (1495) is all we have at present.

Life for the ancient Britons centred round religion and superstition, which are quite different from each other. I have already mentioned the water deities' place in peoples' lives (see the section *Water*, earlier in this chapter). There were other gods and goddesses to whom the people gave homage and offerings: *Borvo* (a god of healing), *Epona* (a goddess of fertility), *Maponos* (a god of youth), *Camulos* (a god of war) and *Toutatis* (a protector of the tribe) are five deities known to have been worshipped by the pre-Roman Britons. Of these, only *Camulos* seems to have come through the centuries to us as a place-name – **Kemble** in Gloucestershire, which must have been one of many places where a shrine in his name would have been sited. The first known written record of **Kemble** is very early (AD 682), though perhaps this lone example is not such a surprising survivor, since war and inter-tribal conflict were a constant theme of the times and adversaries would wish to entreat the god to grant success in their battles and later, to offer him their thanks. Later, the new Roman occupiers of Britain would incorporate this deity's British name into their city name *Camulo-dunum* (modern-day **Colchester**).

A final aspect of the early Britons' community I should briefly mention, as we come to the end of this chapter, is concerned with the rituals following death. British tribes at the turn of the new millennium AD adopted various ways of disposing of their dead. In some areas, burial was the preferred way, in others cremation, followed by the burying of the burnt remains was practised. For some tribes, however, less agreeable practices – at least to our minds – were the custom. The fact that there are many later (Anglo-Saxon) place-name references to 'burial mounds' suggests that these places may have been in existence before the Romans withdrew from Britain at the beginning of the 5th century. The Old English place-names **Barrowden** (Rutland), **Bernwood** (Berkshire) and **Brailes** (Warwickshire) recall the presence of ancient burial sites which may date from early in the first half of the new millennium or even earlier.

In the year 55BC, the Britons became violently aware of a potential cataclysm about to overtake their country and although the southern tribes' military unity exhibited a robust defence, their leaders could doubtless see that there was now a distinct future foreign threat to their island. The following year the same threat materialised in the shape of a greatly reinforced foreign invading force. This time the Britons' resistance was far outmatched by the determination of the aggressors and it seemed that a British defeat was inevitable. However, the invaders ultimately withdrew to Gaul (northern France), taking British hostages with them. Although there was to be no actual conquest of Britain for nearly another century, the island became a 'client kingdom' of Rome, with co-operative British rulers fostering increasing trade links with the continent.

The native Britons must have been unsure exactly what the outcome would be and, for the next three generations, may well have feared the worst – outright conquest.

Nevertheless, when the invasion did materialise, the Britons' traditions would ultimately prove to be strong and greatly resistant to change, so that the military revolution and the accompanying upheavals which were to overtake their country near the middle of the 1st century AD, would not fatally disable their society or its culture, demonstrating a strength that would allow them to survive as a distinct people while under the harsh authority of a new, demanding and stern administrative regime.

So here we must leave our study of the early Britons and the tantalisingly incomplete history of their long occupation of England, leaving our friends the archæologists to fill in as many gaps as they can for us. The interesting, though rather limited, influence which the language and culture of the Britons has had on inherited place-names is a very worthwhile study.

Chapter 2

AD 43 – Invasion – Romans!

BY THE TIME GENERAL AULUS PLAUTIUS led his fleet of Roman ships across the Channel in May AD 43 to invade the soil of Albion (as Pytheas, a Greek explorer of the 4th century BC, had referred to Britain), the islands were populated by a great many native tribes (see Figure 1, page 9) who spoke dialects of a Germanic language. This original language (described as 'Celtic' only in the 18th century) had been brought from Western Europe by settlers, probably throughout the 5th century BC. This latest assault was a true and decisive invasion – unlike the Cæsarean event in 54BC, which achieved no more than a British acknowledgement of Rome's power.

The Romans had not come with the unselfish intention of bringing peace and friendship to the ever-squabbling Britons: their goal was entirely one of material acquisition. Britain's well-reported wealth in metal ores, its temperate climate and good pastureland were what drew the attention of all continental invaders and Rome was keen to incorporate Britain into its extensive empire.

In the decades following the great invasion of AD 43, the Romans steadily and often brutally, imposed their military and administrative authority on the whole of what is now England and Wales. All but the south of Scotland, as it is known today, and its fiercely territorial inhabitants, remained frustratingly beyond the capability of even the expert Roman military strategists. The Emperor Hadrian, in the 2nd century AD, ultimately set the northernmost physical boundary of the Roman occupation between the Tyne and Solway estuaries. For the next three hundred years or so Britannia – that is, England and Wales – functioned as the mighty Roman Empire's north-westernmost, if rather rebellious, outpost.

In order to support their wide-ranging strategies, both military and civil, in the new country, the Romans had quickly to evolve a substantial infrastructure. This, as we all know, produced a network of excellent roads, bridges, viaducts, aqueducts, fortified encampments, magnificent villas and logically planned towns, all built and laid out in ways that must have astonished the native village-dwelling population. Less welcome was the imposition of taxes, for the new Roman bureaucracy was quick to exploit all sources of income. All of this civil administrative structure would be inherited by those Britons remaining after the collapse of Roman authority in the island three and a half centuries later.

Although the 3rd century BC Greek travellers I mentioned in the Introduction had recorded a few of the British place-names and some of the personal names they had encountered on their visits to this island, it was not until three hundred years later, when the Romans were beginning to take a serious interest in Britain and making their presence felt, that we begin to find that notable Roman authors such as Cæsar, Pliny the Elder, Strabo and Tacitus, are making occasional mention in their writings of British places and people. It is to the letters and histories written by these men that we have to turn for most of our information about the early Britons.

The one great difference between the language spoken by the Romans (Latin) and that of the native Britons (Brythonic) was that the British language was very rarely written down. Nevertheless, although Latin was to become the language of government, literature and increasingly, of culture and would gradually become familiar to much of the native population, spoken Brythonic remained a strong survivor and was never lost or displaced and it is this strength and durability that largely explains why modern English people do not now speak a derivative of Latin. Although Latin eventually was to give our vocabulary a significant foundation, this is due to the re-emergence of that language as the official written medium for the later Christian church and subsequent scholarship.

It seems probable that the invading Romans would have included some linguists who were familiar with the Gallic language spoken on the near-Continent, to which the British dialect of the south-east of the country must have been very similar. It would certainly have been of great advantage to be able to communicate directly with the local tribal leaders rather than wholly to rely on force of arms.

Because the native Britons were a largely illiterate people, the names which they had given to their settlements were unwritten. The Roman administrative authorities, therefore, had no option but to create their own descriptive Latin names for native British places. Here are some examples from many hundreds:

	Modern name	**Roman name**
(i)	**Winchester**	*Venta Belgarum* (forum of the *Belgae* – see map)
(ii)	**Bath**	*Aquae Sulis* (waters of the goddess *Sulis*)
(iii)	**Manchester**	*Mamucium* (camp at the breast-shaped hill)
(iv)	**Carlisle**	*Luguvalium* (haven of the god *Lugus*)
(v)	**Lincoln**	*Lindum* (settlement at the pool)
(vi)	**Droitwich**	*Salinae* (salt springs)
(vii)	**York**	*Eboracum* (place of the yew trees)
(viii)	**Salisbury**	*Sorviodunum* (fortress by the quiet river)

It was fairly common practise for the Romans to incorporate elements of the original British name into the Latin version, as can be detected in several of the above examples: (i) – the *Belgae* were a South-west British tribe, (iv) – *Lugus* was a local British deity, (v) – *lindo* meant 'pool' in the native language, (vii) – is thought to have referred to a yew grove, (viii) – two British words *sorvio* – of uncertain meaning, but may possibly have referred to a slow flowing river + *dunu* (a stronghold).

Some gloriously Latin-sounding place-names can still be found on our English road maps: **Ampney Crucis** and **Aston Magna** (both in Gloucestershire), **Rowley Regis** (West Midlands), **Horton-cum-Studley** (Oxfordshire), **Aston Juxta Mondrum** (Cheshire), **Toller Fratrum** (Dorset) and **Ruston Parva** (Yorkshire) are impressive examples, but almost all that we come across are products of much later invention and do not have their origins directly in the Romano-British era. The occupying Romans Latinised hundreds more native British place-names, as we have seen, during their rule in Britain. Nevertheless, despite their overwhelming impact on the society they conquered, their contribution to inherited place-name elements has been surprisingly small. The table below lists the ones that have become most familiar in our place-names:

Place-name element	Latin root	Latin meaning
-caster, -cester, -chester	castra	military camp
-wick	vicus	settlement
Port-	portus	harbour
-port	porta	gate
-pont	pons	bridge
Strat-	stratus	pavement, street
Fos- and -fos	fossa	ditch

Since Yorkshire is the largest English county, it would seem probable that there will be places containing each of the above elements to be found there. With a little persistence I did manage to locate an example of each. There are several '-casters', so let's pick an unusual one – **Acaster Malbis**, a couple of miles south of the city of York. **Acaster** is mentioned in Domesday (1086) and refers to the stronghold of one called *Aca*. **Malbis** is a later addition and recalls a 12th century family who held the manor.

Quite a few places have the suffix '-wick' and from these I have chosen the village of **Giggleswick**. The residents of this attractive little place must long ago have become resigned to the amusement its name seems to elicit, but the name has a long history, for it too is recorded in Domesday (1086) and is a transformation of '*Gikel's wīc*' – identifying the dwelling or homestead of a pre-mediæval resident called *Gikel*.

There are very few places in Yorkshire that begin with '*Port-*' or end with it. I did locate a **Portsmouth**, just inside the West Yorkshire border a few miles west of Halifax (and a long way from the sea!), but I thought **Port Mulgrave**, on the coast, east of Middlesbrough offered a more interesting proposition for, according to Professor Ekwall[1], the word **Mulgrave** is not of Roman origin, but the much later Old Norse '*múli gryfia*' – 'a hollow at the headland'.

Pontefract (often locally pronounced *Pomfret*) is well-known for its sweet liquorice 'cakes' and is first recorded in a mid-11th century document, its original meaning being 'broken bridge'.

Finding an example of the syllable '*Strat-*' in a Yorkshire place-name proved difficult. I could come up only with the derivative **Startforth**, where the '*a*' and '*r*' have exchanged places – a typical English speech peculiarity. **Startforth** is across the River Tees from **Barnard Castle**, the name being derived from **Strat-**

---

1. Eilert Ekwall – Concise Oxford Dictionary of English Place-names. OUP 1960 ed.

ford and referred to a road or track which crosses a river (the Tees in this case) at a ford. It is recorded in Domesday (1086) as *Stradford*.

Finally, we come to the Latin element '*-fos*'. In this case I have chosen the village of **Wilberfoss**, a few miles east of York. Its history shows that it means '*Wilburg's* ditch'. Professor Ekwall[1] tells us that it is first noted in the year 1148 and that, interestingly, *Wilburg* was a woman's name. This place-name has given rise directly to the surname Wilberforce.

An interesting statistical survey would be to count all of the place-names containing these six Latin components in every English county. The resulting distribution chart would give a good indication of both survival rates and any 'hotspots' and would indicate the extent of Roman influence into modern times.

NATURAL FEATURES IN THE LANDSCAPE

WATER

As I have said, there are few Latin words that have evolved into recognisable English place-names. However, it will be interesting to glance first at some water-related Latin words which have given us some of our modern words and then see which place-names are related to them:

Latin word	Meaning	Modern derivative	Place-name
Aqua	Water	Aquatic	–
Caractaca	Waterfall	Cataract	**Catterick** (Yorkshire)
Fons	Spring	Fountain	**Mottisfont** (Hampshire)
Insula	Island	Insulate	Perhaps **Inskip** (Lancashire)
Lacus	Lake	Lake	**Lake** (Wiltshire)
Mare	Sea	Marine	**Mere** (Cheshire)
Rivus	Brook	River	–
Stagnum	Pool	Stagnant	–
Stratum	Pavement	Street	**Strete** (Devon)
Vadosus	Shallow	Wade	**Wadebridge** (Cornwall)

Though at first sight, **Aqualate Mere**, a natural lake near Newport in Staffordshire, would seem a good candidate as a Roman survivor, its appearance in a 13th century document as '*Akilot*', indicates that it derives from the Old English '*āc-gelād*' – 'oak stream'. The second word of the lake's name is of course the derivative of the Latin word '*mare*'. This case shows again that appearances can be deceptive and emphasises the vital importance of the need to consult the earliest possible documents as a guide to meanings.

In Chapter One we met the British word '*isca*', meaning 'water'. The Romans incorporated this native word into their own name for **Exeter**, '*Isca Dumnoniorun*' – 'river of the Dumnonii people'.

Although there seem to be no surviving English place-names based on the Latin word for water, '*aqua*', the Romans themselves included the word in some of their versions of British names: **Buxton** in Derbyshire became '*Aquæ Arnemetiæ*', which incorporates the native British word '*nemeton*' ('sacred grove') and means 'the waters of the goddess *Arnemetia* of the sacred groves'. **Bath**, as already mentioned, became *Aquæ Sulis,* the 'waters of the goddess *Sulis*'.

We might also briefly look at some of the British river-names that appear in their Latinised forms in the works of Roman authors, though the spellings of these can vary according to which author's work is being read. Of course, these rivers would already have had native British names that would sometimes become incorporated into the Roman name:

Roman name of river	Modern name of river
Abbas	**Humber** (Yorkshire)
Alauna Flumen *	**Stour** (Dorset)
Alannius	**Avon** (Wiltshire)
Cauda	**Calder** (Cumbria)
Legra	**Soar** (Leicestershire)
Orus Flumen *	**Ore** (Suffolk)
Sabrina	**Severn** (Worcestershire)
Tamesis	**Thames** (Middlesex)
*Tinea Flumen**	**Teign** (Devon)
Viuidin	**Fowey** (Cornwall)

* '*Flumen*' is the Latin for 'river'.

Hills and valleys

The Latin language has lent us a number of words which are associated with this category: '*vallis*' (a valley), '*vertex*' (a peak), '*culmen*' (a summit), '*tabula*' (a ledge), '*clivis*' (a slope) and '*promontorium*' (a headland). It is easy to see that our familiar words *valley, vertex, culminate, table, declivity* and *promontory* come directly from the Latin words. However, a few Latin words for natural features have entered our place-name list: '*vallis*', in its modified form, '*-vale*', can be found in many place-names such as **Perivale** (Middlesex) – 'pear-tree valley' and **Lilyvale** (Kent). '*Saxum*' (a rock) appears in **Saxham** (Suffolk). This may hint at a hamlet in a rocky place or it may possibly refer to a later Saxon settlement.

The Latin word '*mons*' – a mountain, shows up as a suffix in several place-names: **Beaumont, Egremont** (both in Cumbria) and **Belmont** (Derbyshire). All three are late-comers (12th-13th centuries) via the French, but the original Latin root is clear. The first and third names mean 'beautiful hill'; the second refers to a 'sharp topped hill' (French, '*aigre*').

A place near a ridge or at the edge of a steep slope may have attracted into its name the Latin word for 'edge' – '*ora*'. Such are the two villages called **Oare** (Berkshire and Wiltshire). Both settlements are on the high ground of the Downs, so that their names would have been appropriate. The same Latin root also appears as the suffix in the name **Bicknor**, near Maidstone in Kent. This village too, is placed high on the North Downs and seems to have originated as the location of the dwelling of a 12th century individual called *Bica*.

A word taken directly from the Latin language and often used by geographers and map-makers is '*tumulus*', which is used to describe an artificial mound marking a burial place or other important spot. Although many of these are marked in our atlases, sometimes labelled with the plural word '*tumuli*' and ramblers will be familiar with them, the word itself has not generated any place-names.

FLORA AND FAUNA

As in the case of the hills and valleys, some of the tracts of natural flora of England in the first four hundred years of the new millennium were impressive to the view. A great many miles of forest and heathland still commanded the attention, even though much lowland clearance had been made where waste had been turned over to pasture. Woodland was a common sight and the word '*silva*' was the Romans' word for it. This Latin word has found its way into a few of our place-names, as shown in **Pensilva** (Cornwall) and **Pennsylvania** (Gloucestershire). Trees in general were '*arborēs*' and from this we have evolved the word '*arboretum*', meaning a botanical garden devoted largely to trees. There are several towns with well-known arboretums, including **Walsall** (Staffordshire), **Nottingham** and **Ipswich** (Suffolk). However, there seem to be no place-names that are derived directly from '*arbor*', 'a tree'. **Arborfield** in Berkshire is deceptive and probably recalls the land holding of a 13th century woman called *Hereburg*.

The Roman place *Letocetum* in Staffordshire is another example of where the occupiers would retain an existing British word in their own name for a place: in this case '*ceton*' – 'a wooded place'. The village subsequently became renamed **Wall.**

There are few vestiges of Latin tree-words in our place-names. The most frequently met tree will be the willow in its older form of 'sallow'. This word originates from the Latin name for the tree – '*salix*' – and appears, via the Old English derivative '*sahl*', in **Sale** (Cheshire), **Salford** (Bedfordshire), **Sall** (Norfolk) and **Salwick** (Lancashire).

The pear-tree too, leaves a trace in our place-names. The names **Pirton** (Hertfordshire), **Perivale** (Middlesex), **Parbold** (Lancashire) and **Perry** (Cambridgeshire) recall the Latin root '*pirus*' – a pear-tree – and each refers to the presence of a settlement that was established near to a grove of these trees. However, the names of the more familiar woodland trees – '*quercus*' (oak), '*fraxinus*' (ash), '*ulmus*' (elm), '*taxus*' (yew) and '*fragus*' (beech) – although they were common sights, do not seem to have entered the place-name lists. It would be easy to invent one's own place-names from these Latin tree names, based on the information we have learned so far: Querkham, Fraxton, Ullwick, Tagsfield and Fragford are entirely passable.

Shrubs, grasses, herbs and flowers are absent from Romanised place-names too, with a single, indirect, exception, as far as I am able to detect: a Latin word for 'a plant or grass' is '*herba*' and this word appears, rather shyly, in the Kent village of **Boughton Malherbe**, where it refers (in French) to an 'evil herb' – perhaps the habitat of something unusually poisonous. Although it is a late entry into the inventory of English place-names, with a first recorded reference in 1275 and is clearly associated with the Norman occupation of Britain, I think it deserves a mention here.

Modern English is, of course, greatly indebted to the Latin language for the many elements that have been borrowed and that now form a significant foundation of its vocabulary. An example of this is the following sentence, which contains only Latin-based words:

'Canines plus felines, etc – famished carnivorous animals – avidly consume mature pork daily'.

However, the Latin names of animals, fish and insects have not been preserved in our place-names. Of the common animals, we might have expected that the horse (*'equus'*), dog (*'canis'*), cat (*'felis'*), cow (*'vacca'*) and pig (*'porcus'*) would have earned their places, particularly from the farming and hunting points of view, but it is not the case, though, as we know, many of the words have entered the language as alternatives (equine, canine, feline, vaccinate, pork) to the Saxon-derived words we normally use (*'hors'*, *'docga'*, *'catte'*, *'cū'* and *'pecg'*). Even the wild deer (*'cervus'*), a useful source of meat, fails to feature.

The same is almost true for birds' names. I can locate a couple of place-names which have a strong suggestion of the Latin names of wild birds: **Pica** (Cumbria) and **Gracca** (Cornwall). The Latin word *'pica'* is a magpie and the word *'graculus'* is the jackdaw and it would be entertaining to associate the two places with the birds, but there is no documentary evidence to support this origin.

On the other hand, *'anas'*, a duck, is the origin of several places: **Anmer** (Norfolk – 'duck lake'), **Andwell** (Hampshire – 'duck stream'), **Enborne** (Berkshire – 'duck river') and **Enford** (Wiltshire – 'duck ford').

Places which were usually found to be the seasonal habitats of particular insects – midges, butterflies, bees, wasps and grasshoppers for example – we might consider were worth recording, but, unlike the descriptive names for such fauna that the later Saxon occupiers would use, they were not emphasised in the local feature-names chosen by the Romans. As a matter of interest, the Latin words for those insects mentioned above which might otherwise have claimed a place in local names, were, *'culex'*, *'papilio'*, *'apis'*, *'vespa'* and *'gryllus'*. Try to invent place-names based on these.

HUMAN ACTIVITY

Three great cultural attributes of the Romans were their distinctions in militarism, engineering and administration. Their approach to every new venture was characterised by confidence, imagination and determination, qualities that had enabled Rome to create a vast empire which, at its peak, stretched from Egypt in the south, across the North African borders of the Mediterranean to Portugal in the west, Britain (as far north as the Scottish borders) in the north and then eastwards through Holland, western Germany, Czechoslovakia, Romania and terminating in Syria in the east. Such a military achievement is in itself stupendous, but the administration and control of territories covering a land area of 2½ million square miles must have been a task of such complexity as to be incomprehensible to our modern imaginations, especially when we remember that their means of communication were limited to messengers on horseback and ships at the mercy of the weather. Added to this was the command of the whole of the Mediterranean Sea, the Bay of Biscay and eventually, the (English) Channel, adding about another one million square miles to the total area of the empire.

In Britain, as in every other country that had been overpowered by the Romans, the clearest manifestations of their intentions and endeavours were town planning and road building. The basic Latin words we would expect to find when thinking about a town or city are quite informative, because of the English words we have derived from them:

Latin word	Meaning	An English word
ædificium	a building	edifice
canālis	a gutter	canal
civis	a citizen	civic
domus	a house	domestic
hortus	a garden	horticulture
mercātus	a trading place	market
officīna	a workshop	office
taberna	a shop	tavern
urbs	a town	urban
via	a road	way

None of these, however, seems to have found its way into a place-name.

The Romans' extensive civil and military operations would have required a constant supply of hardware – iron, leather, cloth, wood and stone, as well as foodstuffs from farms – meat, grain and a few vegetables, but almost no trace of the names of the producers or tradesmen was incorporated into their places of work. I have managed to identify only five place-names which recognise the Latin origins of artisans or craftsmen. **Faversham** in Kent recalls the work of the smith, coming from the Latin '*faber*', via the later Old English '*fæfer*'. This individual must have been outstanding in some way for the location of his workplace to have received special mention – perhaps he was the only smith in the district. The earliest documentary record of the place is dated AD 811 and the name is written '*Fefreshám*'.

The villages of **Sutterby** and **Sutterton** in Lincolnshire, though not recorded until 1086 and 1200 respectively, contain an element, '*Sut-*', in their names which goes back to the Latin for a shoemaker, '*sutor*'. This time, however, it is a direct reference to the Latin – the Old English word being '*læstwyrtha*' (a lastwright).

Finally, I will mention the villages of **Sapiston** (Suffolk) and **Sapperton** (Derbyshire). Their claim on our attention lies in their first syllables, '*Sap-*', which originates in the Latin word '*sāpo*', meaning 'soap' and here refers to places where soap was produced. The later, Old English word '*sāpe*' is clearly taken from the Latin, as is our own modern word.

Whether the five places I have mentioned above were established in the Romano-British period is hard to say, but that they record in their names three occupations through the Latin language, makes them significant in this study.

Knowing the dynamic military reputation of the Romans, one might reasonably expect that something associated with this aspect of their endeavours would find its way into place-names, but only two distinctly military-related words that have established themselves in our place-names are from the Latin, if we discount '*stratum*' (a paved way or road), initially intended to make military movements easy. The two words are '*castra*' and '*castellum*'. The first, '*castra*', is perhaps the most well-known Latin import into place-names and signified a military encampment or a fortified place. The second word, '*castellum*', has a slightly different meaning – a defensive stronghold, or a fortress, as we might call it today. The places **Chester** (Cheshire) and **Caister** (Lincolnshire) are simply slightly modified renderings of the original '*castra*', but there are many place-names which incorporate within themselves a variation of '*castra*', sometimes rather disguised: **Lanchester** (Durham) – 'the long camp', **Mancetter** (Warwickshire) – perhaps 'a chariot camp', **Chesterfield** (Derbyshire) – 'field by the Roman encampment', **Casterton** (Rutland) – 'settlement near the Roman camp' and **Bicester** (Oxfordshire) – 'burial place at the camp'. These names have Old English elements as well as the Latin-derived syllable, but show that the Latin word remained an important descriptive component in later, post-Roman centuries.

There are many instances where the word 'castle' (coming directly from the Latin, '*castellum*') forms part of a double name: **Castle Carrock** (Cumbria), **Castle Donington** (Leicestershire), **Bishops Castle** (Shropshire) and **Corfe Castle** (Dorset) and there are just as many where it is incorporated into a single word place-name: **Horncastle** (Lincolnshire) – 'Roman fort on the horn of land (i.e. between two rivers)', **Papcastle** (Cumbria) – 'fort site occupied by a hermit', **Castleford** (Yorkshire) – 'river-crossing by the Roman fort' and **Castlethwaite**

(Cumbria) – 'place near the fort'.

Although other Latin words associated with militarism have been retained in later English vocabulary – '*bellum*' ('war', giving us the words 'belligerent' and 'bellicose'), '*milēs*' ('soldier', giving 'military' and 'militia"), '*adversārius*' ('opponent', 'adversary') and '*victōria*' ('victory'), there seem to be none that have manifested themselves in our place-names other than the two already mentioned – '*castra*' and '*castellum*'. The London district of Victoria is an early 19th century development.

This then, brings us to the end of our search for those place-names that have their origins in the specific era in which the Romans ruled Britain. Looking back and in spite of the impact of the Roman occupation and the prominent place it has come to occupy in Britain's history, their tenure was really rather a short-lived affair and we have seen that its influence on place-names was surprisingly small. Most of the specific Latin inclusions into place-names arose several centuries after the Roman occupation had ended when scholars, both secular and ecclesiastical, turned to Latin as their preferred language of scholarship and communication.

All empires ultimately collapse or fade away and the great empire that the Romans had created began to weaken towards the turn of the 5th century AD, as barbarian forces began to attack the Roman-occupied outposts of Europe. In order to reinforce their far-flung continental armies in an attempt to counter the threats, Roman supreme commanders began to withdraw their forces from Britain, where there was also slowly increasing unrest, until sometime in the year 410, the remaining Roman forces were withdrawn and the Britons were left to manage their own defences and organise their own administration, despite a vain plea to the Roman Emperor Honorius for support. Britain was now effectively abandoned militarily and was no longer held to be a province within the Roman Empire.

Already, during the latter part of the 4th century, there had been attempts at invasion of English borders by Picts, Scots, Irish and Saxons, all of whom the Roman defenders had successfully repulsed. After Rome withdrew its British garrisons at the beginning of the 5th century, it was these nearby antagonists who again presented the greatest foreign threats to England (as I will now call the country).

Once the Roman occupiers had withdrawn from English soil, the native Britons soon discarded many of their Romanised ways and there was a general tendency to return to the old rural-based way of life. Parts of the Roman towns began to fall into decay and some grand villas were neglected and abandoned;

forts were left unmaintained or were robbed of their fabric and the spoken Latin idiom soon declined in common usage. There had been of course, inevitable inter-marriages between Britons and Romans and some Romish customs and practices naturally persisted, but on the whole, the traditional British culture re-emerged.

For the next two generations of Britons there would be a return to a rather dark age and for us and for historians, who wish to know more about those times, there are once again almost no written records to help us out. It was not until the time of the British monk Gildas (c.500 – 570 AD), that a little light is shone into the darkness, though his principal concern was not the recording of contemporary events, but a scathing condemnation of the sins and mismanagement of contemporary rulers.

Chapter 3

AFTER THE ROMANS – ANGLO-SAXONS (PART I)

MANY HISTORIANS BELIEVE THAT after the Roman era, 'England' was quickly subjected to a series of vigorous incursions from Germanic marauders from the near-continent. The depleted native British defensive force which remained after the Roman withdrawal was unable to stave off the greater numbers of newcomers, who were able to overrun the eastern coastal areas and establish their own settlements. These invaders have been identified as mostly Angles, Saxons and Jutes. It is thought too, that Frisians will have been amongst the early settlers, since the new language that became Old English was closely related to that spoken on the North Sea coasts of present-day Netherlands and north-west Germany. An interesting, but small group of place-names towards the east of the country is fairly sound evidence of the early presence of Frisian occupiers: **Friesthorpe**, **Frieston**, **Freiston** and **Firsby** (all in Lincolnshire),

Friston and **Freston** (both in Suffolk), **Frisby-on-the-Wreake** (Leicestershire) and **Friston** (Sussex).

Historians have usually called the new occupiers the Anglo-Saxons – a necessarily portmanteau description of the new wave of occupiers. However, it is interesting to notice that England eventually took its name from the Angles (England = Angle-land), though it might easily have become Jutia, Frisland, Saxland or even Saxonia. The Continental occupiers' numbers continued to increase and their occupation spread northwards and westwards to the extent that their Germanic language took a firm hold in England, to become the dominant tongue of the country: English was born. Cornwall and Wales were remote enough from the centre of the new Saxon power-base to remain resistant for a long time and were able to retain their old Brittonic language.

At this point I think it is important to mention that some historians do not feel that this was the way the early penetration of England occurred. Their interpretation of the evidence, both written and archæological, persuades them that there were no overwhelming invasions, but a steady influx and assimilation of the foreign settlers and their culture and that the Anglo-Saxonising process became naturally self perpetuating.

However, in whichever way the settlement process came about, by the end of the 8th century, English had become the national language, though Cornwall and Wales still held fast to their old Brittonic ('Celtic') speech. Most of present-day Scotland too, except the south-east, escaped the Saxon surge.

As the Anglo-Saxon generations increased and spread ever further afield, seven kingdoms were established with fairly well-defined territories (see the following map, *figure 2*) and we can detect echoes of these ancient provinces today in the familiar county names of **Essex** (*East Saxons*), **Middlesex** (*Middle Saxons*) and **Sussex** (*South Saxons*).

Wessex (*West Saxons*) has not survived as an administrative geographical unit into modern times, though it is widely used informally and the Berkshire Downs are marked as Wessex Downs in some atlases.

The cultural impact of the Anglo-Saxons ultimately proved to be far greater than that of the Romans, for the dissemination across England of the Germanic language which they brought, became total, whereas Latin was never more than an incidental experience for the common Britons and was not widely adopted throughout nearly four centuries of Roman domination. It is to the Anglo-Saxons and their new English language (which we now call 'Old English'!) that we owe most of our place-names.

Although the newcomers would introduce thousands of new words of course,

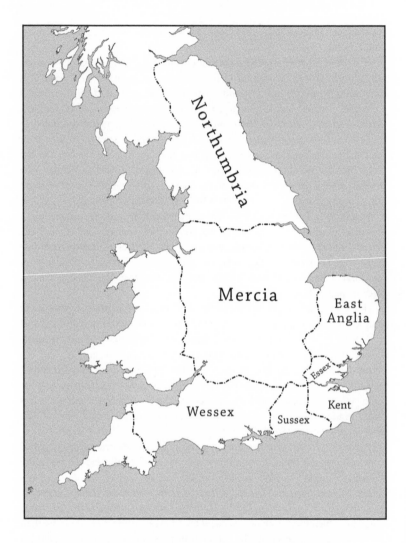

Figure 2 The kingdoms of the Anglo Saxons at the beginning of the 9th century.

many of the old British words were inevitably incorporated into the naming processes. We will still find plenty of the old British '*-combe*' (also '*-comb*' and '*-coomb*'), regularly keeping close company with a new Germanic element: **Yarnscombe** (Devon), '*earn*' + '*cumb*' – eagle's valley; **Winchcomb** (Gloucestershire), '*wincel*' + '*cumb*' – a side valley and **Woolcombe** (Dorset), '*wella*' + '*cumb*' – valley with the stream, while the old British elements '*tre-*' and '*pen-*' proliferate in West Country place-names in combination with other old British syllables.

The familiar Roman ones too ('*-caster*', '*-chester*', '*-cester*', '*-wick*' and '*fos-*', mentioned in Chapter Two) survived the language adjustment, but they too, soon found themselves in company with new Germanic partners: **Bicester** (Oxfordshire, '*byrgen*' + '*ceaster*' – burial mound at the camp); **Shapwick** (Dorset, '*sceap*' + '*wic*' – sheep farm) and **Fosham** (Yorkshire, '*fossa*' + '*ham*' – settlement by the ditch).

The Anglo-Saxons established many new settlements of their own and expanded existing ones, gradually integrating with the native inhabitants, probably a little uncomfortably at first. The newer settlements were of course given names in the new language (which we now refer to as Old English) and it is with these names that we see the beginning of most of the place-names we recognise today. Many of the original words are recognisable to us and their meanings are little different even after more than a thousand years. Here is a list of endings commonly seen in English place-names that derive directly from the Old English spoken by the Anglo-Saxons:

Familiar place-name ending	Old English word	Meaning
-borne, -bourne	*burna*	stream, brook
-bury, -borough	*byrig*	walled or fortified settlement
-cliff	*clif*	slope, cliff
-cott	*cot*	dwelling, cottage
-dale	*dæl*	valley
-den	*denu*	shallow valley
-don	*dūn*	hillside, down
-ey	*īeg*	island
-field	*feld*	cultivated land, plain
-ford	*ford*	ford, shallow crossing
-ham	*hām*	village
-heath	*hæþ**	heathland
-hurst, -hirst	*hyrst*	woodland, wooded hill
-land	*land*	land, disrtrict, country

-ley	*lēah*	lea, meadow
-low	*hlǣw*	mound, hillock, rise
-ness	*nœss*	headland
-shaw	*scaga*	copse, thicket, wood
-stead, -sted	*styde*	place
-stock	*stōc(c)*	place, dwelling, stump, post
-thorp, -throp	*þorp* *	farm
-ton	*tūn*	homestead, settlement
-well	*wiȩll*	stream, spring
-wick	*wīc*	village, dwelling
-wood	*wudu*	wood
-worth	*worþ* *	farm, enclosure

* The mediæval letter '*þ*' (thorn) had the sound of our 'th'.

This is not by any means a complete list of course – there are plenty of other recognisable elements to be found, but they are seen rather less often, though I shall be mentioning some of these others in due course. Although the ones shown in the table are most often found as suffixes, they do sometimes occur as the first elements in names and even in combination with each other, as in **Stockley** (Wiltshire – 'a clearing with tree stumps'), **Cottam** (Yorkshire – 'at the cottages'), **Clifton** (Bedfordshire – 'place near a cliff or slope') and **Hamworthy** (Dorset – 'place with enclosures').

However, as we have seen before, things are seldom straightforward when it comes to interpreting early language and a word will often have been transformed by centuries of regional speech and various spellings into something identical in form to another word with a different origin and meaning. For example, the element '-*well*' in the list above is notoriously unpredictable. In the name **Harswell** (Yorkshire) it refers to '*Hersa's stream*', but in **Wellow** (Isle of Wight), it is a version of 'willow' and in **Wellsborough** (Leicestershire) it is derived from the Old English word '*hwēol*', meaning 'a wheel' and describing a hill with a stone circle. So it is the earliest possible documentary evidence to which we must always turn before reaching any conclusions about the origins of place-names – and even then there is sometimes little in the surviving records to help us. For instance, the small town of **Chickerell,** near Weymouth in Dorset, is recorded in Domesday (1086) as *Cicherelle*, but there is no documentary evidence for the origin of the name. Similarly, **Cheviot**, the name of the northernmost reaches of the Pennines, is without documentary definition.

On looking down the second column of the above table, it's clear that sixteen out of the twenty-six suffixes listed reflect a natural feature of the landscape (flora or geographical), while the remaining ten describe the results of human activity of some kind. These groups, natural features and human activity, are two of the three major sources of English place-names (the third major group is that of places based on a tribal or a personal name).

The majority the English place-names that appear when we open our road maps, have their origins firmly in the Anglo-Saxon period of English history and, considering that this era eventually began to merge with a new phase of Englishness, brought by the Scandinavians, over twelve hundred years ago, these Anglo-Saxon derived place-names have shown an impressive durability – not bad for the period often called The Dark Ages.

Place-names could fall into disuse, however, but only when villages were depopulated for some reason – disease, famine, land clearance, war, flooding by the sea or because of the demise of the inhabitants through old age. The Oxfordshire villages of **Tilgarsley** and **Tusmore** were wiped out by *'the pestilence'* (the Black Death) and were deserted by 1350 and 1355 respectively. There is no trace left of the village of **Tilgarsley** and only the only memory of **Tusmore** today is **Tusmore House** and its park beside the earthworks of the mediæval site. Nor do the names seem to have survived as surnames. On the other hand, the Lancashire **Eccersley** and Worcestershire **Insall** have clung to existence as surnames, but all traces of the villages themselves have long disappeared, leaving even their approximate locations uncertain.

As we have seen, people will always be ready to identify natural features of the landscape by using the simplest and most descriptive way they know, which often means likening them to familiar objects or by simple description. The places **Witcombe** (Gloucestershire), **Catton** (Northumberland) and **Colsterdale** (Yorkshire) nicely illustrate this idea. Each name refers to a valley location: the first is 'wide valley', the second means 'valley of the wild cats' and the third recalls the location of some local charcoal burners. **Bolsterstone** (Yorkshire) and **Cressing** (Essex) are perhaps a little less secretive about their origins. **Bolsterstone**, as it says, recalls a prominent local rock in the shape of a bolster or cushion, while **Cressing** described a stream where watercress grew. This rather pleasing naming process was applied all over the English countryside during the 6th–9th centuries and we can find memories of it in today's place-names which refer to hills, ridges, woods, fords, pools, streams, lakes, islands, headlands and cliffs as well as to farms, enclosures, fields, ditches, roads and a variety of buildings.

MORE FEATURES OF THE NATURAL LANDSCAPE

Watercourses

Proximity to a reliable water supply is of first importance to any community and farming above all, required a source of water which was within easy distance of the pastures and settlements. Springs and brooks could usually fulfil the modest needs of the human dwellers of the community, but for those who kept sheep and cattle, a conveniently close and calm river flowing through the lowland grazing fields was a blessing. England is indeed blessed with thousands of small, quiet rivers, streams and brooks and it is these, together with its pleasant, temperate climate that have helped make the country so attractive to Continental outsiders throughout its early history. So, as in the previous chapters, we should look first at the importance of water in the place-naming process adopted by the new occupiers of the island.

Setting aside for the moment the names of the well-known national English rivers, ten of which I listed in Chapter One, the following list gives a few of the minor water courses from across England and typically, along which pastures, meadows and fields had long been established and close to which settlements had grown up, sometimes taking their names from the water feature itself and sometimes *vice versa* – often called 'back formation'. Although the origins of the greater number of English river names lie in the obscure Brittonic language of pre-Roman times, the following names have their roots in the post-Roman era of the Anglo-Saxon occupation of England, between the mid-5th and mid-11th centuries – probably the most important period of English place-name formation:

Modern river name	Old English	Meaning	Nearby place-names
Blyth (Suffolk)	*bliþe**	*gentle*	**Blythburgh**
Lambourn (Berkshire)	*lām-burna*	*lamb stream*	**Lambourn, Upper Lambourn**
Lud (Lincolnshire)	*hlūde*	*loud*	**Ludney, Louth**
Lugg (Herefordshire)	*lucge*	*bright*	**Lugwardine, Moreton on Lugg**
Lyn (Devon)	*hlynn*	*torrent*	**Lynton, West Lyn, Lynmouth**
Otter (Somerset)	*oter-ēa*	*otter river*	**Otterford, Otterton**
Sid (Devon)	*sīd*	*deep*	**Sidmouth, Sidford, Sidbury**
Waver (Cumberland)	*wæfr*	*wandering*	**Waverton, Waverbridge**

*þ is the long obsolete, but useful, letter 'thorn', pronounced 'th'.

It is quite clear from the meanings of the Old English words in the list that descriptive simplicity was the natural guide when naming rivers. We shall see that this continues to be the case throughout the landscape when hills, valleys and other major features received attention.

The names of ten of the major English rivers were dealt with in Chapter One, together with twelve of the smaller ones. A little investigation into river-name origins shows that the majority of them have retained their most ancient names throughout the subsequent centuries. A significant exception to this, however, is the **Mersey** (*'mæres-ēa'* – 'boundary river'). This word has its root in Old English, rather than in the ancient Brythonic language, and arises from its importance in dividing the Saxon kingdoms of Mercia from Northumbria. Nowadays, it forms the border between Cheshire and Lancashire. Two place-names that incorporate the name of the river are **Ashton-upon-Mersey** and **Heaton Mersey**, both now within the urban precincts of the city of Manchester. (The metropolitan county of Merseyside came into existence in 1974 as a result of the Local Government Act, 1972).

The **River Idle**, which flows through Nottinghamshire also has an Old English origin – *'īdel'*, meaning 'slow', though, in spite of its long and winding course, there are no place-names along its length which are derived from its name. **Idle**, the well-known suburb of Bradford (Yorkshire) has no historic connection with the Nottinghamshire river.

There are several rivers by the name of **Swale**, which has an Old English word, *'swillan'*, meaning 'washing or swirling', at its root. The Yorkshire river of this name has a collection of place-names along its length, of the '*X-on-Swale*' pattern: **Myton-on-Swale, Skipton-on-Swale, Morton-on-Swale, Bolton-on-Swale** and **Brompton-on-Swale**. The first name in each of these triples is also of Old English origin: **Myton** is *'gemyþ-tūn'* – 'settlement or dwelling at the meeting of streams'. The village is indeed within a few hundred yards of the confluence of the **River Swale** and the **River Ure** and crop marks suggest that the original village may have been located closer to the river. **Skipton**'s name is from *'scēap-tūn'* – 'sheep farm'; **Morton** is simply *'mōr-tūn'* – 'the village near the marsh'. The modern terrain near the village certainly looks potentially marshy, especially if the river is swollen. *'Bōþl-tūn'* is the source of **Bolton** and means 'the settlement with a farmhouse'. **Brompton** (*'brōm-tūn'*) refers to the 'place where broom grew'. Each of these places ends with the common Old English suffix *'-tūn'*, which eventually developed a rather variable meaning: enclosure, farmstead, cottages, hamlet, village and, in its guise as *'-ton'*, it is one of our most familiar place-name endings.

We can now move from the names of specific rivers to generic words for rivers, streams, springs and brooks which appeared during this period as suffixes and occasionally, as prefixes. There is a surprising number of these and one of the most familiar is derived from the Old English word '*burna*' – a stream or river – and usually manifests itself in river names as '*-bourne*', '*-bourn*' and '*-burn*', this latter especially in Scotland. Here is a selection of water-related place-names belonging to this group from across the country, together with their meanings and the watercourse with which they are today associated:

Place-name	Meaning	Nearby watercourse
Albourne (Sussex)	'river beside the alders'	Cutlers Brook
Bradbourne (Derbyshire)	'broad stream'	Haverhill Dale Brook
Bournheath (Worcestershire)	'stream on the heath'	Hockley Brook
Burnham-on-Sea (Somerset)	'river meadow'	River Parrett
Colburn (Yorkshire)	'cool stream'	Colburn Beck
Holybourne (Hampshire)	'sacred stream'	River Wey
Morborne (Cambridgeshire)	'marsh stream'	Billings Brook
Welbourn (Lincolnshire)	'welling spring'	The Beck

A London stream belonging with this group and having an interesting history is the **Tyburn**, which rises in Hampstead and now flows beneath St James's Park and into the Thames at Pimlico. The stream originally flowed over-ground and marked the western edge of the lands belonging to 10th century Westminster Abbey. Its name meant 'boundary stream' (from '*tȳnan*' – 'to enclose'). The village of **Tyburn** occupied an area at the western end of London's Oxford Street around the site of today's Marble Arch. In the 16th century, a public gallows ('Tyburn Tree') was erected here, imparting an abiding grimness to the name of **Tyburn**.

However, we must be cautious when examining places which include the first element '*Burn-*', for it can often be the result of an abbreviated ancient personal name, as in **Burneside** (Cumbria), **Burnaston** (Derbyshire) and **Burnsall** (Yorkshire). In the first two, the central '*-es-*' and '*-as-*' and the solitary '*-s-*' in **Burnsall**, are suggestive of ownership and indeed both **Burneside** and **Burnaston** refer to an early mediæval land holder called *Brūnwulf* – '*Brūnwulf's* hillside' and '*Brūnwulf's* dwelling', while **Burnsall** is '*Brȳni's halh*' – 'the place of one, *Brȳni*'. It is only from their appearances in the earliest written records that we are able to determine this.

Other commonly seen elements in place-names with a flowing water connection are '*-brook*' and '*-well*', of which there are hundreds of examples. The Old

English origins of these are in the words '*brōc*' and '*więll*'. If ever there was a water-word to rival, for sheer versatility, that other natural feature word '*-combe*', which we first met in Chapter One, it has to be '*-brook*'. Brook itself is a common surname of course and recalled one whose dwelling was near a brook or spring. As an independent place-name, **Brook** is listed in my road map a total of 9 times in England: 2 in Surrey, 2 in Hampshire and 1 each in Rutland, Kent, Wiltshire, Devon and Isle of Wight. The name is very versatile and has attracted a number descriptive and helpful additions, as in **Brook End** (in 7 counties), **Brook Street** (in 4 counties), together with a **Brook Bottom** (Lancashire) and a **Brook Hill** (Nottinghamshire). The prolific resourcefulness of **Brook** continues with **Brooke** (Norfolk) and a host of names in which the word is only one syllable of the place-name: **Brookhampton** (Somerset), **Brookfield** (5 counties), **Brookfoot** (Yorkshire), **Brookgreen** (Isle of Wight), **Aldersbrook** (Essex), **Quabrook** (Sussex), **Bolingbroke** (Lincolnshire) and even **Coalbrookdale** (Shropshire – meaning 'valley with a cold brook'), together with very many others in which the word is clearly identifiable. Less obvious though, are **Brogden** (Yorkshire – 'brook valley') and **Broxfield** (Northumberland – 'field with a brook').

To illustrate the frequency with which the syllable '*-well-*' (or occasionally '*-wel*') occurs in English place-names, I have put ten of them into the table below. In most cases, its meaning can be 'stream', 'spring' or 'brook':

Place-name	County	Meaning	Earliest record[1]
Well	Kent	Spring	1086
Wells	Somerset	Springs	1050
Wellesbourne	Warwickshire	*Wealh's* stream	840
Welton	Yorkshire	Place by the spring	1080
Sywell	Northamptonshire	Seven springs	1086
Digswell	Hertfordshire	*Dicca's* stream	1086
Bywell	Northumberland	Spring in the river bend	1104
Framwellgate	Durham	At the gushing spring	1352
Ashwellthorpe	Norfolk	Farm by the ash stream	1066
Boxwell	Gloucestershire	Stream near the box trees	1086

Wellesbourne (third in the table) illustrates how we might easily be deceived, for the first syllable is actually from a personal name and not a reference to water at all. I have included the earliest record column in this table for two reasons: firstly to show that many of the earliest written records of place-names come from within a century or so of the Domesday register of 1086 and secondly, to

---

1. Eillert Ekwall *Concise Oxford Dictionary of English Place-names*. OUP 1960 Ed.

remind ourselves that such names must have been in existence for a considerable time before their appearance in that written archive.

Like '*brook*', the element '*well*' can appear at the beginning, middle and end of place-names, as well as in doubles such as **Jacob's Well** (Surrey), **Malvern Wells** (Worcestershire) and **Well Street** (Kent), making it too, very adaptable and giving good service to the place-name catalogue. As I have pointed out, its root is in the word '*wiell*', which is of course the origin of our modern word 'well'. The Anglo-Saxons, however, usually used the word '*pytt*' to describe a water-well.

As I mentioned earlier, there is an unexpected variety of words describing moving water, so this might be a good point to summarise the elements derived from Old English that refer to streams and similar moving water:

Old English	Place-name element	Place-name examples
burna	-bourn(e), -born(e), -burn	**Camborne, Newbourne, Burnby, Welbourne**
brōc	-brook(e), -broke, -brock	**Shottesbrook, Brockweir, Ladbroke**
wiell	-well, -wall	**Welham, Bradwell, Bradwall**
ēa	-ea, -ey	**Eton, Ealand, Andersea, Arlesey**
flēot	-fleet, flit-	**Fleet, Fleetham, Benfleet**
lacu	-lake, -lock, Lack- Lay-	**Standlake, Wheelock, Lackham, Layton**
læcc	-ledge, Latch-, Lash-	**Latchbrook, Lashbrook**
bæce	-batch, -beach, -bach	**Colebatch, Waterbeach, Comberbach**
lād	-lode, -late	**Evenlode, Whaplode, Shiplate**

Although I have not included all variations of the elements and all of the place-names by any means that are derived from the Old English elements, it is clear that the variety is great. I will discuss some of them in the paragraphs that follow.

The reader may have noticed the absence of the fairly familiar water-word '*beck*' from my list. I haven't forgotten it; I have postponed its inclusion until Chapter Five because its origins lie in an Old Danish word, '*bæk*' – suspiciously similar to the Anglo-Saxon word '*bæce*' in the list above – and the Danes have yet to make their appearance in our place-name story.

We first came across the ending '-*ea*' in its modified form '-*ey*' as the suffix in the river name **Mersey** ('*mæres-ēa*'). However, there can easily be confusion between the almost identical '-*ea*' and '-*ēa*' and differing slightly only in sound, the former of which stems from the Anglo-Saxon word '*īeg*', indicating an island, as we shall see later. Each has often become reduced to '-*ey*' in its place-name form. It seems likely that '*ēa*' is a battered relic of the Latin word for water, '*aqua*' and is a relation, once removed, of the French '*eau*'. As an independent river name, our slippery '*ēa*' shows up in **Rea**, the name of three rivers in the counties of Cambridge, Warwick and Shropshire. However, this river name illustrates an interesting peculiarity of early misspelling following a typical English pronunciation mannerism. By the 1450s, the river was appearing in records as the Ree, whereas only a few years before, it had not acquired the initial 'R'. The explanation is that, speaking the words '*atter Ēa*' ('at the Ēa'), inevitably leads to a collision of sounds where the final '*-r*' of '*atter*' becomes attached to the beginning of the next word '*Ēa*', resulting in the birth of the new word 'Rea'. The same mannerism persists in Buckinghamshire's **River Ray** ('*atter Ēe*'). The same oddity can also be seen in some surnames, for example Roake ('*atter oak*'), Nokes ('*atten oaks*'), Nash ('*atten ash*') – all recalling one who dwelt near a prominent oak or ash tree. Leicestershire, however, has a **River Eye**, where the pronunciation peculiarity has not intruded into the spelling, though there is a duplication of sense ('River River'), in the same way as is seen in River Avon (see page 13).

In doing its service in place-names, rather than purely river names, our little river-word, '*ēa*', is to be found quietly doing duty in **Eathorpe** (Warwickshire), **Eythrope** (Buckinghamshire) **Ewart** (Northumberland), and **Eyton** (Shropshire).

If '*beck*' is a Scandinavian borrowing (see Chapter Five), then **Fleet** is firmly Old English and derives from the word '*flēot*', a very adaptable word, which could mean anything from an estuary to a creek and a stream. **Fleet** occurs as a 'stand-alone' place-name in several counties and as the **River Fleet** which now flows beneath the City of Westminster in London. In the 10th century, this stream, which flowed above ground at the time, marked the eastern boundary of Westminster Abbey's estate and flowed into the Thames at Blackfriars.

The Bedfordshire villages of **Flitton** and **Flitwick**, together with **Old Fletton** in Cambridgeshire, also recall the root-word '*flēot*', the first two being on the **River Flitt**, while **Old Fletton** nestles beside the **River Nene** within the conurbation of Peterborough. The villages of **East** and **West Fleet** (Dorset coast), however, illustrate '*flēot's*' allusion to a cove or inlet rather than to a river or a stream.

The Old English word '*lacu*', which generates some place-names having the ending '*-lake*', is certainly sometimes the father of the word 'lake', but usually the original record refers to a stream – **Mortlake**, a mediæval Thames-side village, **Bidlake** (Devon, on the River Lew), **Cocklake** (Somerset, beside the River Axe) and even **Fishlake** (Yorkshire, next to the River Don) all lie near rivers and streams. **Hoylake**, however, is on the tidal reach of the Wirral peninsula on the Cheshire coast and probably did not recall a strictly river-side situation.

The word '*bæce*' has given us quite a variety of place-names associated with streams: examples of place-names having the suffixes '*-batch*', '*-beach*' and '*-bach*' have already been mentioned in the table above. However, in the mouths of Englishmen, the word '*batch*' lends itself to several shades of pronunciation and therefore spelling, as in **Beccles** (Suffolk) and **Beighton** (Yorkshire), while **Burbage** (Wiltshire) also, surprisingly perhaps, utilises the Old English word. Each place nestles beside its respective watercourse, respectively the River Waveney, the River Rother and Deane Water. **Hazlebadge** too, in the Derbyshire Dales, is a surprising member of the group.

The rather rarely occurring old word '*lād*', indicating a stream, in place-names can be detected in **Oxlode** (Cambridgeshire) and **Framilode** (Gloucestershire), as well as in **Lode** (Somerset) and **Load** (Cambridgeshire). The above table gives three more instances.

Finally, the interesting Old English word '*læce*' was usually applied to a stream which rose from, or drained a wetland of some sort: a marsh, fen, swamp or bog. Each of these wet areas has a slightly different constitution and geological explanation and their streams can have variable chemical natures, giving rise to flora which thrive in specific conditions – sedges, reeds, rushes, mosses and so forth. '*Læce*' seems to have been a general name for these wetland streams and has generated a number of place-names: **Letchmore** (Hertfordshire – 'a boggy heathland' which lies near to a stream called Tykes Water), **Latchford** (Oxfordshire – 'a crossing over a stream' – a tributary of Haseley Brook) and **Lechlade** (Gloucestershire – 'crossing at the River Leach').

Dwellers in the ancient English countryside were always ready to give descriptive names to the natural things around them and local watercourses would be nicknamed according to how fast they flowed, the noise they made, whether their courses were winding, the smoothness of the surfaces, the colour of the water, its depth, width and the wildlife that frequented the banks – an entirely natural and practical idea. Our good fortune has been to inherit a whole range of evocative place-names originating in these expressive and sometimes colourful descriptions. The village of **Oborne** ('*wōh*' – 'crooked') in Dorset takes its name from the winding **River Yeo** ('yew-tree river') which passes through the village. A river with a noticeably shallow and sandy bed might easily be called **Sandbach** (Cheshire), while a fast flowing, noisy stream would soon be known as **Loudwater** (Buckinghamshire). The two watercourses remembered in these last two names are the **Rivers Wheelock** and **Wye**.

Clear waters with unusually sparkling surfaces could attract appropriate descriptions: **Leeming** (Yorkshire, *'lēoma'* – 'shining'), **Brightwell** (Suffolk, *'beorht'* – 'bright'), but on the other hand, a muddy crossing is indicated at **Mudford** on the **River Yeo** in Somerset. There must have been something distinctly disagreeable about the **River Windrush** in Oxfordshire, where it skirts the village of **Fulbrook**, for the village's name means 'foul stream'. There are other places too, labouring under this ancient burden: **Fulwell** (Durham), **Fulready** (Warwickshire – *'fūl-rīþig'*, foul stream) and **Fulford** (Staffordshire). One hopes that the waterways concerned are now cleaner!

Wildlife of all sorts was seen to frequent rivers and streams in pre-mediæval centuries and many of the animals were sources of food, fat and skins to those early Englishmen. A common sight in some places was the beaver, though sadly a rarity today. This pleasant aquatic mammal is remembered in the place-names **Beversbrook** (Wiltshire) and **Beverley** (Yorkshire), where the streams concerned are **Fisher's Brook** and the tributaries of the **River Hull**. Otters too, were noticed in the **River Itchen** in Hampshire and gave the nearby settlement **Otterbourne** its pleasing name. Badgers must have been familiar visitors to the river's edge at **Broxbourne** in Hertfordshire to earn a memory in its place-name, while **Catford** (Kent) recalls the rather curious spectacle of shy wild-cats seen drinking at the water's edge.

All animals need to frequent the riversides as a source of drinking water and deer represent one of the bigger species that were often seen to come to the stream's margin. **Roeburn** (Lancashire) and **Harford** (Cheshire) are places where these beautiful, but nervous creatures would have been seen to drink.

The enemy of such creatures, as I have mentioned previously, but one which was long revered for its fearless courage, was the wolf and there may be a memory of this creature in the place-names **Little** and **Great Wolford** in Warwickshire, where the animal was perhaps seen at the nearby **Nethercote Brook**.

Many birds and fish feature, as one would expect, in place-names ending in '-*bourne*' and '-*brook*' – a variety of birds in **Birdbrook** (Essex), cuckoos in **Exbourne**, (Devon – *'gēacs-burna'*), various fish in **Fishbourne** (Sussex). Eels could be taken from Auburn Beck in the now vanished Yorkshire village of **Auburn** and pike were to be found in **Pickburn** (Yorkshire). **Beaford** (Devon), however, sustains the questionable distinction of harbouring that seasonal plague of all livestock, the gadfly (known as the warblefly in some districts). The place-name is based upon the Old English word for a horse-fly, *'bēaw'*. Doubtless the amphibian that has bequeathed its name to **Polebrook**, (the frog, '*pocce*'), in Northamptonshire, could have dreamt of a grand time swallowing the summer gadflies in **Beaford**.

And so we reach the end of our journey in search of place-names along the many flowing waters of Anglo-Saxon England. The variety is astonishing, as we have seen and I have dealt with only a modest fraction of the possible places associated with the old stream and river words. But it is time to move on to another watery aspect of the English landscape, the lake and to look at the Anglo-Saxon treatment of its place-names.

LAKES

The locations of England's natural lakes are not immediately obvious when one opens an atlas to the map of the British Isles and it takes quite close scrutiny to locate the country's major expanses of still water. The largest and most familiar stretches of calm water are to be found in modern-day Cumbria – formerly the north-western counties of Westmorland and Cumberland, together with parts of Lancashire and western Yorkshire. The Dales of Yorkshire and Derbyshire have their collections of small lakes too, but it is to Cumbria that we must turn for the most important of England's natural lakes. The uniqueness of such a national feature as the Cumbrian lakes has long been celebrated by naming its location 'The Lake District' and recognising the value of its setting by establishing the whole region as a National Park in 1951. Aside from the outstanding natural beauty of the country and its special literary associations (Wordsworth, Taylor Coleridge, Southey and the other 'Lakes Poets'), the names of the lakes are illustrious and abide in the memory as clearly as their vistas remain in the mind's eye. The rugged, mountainous terrain, with its deep valleys and high bowls ('cirques') is a perfect natural environment for lakes of all sizes to have formed after the last glacial age. There are about twenty large lakes and over seventy smaller ones, many of which are called 'Tarns'. However, although England's largest lake, Windermere, is often known as 'Lake' Windermere, only one of the major lakes officially incorporates the word 'Lake' into its name – **Bassenthwaite Lake** – while no fewer than fourteen of the rest are called 'Water'. Four of the larger lakes' names incorporate the suffix '-*mere*', an adoption into Old English from the Latin '*mare*', originally meaning 'the sea', but almost always by this period, referring to a lake or pool. Of the four '-mere' names – **Buttermere**, **Grasmere**, **Thirlmere** and **Windermere** – only **Thirlmere** lacks a village partner of the same name. Interestingly, Wiltshire too, has a tiny hamlet called **Buttermere**, a few miles south of Hungerford and which lies high on the Downs. The village still has a modest pool, called Buttermere Pond, which may have been the progenitor of the place-name, though the village's history stretches back into early mediæval times and there may have been something larger than the present pool a thousand years ago. At any rate, such a descriptive place-name as **Buttermere** suggests that both villages must have had reassuringly rich pastureland for their milking cattle or perhaps the margins of each were bedecked with seasonal butter-yellow flowers – marigolds, daffodils, buttercups.

Clearly, the word 'mere' was a commonly used title for any body of water, no matter of what size – from a modest pool to a great lake, whereas the word 'lake' seems usually, though not quite always, to have been applied to the more substantial natural stretches of water.

Of the many Cumbrian Lakes whose names include the word 'water', only a few have a village of a similar name: **Coniston, Elterwater, Rydal** and **Loweswater** for example and of these four, only **Rydal** is of a strictly Old English origin – 'rye hill', the others each having a Scandinavian component (see Chapter Five).

If we were to look through a list of England's 'lakes', we would be struck by the huge number of these waters that are now called 'reservoir'. This is not surprising really for, as the need for industrial and domestic supplies of water grew between the 18th and the 20th centuries, huge volumes had to be stored and artificial lakes had to be created, often from small 'meres' lying in shallow valleys and usually to the annoyance of nearby communities, who sometimes had to forsake their homes as their valleys were commandeered for the building of dams and the subsequent flooding.

Another feature of the list of English 'lakes' that would emerge on careful investigation, is that many have been formed as the result of mans' other activities such as the establishment of canal feeder reservoirs, like **Chasewater** in Staffordshire, the flooding of pits after gravel extraction, such as **Caversham Lakes** in Berkshire, the creation of ornamental lakes on grand estates and latterly, the building of leisure activity centres – often incorporating nature-reserves like that at **Rudyard** (Staffordshire).

Man has always made the most of his local resources and twelve-hundred years ago, lakes would have been a useful source of fish for his modest cottage table, as the place-names **Fishmere** (Lincolnshire), **Fishlake** (Yorkshire) and **Pickmere** – 'pike lake' (Cheshire) surely confirm. There is no lake now at either **Fishmere** or **Fishlake**, but the small lake called Pick Mere still lies on the edge of the village of **Pickmere**, not far from the town of Northwich in Cheshire.

Lakeside birds too, could be taken by artful villagers, for their cottage cooking pots. **Fowlmere** (Cambridgeshire) still has a small nearby area of wetland where wild birds can be found; **Enmore** (Somerset) also retains its comma-shaped pool and was a place to catch ducks ('*ęned-mere*' – duck-lake). **Elterwater** and neighbouring **Eltermere** (Cumbria) were places to encounter swans ('*ięlfetu*') and would assure a hungry 11th century family a good meal or two.

Animals stepping down to sip at the water's edge might also find themselves unexpected quarry for poachers. Wild cats were seen by 10th century cottagers to make cautious visits to a pool near **Catmere End** (Essex), just a few miles from **Fowlmere**, mentioned in the last paragraph. Maps show the position of an ancient 'fish pond' on the edge of the village. A small mere at **Catmore** in Berkshire must also have been a frequent watering place for wild cats. This pool is now probably rather smaller than in the old days, but it still exists. Cats may not seem to have much to offer, but rotting cat flesh was often used as a lure for other, more serviceable creatures, especially by the eel catchers of the Fens.

Woolmer Forest and **Woolmer Down** ('wolf-mere *hill*') in Hampshire recall that most revered of wild animals, the wolf, which obviously had been seen to come down to the pools to drink. **Barmer** in Norfolk may possibly hold the rather alarming distinction of recording in its name a small lake at which bears had been seen. However, given the English location, '*bār*' – a boar – may perhaps seem a more likely candidate than a bear, if it weren't that early documents record the place-name as *Beremere,* indicating that its origins do indeed lie in the Old English word for a bear, '*bera*'. **Barmere** in Cheshire may also have the same origin, though there is no sufficiently early written evidence traceable at present to verify it. Only a trace of the site of a pool can be seen near the Norfolk **Barmer** today, but my road map shows that the Bar Mere is still in place in Cheshire.

Less fearsome, but perhaps also less expected creatures that have given their names to English lakes and meres are the hedgehog, giving the name **Ilmer** (Buckinghamshire, from '*igil*' – a hedgehog) and the gnat in **Pymore** (Dorset – from '*pīe*' – a biting insect). **Ilmer** now seems to have only a few tiny pools remaining, but **Pymore** has retained a variety of small meres.

Fenemere, a small lake a few miles north of Shrewsbury, will no doubt have had its share of visiting wild life, but another, unexpected quality gave rise to its name, for '*fynig-mere*' meant 'stale-smelling lake'.

If there was little else to distinguish a local mere, its shape might suffice. **Widmerpool** (Nottinghamshire) meant simply 'wide mere-pool' and **Bradmore** and **Bradmer**, both also in Nottinghamshire, were each 'the broad mere'. The village of **Ringmer** (Sussex) must once have possessed a 'round pool', though the only nearby water today is adjacent to a works half a mile to the north.

Before leaving the natural lakes and meres of England, I'd like to allow the final bow to be taken by a couple of pleasant small ones – a 'Mere' and a 'Lake'. **Hornsea Mere**, close to the Yorkshire coast, derives its name from its angular shape and a small neck of land projecting into the lake from its eastern bank, perhaps reminding those early English observers of an animal's, or perhaps even a musical, horn. **Fonthill Lake** in Wiltshire, in a delightful setting, roughly between Warminster and Shaftesbury, has the Old English word '*font*' (a spring) as the first element of its name. The second element, '*-hill*', may originate in the Welsh word '*iâl*', meaning 'an upland pasture', which seems to make good sense when one looks at the attractive nearby countryside.

WEIRS

After the discussion on rivers and lakes, it would seem sensible next to deal with a man-made feature so closely associated with flowing water that it too has contributed to the names of many riverside villages throughout the country. The weir, or dam, is an ancient idea that can be traced back at least to the Roman era in Britain. Initially, its purpose was to create a water trap to hoard river fish and prevent their freedom of movement downstream. A barrier of wooden posts would be driven into the bed of the stream, or a dam of stone would be built across a gently flowing stream or river at a point chosen to allow a reasonable depth of water to back up without flooding the surrounding land, thus raising the level of the water on the upstream side. A steady, but shallow overflow would be allowed to breach the dam so that the water would continue to flow downstream, but no fish of useful size would pass over the barrier. Because of the continuing current, most fish would be confined to the weir pool thus created and could be caught easily. In order that settlements further downstream would not be starved of river fish, many weirs were of a funnel pattern, the narrow outlet being blocked by a stout wooden gate whenever fish needed to be taken. The gate would then be pulled clear to allow the river to return to its normal flow.

In a later period, side-channels would be dug and rivers would be divided so that the side stream could be dammed and no interruption to the main flow would be suffered by villages further downstream. Later still, these side streams would drive watermills as well as becoming fish pools.

A more descriptive place-name could hardly be imagined, in our present context, than that of the Shropshire village of **Weirbrook**, which lies against the Weir Brook. Reversing the syllables of this place-name, we obtain **Brockweir** in Gloucestershire, on the River Wye. Each place clearly had its ancient fish-weir.

Among other place-names which contain variations of the word 'weir', are **Weare** (Somerset), **Ware** (Hertfordshire), **Wargrave** (Berkshire) and **Edgware** (Middlesex). All are very close to the streams on which their mediæval weirs were constructed. The first three are listed in Domesday (1086), while **Edgware's** earliest record dates from AD 972 and refers to its landholder, one *Ecgi,* thus making it '*Ecgi's-weir*'.

On the banks of the **River Wear** in the city of Durham and in the grounds of present day Kepier Farm, is the site of an ancient monastery (**Kepier** – originally Kypier). Twelve hundred years ago, the river must have provided the monks with a good supply of fish since the word **Kepier** comes from the Old English '*cȳpe*', meaning a basket of woven sticks for catching fish and placed across a weir.

An obvious alternative word for weir is 'dam' and there is a handful of place-names which include this element. In **Burleydam** (Cheshire), the '*-dam*' suffix is a later addition to the name Burley, but is clearly a reference to a weir constructed on the nearby tributary of **Bennett Brook**. **Damgate** in Norfolk, **Dam Side** and **Dam Head** in Lancashire each suggest the presence of weirs, all three being sited on a stream.

Finally, **Yarm** (Yorkshire) and **Crewe** (Cheshire) make unexpected reference to weirs. **Yarm's** origin lies in the Old English word '*gear*' (pronounced 'yar'), meaning 'a fish enclosure', which must have operated in the **River Tees** or in its tributary the **River Leven,** adjacent to the village. We see the same idea at work in **Yarpole** (Herefordshire – 'fish enclosure'). The familiar place-name **Crewe**, although probably from the Welsh '*cryw*', also recalls a weir-like structure with stepping stones on which to cross the water – either the **River Weaver** or the **Valley Brook** in this case.

If ever the reader passes through the Warwickshire village of **Wootton Wawen** on the Birmingham to Stratford-on-Avon road, an impressive weir can be seen at close quarters as the road passes over the **River Alne**, flowing through the grounds of the 17th century Wootton Hall.

So here we can readily pass from our brief look at England's ancient weirs and on to a closely related topic.

POOLS

It may be that the reader's first thought is that a simple pool has little of interest to offer by way of historical relevance. However, what we now think of as the village pond is usually not the 'pool' that gives some places their names. The ancient pool in question will have lain just outside the boundary of the village dwellings and will have been an entirely natural feature of the landscape. It may have been no more than the size of the village itself in area, or it may have been many times that, but if it was well served with both a feeder and a relief stream, it was an invaluable resource for the small community, providing water for grazing animals, as well as for humans. It was therefore, in everyone's interests that it should be kept in good order and indeed, a villager whose cottage was close to the pool might be expected to keep it free of overgrowth and weeds and ensure a good flow of usable, clean water. Such a man would doubtless be called 'the poolman', a nickname that would eventually stick and, in the 12th or 13th centuries, would become a permanent surname – Pullman. In some localities, other nicknames might be used, like Poole, Pooler, Pooley, and sometimes Poll. These would follow suit and become English surnames in their own right too.

Not all villages of course, were blessed with an adjacent natural pool, though most habitations would not be far from a river, stream or brook. It was therefore, a sensible step for early English peasants to divert a nearby stream closer to the village and into a prepared hollow, lined with waterproof clay if possible, the relief stream returning to the main bed outside the village.

Even the poorest villeins knew the dangers of drinking unboiled water, for in every community there were occasional deaths from typhoid, cholera and other water-borne infections, especially in the children. It was not until the 20th century that the last of England's remote settlements were able to draw on clean mains' water and had, until then, still to rely on springs, brooks and wells for their supplies. Many, though by no means all, of the ornamental pools we like to see in our country villages, are the vestiges of the ancient village water resource now turned into attractive and characteristic features of the English village.

By the 10th century, two words were commonly used for a pool – '*pōl*' and '*pull*' – and we see these in a variety of forms in English place-names. The pool's most obvious appearance of course, is in the common place-name **Poole**. Places of this name, sometimes spelt **Pool**, are to be found in Dorset, Wiltshire, Somerset, Devon, Gloucestershire and Cheshire. Many settlements had a pool within their boundaries, so it is rather surprising that such a common local feature should be the source of so many place-names. If the village pool were exceptional in some way – deep, broad, circular, long or full of weeds – it might be expected to receive notice in an elaborated description such as **Radipole** (Dorset – 'reedy pool'), **Liverpool** (Lancashire – 'dirty pool'), **Bradpole** (Dorset – 'broad pool) and **Blackpool** (Lancashire – 'pool of dark water'). Pools are magnets for birds of course, and **Cople** in Bedfordshire must have been particularly attractive to them, for it means 'cock's pool', '*cocc*' being the common word for water birds. If the pool belonged to a particular landholder, it might be known after him – **Hampole** (Yorkshire – '*Hana's* pool') and **Walpole** (Suffolk – 'the Welshman's pool').

An interesting pair of descriptive pool-names is **Melplash** (Dorset – 'mill pool') and **Fulledge** (Lancashire – '*fūl-lœcc*' – 'foul pool'). One can only guess at the justification for conferring such an unflattering name on a pool, though it must have been given by those living close by. **Claypole** (Lincolnshire) tells of a pool, less objectionable perhaps, but still lacking clear water, for it means 'clay-pool' ('*clœg-pōl*'). Pools could become stagnant in hot weather and were easily susceptible to contamination from wildlife and cattle. The two **Harpoles** (Kent and Northamptonshire) have suffered the same misfortune, for this name is directly from the Old English '*horh-pōl*' – dirty pool. The Northamptonshire village of **Harpole** still has a significant nearby pool called The Lake and water meadows beside the **River Nene**, either of which might have given rise to the description, which dates from before Domesday (1086). The nearest standing water to the Kent hamlet of **Harpole** today is a small pool half a mile away and may not relate to the name.

Islands

When the word 'island' is mentioned, most people tend first to think of something lying offshore – the **Isle of Wight** perhaps, England's biggest coastal island and called *Vectis* by Pliny, the 1st century Roman author, or perhaps they will think of Lundy Island off the Devon coast. However, a land as criss-crossed by rivers as is England, is bound to have hundreds of river-islands as well as hundreds more of the type which rise only a few feet above marshes and fens. If asked to name a non-coastal English island, many people will have to scratch their heads for some time and, unless they live close to an example, they may not be able to give an answer at all. The **River Thames** has almost one hundred named islands in its 215 mile length and a glance down a list of their names reveals that 14 of them are termed '*Eyot*' rather than 'Island' – **Appletree Eyot**, near Reading in Berkshire, **Rod's Eyot** at Henley, Oxfordshire and **Headpile Eyot** at Bray in Berkshire are some of them. No fewer than 16 Thames islands are termed '*Ait*'– for example, **Garrick's Ait** at Hampton in London, **Bush Ait** at Windsor and **Lot's Ait** at Brentford in London. One other variation on this theme is to be seen in the Thames-island name, **Sonning Eye** in Berkshire. This curious naming pattern ('*eyot*', '*ait*', and '*eye*') derives from a local pronunciation of the Old English word for an island, '*iēg*' (pronounced 'yay').

A look at the map of **Sonning Eye** will show that it is bounded on all sides by flowing streams and is a true island, though it does not lie in the main Thames channel. This form of island is very common and is remembered in many names ending in '*-ey*', '*-ea*' and occasionally '*-y*', '*-ay*' and '*-oy*'. Here is a selection of twelve from across the country, showing all of these suffixes:

Island name	County	Original form	Meaning
Battersea	Surrey	Badrices ege	Island of *Beaduric*
Brightlingsea	Essex	Brictriceseia	*Brihtrīc's* Island
Campsea	Suffolk	Campeseia	Island with an enclosure
Eastrea	Cambridgeshire	Ēastor-ēg	Eastern part of the island
Godney	Yorkshire	Godeneia	*Gōda's* Island
Longney	Gloucestershire	Longanege	Long island
Osney	Oxfordshire	Osanig	*Ōsa's* Island
Bunny	Nottinghamshire	Bonei	Reed island
Denny	Cambridgeshire	Daneya	Island of the Danes
Bungay	Suffolk	Bongeia	Island of *Buna's* people
Wormegay	Norfolk	Wirmegeie	*Wyrm's* Island
Chedzoy	Somerset	Chedesie	*Cedd's* Island

The 'islands' which are shown in the table to be in the Fen counties, that is Cambridgeshire, Norfolk and eastern Suffolk, were indeed islands amid the surrounding marshlands of the Fens until the area was drained in the 18th century. Nowadays, the villages are 'dry', though usually within sight of streams and channels.

Some islands were named for the very distinct purposes for which they were habitually used by the landholder: **Goosey** (Berkshire) was an island where geese were kept, **Horsey** (Norfolk) and **Horse Eye** (Sussex) were homes to horses, while calves were safely pastured on **Chalvey** ('*cealf-iēg*') in Buckinghamshire. Early farmers, who chose to live and work in fenland and other extensively marshy areas, had little option but to allocate 'islands' a few feet above the waterline to their livestock. It is not a surprise therefore, that such spots were referred to by the name of the animals commonly grazed or penned there.

Sometimes islands became nicknamed after the familiar wild visitors seen to frequent the places: **Henney** (Essex) and **Foulney** (Lancashire) were islands where wild fowl were usually seen, swans were to be found at **Iltney** in Essex ('*ielfetu*' – a swan); **Selsey** (Sussex), although at a coastal location, was frequented by seals; **Corney** (Cumbria) harboured wading birds called cranes, while bees seemed to have taken a distinct liking to **Dorney** in Berkshire ('*dora*' – a humblebee). **Kersey** (Suffolk), however, was clearly notable for its watercress.

So it's clear that there is rather more to the word 'island' than might have been thought at first: an area of land, sometimes quite large, but bounded on all sides by watercourses, often earned itself the name '*iēg*' – an island – and after twelve hundred years, many of their names, amazingly, are still with us.

Bays and coves

As part of a greater island, England's coastline has its share of bays, coves, creeks and inlets, though only on a modest scale when compared with Scotland. The word 'bay' itself is a 14th century introduction, having come from the French '*baie*' and by far outnumbers the alternatives in England's place-names. Our 9th century forebears of course, had a word, '*cofa*', to describe the coastal feature we now usually call a bay. The natural hardening of the letter 'f' to 'v' in speech, has brought us the useful word 'cove', which appears as a separate word in names of inlets around the coast: **Church Cove** and **Mullion Cove** (near The Lizard in Cornwall), **Lulworth Cove** (Dorset) and **Countisbury Cove** (Devon). The villages of **North** and **South Cove** in Suffolk look as though they were, at one time, close to a small cove which has now disappeared as the sea has retreated. Of the two other places called simply **Cove** (Devon and Hampshire), the Devon village illustrates the other meaning of '*cofa*' – a recess in a steep hillside – in this case, a long way from the sea. **Discove**, near Bruton in Devon, also demonstrates this alternative inland feature.

Covehurst Bay (Hampshire), **Covehithe** (Suffolk – 'landing place at a cove'), **Wilcove** (Cornwall) and **Coverack** (Cornwall) well illustrate the familiar idea of a coastal cove.

Lastly on this topic, a curious case of a probable error by a clerk writing in a court record in the year 1252. It seems likely that he misread the name *Rumcua* in an earlier document from which he was copying and writes *Runcore*, which eventually becomes spoken as **Runcorn** (Cheshire – '*rūm-cofa*' – an open bay).

WETLANDS – MARSHES, SWAMPS, BOGS AND FENS

Patches of marshy ground can be found all over the country of course, but the largest areas of wetland are the **Fens** and the Broads in the areas around The Wash on the east coast, where many thousands of acres of land are below sea level and very little rises more than about thirty feet above that level. The Somerset Levels and **Romney Marsh** (Kent) are notable wetlands with their own characteristic environments. Such difficult natural conditions made early habitation and agriculture extremely difficult and these areas of the country were very sparsely populated as a result. However, districts of generally much more favourable surface types could still have small areas of marsh and boggy ground where local natural drainage was poor, thus rendering the terrain hazardous to humans and quadrupeds.

There was a rather surprising number of words available to local 9th century Englishmen who wanted to describe this sort of waterlogged ground: 'fen', '*mersc*', '*mor*', '*mos*', '*slōh*', '*wæsse*' and later, in the so-called Middle English period, '*kerr*' and '*mire*'. It is easy to see that the first three in the list gave rise to our words 'fen', 'marsh' and 'moor', while '*slōh*' is the precursor of the old word 'slough' (pronounced 'slow' and meaning a marshy hollow). '*Mire*', a later addition, has remained unchanged as 'mire', but the others have not made themselves into words we can easily recognise today, though they are present in a number of our place-names.

Romney Marsh on the south coast of Kent, is a good place to begin our discussion because, within its current area of about 100 square miles, lie two other named marshes, **Walland Marsh** and **Denge Marsh** (that is, 'dung marsh') and two villages whose names include the word marsh, **Burmarsh** ('marsh belonging to the townsfolk') and **St.Mary-in-the-Marsh**. **Romney** itself, is mentioned in the Anglo-Saxon Chronicle for the year 1052 and appears in that record as *Rumenea* (probably meaning 'broad water').

Anyone who lives in the Shropshire villages of **Bagley Marsh**, **Edgmond Marsh** or **Maesbury Marsh**, will probably appreciate the reason for their village's name, for there are nearby rivers and their tributary streams running across the local relatively low-lying land, which must have turned the ground into a quagmire in mediæval times. There are many place-names that incorporate the name Marsh, either as a second word, as in those just mentioned, or as the principal word – **Marsh Benham** (Berkshire) and **Marsh Gibbon** (Buckinghamshire) for example.

There are indeed places called simply **Marsh** or **The Marsh** in several counties and a look at a detailed map will show that almost all lie within the influence of one or more nearby streams that would very probably have been the origin of the waterlogged ground recalled in their names. However, one or two places are on rather higher ground than one might expect and the explanation may well be that the local water table meets the surface at that point and so saturated the surrounding land surface. Of course, there are many instances of single-word names where 'marsh' is found both as prefix and as suffix: **Marshfield** (Gloucestershire), **Marsham** (Norfolk) and **Stodmarsh** (Kent – 'marsh where horses are kept'), for example, but there are also cases where the word is heavily disguised. Would you have guessed that **Marske** (Yorkshire) concealed the word and meant 'place at the marsh' or that the word is deeply hidden in the place-name **Lamas** (Norfolk), which means 'lamb marsh'?

It's probably no surprise that a great many place-names containing the word '*fen*' are to be found in the counties of Cambridgeshire, Lincolnshire and western Norfolk, for this is the area of England known as **The Fens**. However, unlike the name **Marsh**, I am unable to locate a place called simply Fen or Fenn, though there are many farms and other small local sites which include the word in their names. Fenn of course, is also an established surname. The place-name nearest in its simplicity, seems to be **Fen Bog** in Yorkshire, a name that rather waggishly describes its situation in duplicate. It is not a village name, however, but a genuine bog, which stretches for nearly a mile beside the North Yorkshire Railway Line as it traverses Goathland Moor, about ten miles south of Whitby. A glance through a gazetteer will reveal dozens of other place-names based on the word 'fen', most of which recall their ancient wetland situations.

My final inclusion is again a case of effective concealment. Who would have thought that **Vange** (Essex) is really a curious transformation of the word 'fen'? It is true, for its origin lies in the Old English '*fen-gē*' – 'fen district' and is recorded as *Phenge* in Domesday (1086). The nearby area is low-lying and is indeed marshy and is called Vange Marshes which, together with the adjacent Fobbing Marshes, cover an area of about three square miles. Apart from any other considerations concerning the name **Vange**, it has the small distinction of being one of very few English place-names that begin with the letter 'V'.

Moors are usually thought of as being wide, almost featureless stretches of heathland with poor soil and little but a few rocks to relieve the monotonous vista, but the word *'mor'* was sometimes used to indicate an area of boggy terrian, whether on uplands or in low-lying districts. **Morborne** (Cambridgeshire) is fairly clearly 'marsh stream', while the Shropshire village of **More** lies in a fen-like area beside the **River West Onny**. **Morden** (Surrey and Dorset) must once have been 'the hill in the marsh'. Of course, many of the place-names which end in *'-more'* or *'-moor'* will have been applied to a moorland settlement with no suggestion of poorly drained ground. **Blackmore** (Essex – 'black moor') and **Moorsholm** (Sussex – 'dwelling on the high moor') demonstrate this. The situation is complicated further when one finds that the suffix *'-more'* has, in some places, become a spoken variation of *'-mere'* – a lake – in some cases, such as in **Colmore** in Hampshire, which means 'cold lake'. **Catmore** (Berkshire), mentioned earlier in the chapter, is really 'cat-mere'.

We should remember too, that Moor, Moore and More are fairly common surnames, given originally to one whose dwelling was on a moor or near to a patch of upland boggy ground – that is unless he had not already been nicknamed Marsh, Fenn or Moss by his fellows.

A common element in English place-names is *'mos'* (a morass or swamp) and shows itself in several forms as varied as **Moss** (Yorkshire), **Moze** (Essex), **Moston** (Shropshire) and **Mozergh** (Cumbria), as well as in doublets like **Moss End** in Berkshire and **Hesketh Moss** in Lancashire. Two districts particularly rich in *'moss'* names are the Yorkshire Dales and the Peak District of Derbyshire, where they describe areas of local swampy ground rather than settlements.

Less commonly applied, but nevertheless an important feature of place-names found in marshy landscapes, were the words *'slōh'* and *'wæsse'*. A couple of examples of each are interesting: **Slough** (Buckinghamshire) itself, is a later rendering of the word *'slōh'* while **Polsloe** (Devon – 'marsh with, or near a pool') shows it as a suffix. Place-names featuring the word 'wash', the modern form of *'wæsse'*, can sometimes refer to marshy locations. However, it is thought likely that the wide bay known as **The Wash** (East Anglia) derived its name more from the 'washing' motion of the sea, than directly from the old word *'wæsse'*. **Washingley** (Cambridgeshire) indicates a swamp close by, perhaps associated with the existing small, nearby pool and several small streams. **Wass** (Yorkshire) is also the embodiment of the old word *'wæsse'*, for it lies in a valley where several streams drain from the heights of Wass Moor.

Wass, incidentally, is not a rare surname – the mainland telephone books record several hundred holders of the name countrywide, though it may also be a foreign name in some cases.

Although we shall be jumping ahead a little in time by doing so, we should perhaps briefly look at the two later words related to wetlands that appear in place-names – '*kerr*' and '*mire*'. Both words are related to Old Scandinavian words which had filtered their way into English later on in the 10th century. '*Kerr*' most often referred to a patch of marsh which was overgrown with scrub. **Bescar** (Lancashire – 'birch marsh') and **Ellerker** (Yorkshire – 'alder marsh') actually name the prevalent vegetation, while **Broadcar** (Norfolk – 'wide marsh') and **Holker** (Lancashire – 'bog in a hollow') are more general descriptions.

'*Mire*' is one of those annoyingly deceptive elements when it appears in a place-name, for it can simply be a regional transformation of '-*mere*' – a lake or pool – so we must be cautious. **Redmire** (Yorkshire) looks promising, but its Domesday (1086) entry (*Ridemare*) shows it to mean 'a reedy lake'. However, a few names do retain the original meaning of '*mire*': **Myerscough** (Lancashire – 'marshy wood') and **Birkett Mire** (Cumbria – 'marsh at the birch copse'), for example. Of course, our useful word 'quagmire' originates in the old word too ('*quag*' also meaning a marsh).

To end with, a few place-names that recall ditches and dykes (both of these words coming from the Old English word '*dīc*'). Ditches, as drainage features, are very familiar to us, but a dyke – an earth bank, sometimes strengthened with stone, the purpose of which is usually to hold back or channel a body of water – is perhaps less often encountered these days. The wetlands, especially in the east and south-west of England, were always prone to flooding and dykes and ditches became essential to prevent isolated habitations and trackways from being submerged or washed away. As such, these were important man-made features and were subjected to careful maintenance. Their local significance has ensured their survival in place-names. **Ditton** (Buckinghamshire – 'settlement near the ditch') and particularly **Fen Ditton** in Cambridgeshire, are reminders of the value placed on the dyke. Yorkshire has several places which include the name **Deighton**, signifying a settlement that had a protective embankment or dyke. The place-name **Dyke** itself, exists in both Lincolnshire and Devon. **Car Dyke**, a name that crops up in several counties, usually describes a water feature. The Lincolnshire **Car Dyke** ('dyke of one called *Kārr*') is typical of the drainage dykes that remove surface water from low-lying pastures in that area. **Biddick** (Durham) and **Dickley** (Essex) tell of settlements beside significant local ditches. Finally, I might mention a dyke whose construction is either mysteriously attributed to the god *Woden*, or perhaps more likely, was dedicated to him. This is **Wansdyke** ('*Wodnes dīc*'), which runs through Wiltshire and into Somerset.

FORDS

The ford has given us one of the most familiar elements to be found in English place-names. It is most often seen as a suffix and usually appears as either '-ford' or '-forth'. As a consequence of its frequency, most of us will be able to think of someone whose surname begins or ends with *'ford'* as well as recalling several place-names containing the word. It is perhaps understandable why it has become such a common syllable in place-names, for the river-crossing place was an important and well-used spot near most villages. Shallow river beds were easy crossing places and saved the villagers the trouble of constructing bridges. The importance of this natural resource is reflected in the fact that the name **Ford** occurs as a 'stand-alone' place-name in no fewer than fourteen English counties. The location or nature of a ford would be certain to attract nicknames: if it were an especially broad crossing, **Bradford** (found in nearly a dozen counties) would be a likely name; a ford under the alder trees would be called **Allerford** (Somerset), or if it were in an ash grove, it would inevitably be the **Ashford** (Devon, Derbyshire); a dirty or muddy crossing might acquire the name **Fulford** (Staffordshire – 'foul ford'), while a sandy crossing-place would earn itself the nickname **Sandford** (Shropshire, Oxfordshire, Cumbria, Devon). There are place-names recalling shallow fords, long fords, noisy fords, stony fords, chalk fords, harvest fords and even double fords – **Twyford** (in at least eight counties); the possibilities are very numerous.

Many of England's fords are called after creatures that were found nearby or which, under the bidding of their human masters, would regularly pass across a certain ford. I've listed a dozen of these in the table below:

Place-name	County	Meaning
Beaford	Devon	Gadfly ford ('*bēaw*')
Catforth	Lancashire	Wild-cat ford ('*catte*')
Cornforth	Durham	Crane ford ('*cranoc*')
Durford	Sussex	Deer ford ('*dēor*')
Enford	Wiltshire	Duck ford ('*ened*')
Gateford	Nottinghamshire	Goat ford ('*gāt*')
Gosforth	Cumbria	Goose ford ('*gōs*')
Hartford	Cheshire	Stag ford ('*heorot*')
Horsforth	Yorkshire	Horse ford ('*hors*')
Ketford	Gloucestershire	Kite ford ('*cȳta*')
Lostford	Shropshire	Lynx ford ('*lox*')
Oxford	Oxfordshire	Oxen ford ('*oxa*')
Swinford	Berkshire	Pig ford ('*swīn*')

Some river crossings were named after a person who lived at that location, or on whose land holding the ford was situated. **Alford** is a village which lies on the **River Brue** in Somerset and rather unusually, takes its name from a woman who had some connection with that place. The Domesday (1086) scribe records the place as *Aldedeford* and it is known that the woman's name was *Ealdgȳþ*. The hamlet of **Bickford** in Staffordshire recalls the name of a man, *Bica*, who was somehow associated with a nearby crossing of **Whiston Brook**. There is still a ford in existence across the Brook. In some places, a family or a settlement of people under the leadership of a head man may be remembered in the name. **Wallingford** (Oxfordshire) is one of many such places and means 'the ford (over the River Thames) of *Wealh's* people'. In almost all of such cases, we will have no other information about the man, or woman, than his or her personal name, which has lived through the centuries by virtue of the survival of the place-name. This is certainly true for the woman *Ealdgȳþ*, mentioned earlier. How fascinating it would be to know more about the people whose names are now all that we have.

The word 'ford' makes an appearance at the beginning of a number of place-names too. **Fordingbridge** (Hampshire) is an appropriate example, for its central syllable, '-ing-' points to a place associated with a group of people, as in **Wallingford** above. In this case it means 'the bridge of the people living near the ford'. The Domesday (1086) entry for **Fordington** (Lincolnshire) – *Fortintone* – shows that this too, refers to 'the settlement of the people who dwell at the ford'. A road bridge now crosses the stream where that ancient ford probably lay.

Lastly, five of the English counties include the element '-ford-' as the middle element of their names: **Bedfordshire, Herefordshire, Hertfordshire, Oxford-shire** and **Staffordshire**. In that order, we have, 'the district around *Bīeda's* ford', 'the shire of the army's river-crossing-place', 'the county of the stag crossing', 'the district around the oxen ford' and 'the shire of the ford with a landing place'.

At this point, I think we can comfortably bring to an end our investigation into the variety of water-based natural – and a few man-made – features of the countryside and pass on to look at another powerful geographical component of the English landscape.

Uplands and lowlands

It would seem that the 5th and 6th century Angles, Saxons, Jutes, Frisians and maybe the Franks, made landfall on the British coast closest to their continental departure points – the east and south-east coasts. Although these peoples spoke dialects of the same Germanic language, their natural inclination to maintain their separate tribal cohesions, once in their new territory, prompted them to migrate in different directions. The Saxons moved to the west and south – hence the long-surviving districts of **Essex**, **Sussex**, **Wessex** and **Middlesex**, meaning East, South, West and Middle Saxons. The Angles swung northwards to occupy **Norfolk**, **Suffolk** (now known of course, as East Anglia – that is 'the east Angle-land'), **Lincolnshire** and the east Midlands (to be named Mercia) and eventually into Northumberland. The Jutes quietly settled in the south east (**Kent** and **Hampshire**).

Expansion westwards was relatively rapid and by AD 600, about three-quarters of England was occupied and controlled by the descendants of the new settlers. Wales, Scotland, western **Cumberland** (now **Cumbria**) and the West Country, that is **Devon** and **Cornwall**, however, had not been subdued.

From their adopted homelands in the eastern quarter of England, the four or five generations of westward-bound Saxons would have encountered such uplands as the **Chiltern Hills**, the southern reaches of the **Cotswolds**, the **North** and **South Downs**, the **Berkshire Downs**, **Salisbury Plain** and the **Mendips**. None of these terrains would have presented any difficulties to the roving Saxons. However, the Angles, in their passage north and north-westwards, would have rather different experiences: firstly, they would have encountered the marsh-covered fenlands of Lincolnshire at one extreme before, at the other extreme, the mountains we now call the Pennines, stretching northwards for over two hundred and fifty miles and increasing in ruggedness all the time. The Angles, nevertheless, were not discouraged in their thrust northwards. The Jutes seemed to be content with their modest southern territories until the western Jute tribes of **Hampshire** and the **Isle of Wight** became absorbed into the Saxon advance westwards, leaving **Kent** as their only remaining domain. The Frisians and any Franks that were among the new occupiers of 6th century Britain appear to have become assimilated into the Saxon fold and have left little trace in place-names (but see the opening paragraph of this chapter for mention of six known early Frisian settlement names).

As the Saxons moved west in their searches for more good pasture, fertile soils and land on which to establish their settlements, it would not be long before the words '*dūnland*', '*denu*' and '*dæl*' would have been on the lips of the leaders, for these were the words for 'hilly country', 'shallow valley' and 'deep valley'. It is from these Saxon words that our 'down', 'dean' and 'dale' have descended. Our road maps will show us the **North** and **South Downs** and the

Wiltshire Downs and any number of place-names ending in '-*don*', indicating some association with a nearby hill. Both 'dean' and 'dale' have also attached themselves to countless words to make hundreds of village and town names. As I have mentioned before, the passage of time and the mannerisms of regional speech often disguise forms and therefore meanings. Place-names originally ending in '-*den*' or '-*don*' will easily sound the same in everyday speech and their spellings therefore, will often be misleading if we are searching for their origins. So it is essential to look back at the earliest available written documents to try to decide whether the name refers to a valley or a hillside. An example of this blurring effect of meanings is to be found in the name **Basildon**. There are two places of this name. The Essex town's Domesday (1086) entry is *Berles-duna*, which clearly refers to a hill ('*Beorhtel's* hill'), while the Berkshire village of **Basildon**, to the west of Reading, is recorded as *Bastedene*, which must relate to the valley inhabited by one named *Bæssel*. **Ballidon** (Derbyshire) presents a similar case: Domesday tells us that it was pronounced *Belidene*, thus giving it the meaning of a 'bag-shaped valley' ('*bælg*' – a sack). Domesday (1086) is a fascinating and invaluable interpretative and definitive tool in the repertoire of place-name investigators.

Dundon, (*Dondene* in Domesday, 1086), a delightful village in Somerset, may represent roughly the furthest point west to which the first wave of Saxons would advance for some time. It lies beside a picturesque hill and its name reflects this – 'at the bottom of a hillside slope'.

The above examples again show that people continued to be inventive and logical in their naming of natural features and would name nearby hills and valleys according to their shapes or after the person who held the land or by its particular vegetation or the animals seen to frequent the land. There are no English examples of a habitation place-name Don or Dun (though **Dun Street** can be found in Kent), but the name **Dean** can be found in seven English counties.

Many ranges of hills and high ground from Shropshire southwards have a tendency to be called Down or Downs, or to incorporate '-*down*' as a suffix. There are not many places north of Shropshire that use this nomenclature, which indicates that the Saxon movement was limited to the Midlands and the South-West and shows the specific influence of Saxon naming preferences. Apart from the vast downlands of Berkshire and Wiltshire, smaller upland features like **Chavey Down** (Berkshire), **Horsey Down** (Wiltshire), **Bishop's Down** (Dorset) and **Berkley Down** (Somerset) also reflect the wide use of the useful and evocative word.

The initial territory of the Angles – Suffolk, Norfolk, Cambridgeshire and the southern part of Lincolnshire – was almost wholly bereft of high ground. It was not until twenty miles had been covered, north from the River Welland's estuary at The Wash, that a sight of significant rising ground would have greeted them. Here, a long swathe of low hills, extending about thirty miles northwards, almost to the mouth of the River Humber, is known as the Lincolnshire Wolds ('*wald*' – a wooded upland). However, a glance at a road map of the area will quickly reveal hundreds of place-names ending in '*-by*' – an important legacy of a later invasion by yet another near-continental race and which we shall examine in Chapter Five.

Sixty miles to the west of the Lincolnshire Wolds lies the **Peak District**. This extensive area possesses hills far higher than the modest Lincolnshire summit called Wolds Top, which rises to 550 feet and is found a little to the north of **Normanby-le-Wold** (Lincolnshire). The Peak District's **Kinder Scout** is 2088 feet above sea level. The name Kinder is probably a very old British name and Scout derives from an Old Norse word for 'an overhanging rock'. However, it is to the word 'peak' that we must turn, for its origin lies in the Old English '*pēac*' – a pointed hill. Only one **Peak District** hill possesses the name 'peak' – **Calver Peak**, though three others have embraced the name 'pike' ('*pīc*' – a point) – **Eccles Pike**, **Pikenaze Hill** and **Pike Low**. Majestic as they are, these hills do not really qualify as mountains, though their beauty and the landscape must have appealed to the senses of the advancing Angles, for many settlements were established across the region during the 7th, 8th and 9th centuries. The upland nature of the terrain is reflected in the many Derbyshire settlement names having the '*-low*' suffix, from Anglo-Saxon '*hlāw*', meaning simply a hill: **Hucklow** (hill of *Hucca*), **Grindlow** (green hill), **Wardlow** (lookout hill) and **Baslow** (*Bassa's* hill).

To end with, there are one or two other similar names which refer to locally distinct hills: **Callow** (Herefordshire) described a hill bare of significant vegetation ('*calo-hlāw*' – bald hill), **Kelloe** (Durham – '*celf-hlāw*', calf hill) must have been applied to hillside where calves were grazed in the warmer months, and **Harlow** (Essex – '*here-hlāw*) was a hill where people gathered for meetings or even where an army ('*here*') had once been assembled.

The last of the many varieties of high ground we shall meet in this chapter centres on what would certainly have been a familiar sight to the new Englishmen in the 8th century, especially in the Midlands and South of the country – the '*hyrst*'. This was a wooded hill and even today there are many of these distinctive features still to be seen across the English countryside. This Old English word has become mildly transformed into '*hurst*' and '*hirst*' in our place-names and will be most familiar to us as the suffix in the name of a settlement close to the site of its companion wooded hill. The first element in these place-names is often the particular type of tree which grew on the hill or else some noticeable wild life to be seen amongst the trees: the villages of **Ashurst** in Kent and Sussex are still near to their '*hyrsts*', which may still include the ash trees; **Lyndhurst** (Hampshire) may also have its lime tree '*hyrst*' nearby; **Crowhurst** (Surrey) was home to flocks of crows and **Brockhurst** in Warwickshire must have been notable for its families of badgers.

There are, however, plenty of examples of the word 'hurst' as part of a doublet: **Cold Hurst** (Lancashire), **Hurst Hill** (Oxfordshire), **Rodd Hurst** (Herefordshire) and **Mill Hirst** (Yorkshire). Each of these places still lies next to its Mediæval wooded hill. The simple name **Hurst** itself, occurs in at least six counties from Kent to Cumbria.

We must not, however, forget the well-known and universally applied word 'hill' (Old English, '*hyll*'), which needs little comment: we can all name a dozen or more place-names containing this useful word.

A valley-word carried north by the Angle settlers was '*clōh*' and is a characteristic component of many place-names in the hilly districts in the north of England. Its direct derivative, **Clough**, is a place-name in Cumbria, Lancashire and Yorkshire and in each case the settlement lies in or near a steeply sloping valley. **Deepclough** (Derbyshire) and **Broadclough** (Lancashire) tell their own stories and **Wildboarclough** (Cheshire) seems to be self-explanatory too, though its first recorded mention is in the later Middle Ages (*Wildeborclogh*, 1357).

Another frequently met north-country valley-word from the Old English of the Angles, is '*dæl*' ('dale' in its modern guise) and a gazetteer of the northern counties will list many place-names incorporating this word. Perhaps the best known dales are in Yorkshire and the Lake District: **Wharfedale** ('valley of the River Wharfe') and **Langdale** (Cumbria – 'the long valley') are typical, while **Uldale** in Cumbria has the interesting distinction of being the 'wolf valley'. A small number of 'dales' are to be found in the south of England – Sussex has **Camelsdale** and **Dale Hill**, Surrey has **Forestdale**. **Colindale** is found in Middlesex, while **Crundale** is to be found in Kent. In the east of England there are **Botesdale** (Suffolk) and **Burnham Deepdale** (Norfolk), though both are villages in only very shallow valleys.

The suffix '*-hope*' and its abbreviations '*-op*', '*-ap*', '*-up*' and the occasional '*-pe*' can also indicate a valley setting. **Harehope** (Northumberland) and **Harrop**

(Yorkshire) each record a 'hare valley', while **Cowpe** (Lancashire) means 'cow valley'. **Bacup**, also in Lancashire, signifies a valley beneath a distinctive ridge ('*bæc*' – a back or ridge).

An unusual Old English word of dual meaning that was occasionally applied to small, shallow trackways that had been worn up a hillside, was '*pæþ*' (pronounced 'path', with the flattened 'a' sound as in 'hath'). We see this in **Horspath** (Oxford-shire – 'a sunken path for horses'), **Bagpath** (Gloucestershire), perhaps meaning 'badger's track' and in a gruesome recollection in **Morpeth** (Northumberland), where it recalls a 'murder path'. In **Sticklepath** (Somerset), however, it probably refers to no more than a steep track ('*sticol pæþ*').

'*Vale*' too, continued to give long and faithful service to our place-name inventory throughout the current era, though its roots lie in the Latin ('*vallis*') of the 1st century Roman occupiers of England (see Chapter Two).

At this point in our history we seem to have descended to the lower reaches of the upland story, but before we arrive at the moorlands, there is one more feature that I ought to mention, though it is to be found at the tops of the hills. It is the ridge. As early as Mesolithic times, wandering travellers often followed the tops of hills to traverse the countryside and the ridges were important components of these ancient trackways. Today, The Ridgeway is a length of a once much longer hilltop route across the southern half of England and the ancient Icknield Way follows the ridges of the **Chiltern Hills** for part of its route. The Old English word for a ridge was '*hrycg*' and can be found as both a prefix and a suffix in place-names. **Bledlow Ridge** (Buckinghamshire) and **Chobham Ridges** in Surrey mark the lines of two ancient trackways. Villages near to prominent local ridges often emphasise their location in their names: **Boveridge** (Dorset) lies high on a ridge, **Chartridge** (Buckinghamshire) lies along a Chiltern ridge and **Burridge** in Devon is over 600 feet high up on a ridge. Though not a ridge in name, **Harnage** (Shropshire) tells of a nearby steep or rocky edge ('*hār-ecg*' – grey edge).

Uplands across the whole of England are peppered with the name 'moor', often as the second word of a doublet. Derbyshire and Yorkshire are particularly richly served by this name, as a close look at a good map will show – **Horton Moor, Walden Moor, Carlton Moor, Cragdale Moor, Bradwell Moor, Cowms Moor, Blackden Moor . . .** there are dozens of them in these two counties alone. **Dartmoor** and **Exmoor** (Devon) tell of their association with the Rivers Dart and Exe, while **Otmoor** near Oxford was originally a marshy expanse – '*Otta's fen*', though it is now mostly drained and fertile.

Heaths too, were a distinct feature of higher ground where the soil was too poor or thin to support anything more than heather and gorse. Nevertheless, heaths themselves have generated a good many place names, often in the form of doublets – **Hampstead Heath** in London, **Bexley Heath** in Kent and **Balsall Heath** in Warwickshire are three well-known examples. Many places of course, incorporate the word 'heath' into a single name – **Blackheath** (Kent) described the dark nature of the foliage, **Broadheath** (Worcestershire) is self-explanatory and **Heathcote** (Derbyshire) tells of a cottage dwelling located high on the heathlands of the Peak District. Gorse and heather are components of a number of place-names, though not necessarily indicative of a heathland setting. **Gorsley** (Gloucestershire) was descriptive of a 'gorse-covered clearing', while **Fersfield** (Norfolk) and **Fresden** (Witshire) refer to furze, an alternative name for gorse. Yet another old gorse-name is '*whin*' and this occurs in the names **Whinburgh** (Norfolk – 'gorse-covered rise') and **Whinfell Beacon**, a Cumbrian peak. Heather itself features fairly strongly in our place-names too. **Heathfield** (Somerset), **Hadleigh** (Essex), **Headlam** (Durham) and **Hothfield** (Kent) demonstrate how diverse the spellings have become. Heather has also been a pleasant personal name for girls from about the 1880s.

At this point, after mentioning in this chapter about five hundred and fifty place-names deriving from natural features of the landscape, it's quite clear that we owe a huge debt to this fertile period of English history. But of course this is by no means the end of our study of the Anglo-Saxon era of English place-name formation, for we now must turn to the important impact on place-names made by the flora and fauna of the countryside, followed by the activities of the people themselves and these will need a chapter of their own.

Chapter 4

After the Romans – Anglo-Saxons (part ii)

Flora and Fauna - their importance in place-names

Trees

DURING THE WHOLE OF THE ANGLO-SAXON period of our history, woodland and heathland were being cleared and other wasteland reclaimed for the purposes of extending grazing pasture and expanding arable farming, in much the same way as it had been in the previous Romano-British era. This was an essential means to an end, for the population was increasing steadily and settlements were gradually growing in both number and in inhabitants. The ash-wood, the oak-lea and the elm-hurst were likely to become necessary casualties of the development, as the requirement for wood for building and for domestic fires was also increasing apace. Despite the needs, the natural resources could easily sustain the demands placed upon them, for the population's requirements were still small when compared with those of a millennium later, when the accelerating natural fuel consumption of the 'Industrial Revolution' began to threaten the supply of these environmental resources.

Woodlands were, of course, a conspicuous feature of the English landscape in the era we are considering and were the source of many types of wood, each with its own value. Each wood had special qualities which made it useful for building structures and making tools, utensils or weapons. Wood has been the most versatile of nature's provisions to man and cannot yet be said to have been wholly superseded by anything synthetic.

There are well over twenty species of tree and a dozen or so different shrubs and bushes that make an appearance in the English place-name inventory, which must indicate that the common people of the times could identify everything that grew around their localities. The oak-tree, of course, was an indispensible source of strong timber and its importance is reflected in the huge number of place-names it has generated. **Oakhill** (Somerset and Sussex), **Oakhanger** (Cheshire and Hampshire – meaning 'oak slope'), **Oakham** (Rutland and Worcestershire), **Oakley** (in at least seven counties) and **Oakwood** (again, in at least seven counties), attest to its importance. There are, of course, hundreds more place-names that include the word 'oak' in its various guises and, knowing the typical Anglo-Saxon elements of place-names as we now do, one could readily invent one's own village names.

As well as the basic word 'oak' and its easily recognised variation 'ock', the tree appears in many other teasing guises in place-names: **Aughton** (Lancashire), **Each End** (Kent), **Noke** (Oxfordshire), **Bradninch** (Devon) and **Oxted** (Surrey) are some of its clever camouflages. **Dethick** (Derbyshire) has a macabre tale to tell, for it means 'death oak', that is the tree where felons were hanged. If some of these place-name meanings seem unlikely, it is because Old English was an inflected language (a burden we are now thankfully almost wholly spared) and very often the dative case is used in some applications of words, as in **Each End** and **Bradninch** above, where the dative 'æc' is the source instead of the nominative 'āc'. It looks as though the dative case crops up again in **Eachwick** (Northumberland), but the earliest record of this village (1160) notes its name as *Achewic*, suggesting that a regional speech transformation may be responsible for the later spelling.

Other familiar trees feature strongly in place-names – the elm, ash, beech, willow and even the plum and pear. For clarity's sake, I have tabulated them all below, together with some of the place-names derived from each:

Tree name	Old English	Place-names
Alder	*alor*	**Arle** (Glos), **Ellerton** (Yorkshire), **Ollerton** (Cheshire)
Apple	*æppel*	**Apley** (Shrops), **Eppleton** (Durham), **Apperknowle** (Derbys)
Ash	*æsc*	**Askern** (Surrey), **Axford** (Wilts), **Prinknash** (Glos)
Aspen	*æspe*	**Aspall** (Suffolk), **Espley** (Northumb), **Aspenden** (Herts)
Beech	*bēce*	**Beechburn** (Durham), **Beckwith** (Yorks), **Bitchfield** (Northumb)
Birch	*birce*	**Birchanger** (Essex), **Bartlow** (Cambs), **Bircholt** (Kent)
Box	*byxen*	**Bix** (Oxon), **Bexley** (Kent), **Buxted** (Sussex)
Elder	*ellen*	**Elstead** (Surrey), **Elingdon** (Wilts), **Elstob** (Durham)
Elm	*elm*	**Emley** (Yorks), **Elmham** (Norfolk), **Ilmington** (Warwickshire)
Hawthorn	*Haguþorn**	**Hackthorn** (Lincs), **Hagley** (Worcs), **Haughley** (Suffolk)
Hazel	*hæsel*	**Halberton** (Devon), **Haselor** (Warwicks), **Haseley** (Oxon)
Holly	*holegn*	**Holne** (Devon), **Holnest** (Dorset), **Olantigh** (Kent)
Lime	*linde*	**Limber** (Lincs), **Lindeth** (Lancs), **Lympsham** (Somerset)
Maple	*hlyn/ mapuldor*	**Linford** (Bucks), **Maperton** (Somerset), **Mappowder** (Dorset)
Pear	*pirige*	**Parham** (Suffolk), **Spurshot** (Hants), **Hartpury** (Glos)
Pine/spruce	*sæppe*	**Sabden** (Lancs), **Sapley** (Cambs)
Plum	*plūme*	**Plumley** (Ches), **Plymstock** (Devon), **Puncknowle** (Dorset)
Sloe	*slāh*	**Slaithwaite** (Yorks), **Slaugham** (Sussex), **Slaughterford** (Wilts)
Spindletree	*lūsþorn**	**Lushill** (Wiltshire)
Willow	*salh*	**Saighton** (Ches), **Selwood** (Somerset), **Zeal** (Devon)
Yew	*īw*	**Iwade** (Kent), **Uley** (Glos), **Ifield** (Kent), **Ewshott** (Hants)

* þ was the useful letter 'thorn' and was pronounced 'th'.

The poplar is one tree notably absent from my list. Although the London borough of **Poplar** is well-known, the word has probably come down to us from Old French (*le popeler*) via Middle English, though the word, *'popul'*, may have existed in Old English. **Blackthorn** (Oxfordshire) too, is missing from the list above because its fruit is the sloe and that is shown lower down in the table. There are many place-names which are derived from the word 'willow' – **Weeley** (Essex), **Wilden** (Bedfordshire), **Willen** (Buckinghamshire) are some of them, but the Old English word for the willow-tree was *'salh'*, giving us 'sallow', the alternative name for the tree.

The wych elm (*'wice'*), a species of elm, common especially in the north of England at the time we are discussing, has also lent its name to a number of places. **Horwich** (Lancashire), **Wicklewood** (Norfolk), **Wickford** (Essex) and **Witchford** (Cambridgeshire) hold memories of nearby ancient wych elms.

This is not quite an exhaustive list of tree place-names, but it does serve to show how important trees of all sorts were to the new Englishmen of the first millennium, no matter where in England they lived.

Having now detailed so many trees in our place-names, it will not be surprising to find that unnamed trees too, found a place in the early local consciousness. It was nearly always due to a conspicuous feature of the tree that earned it a mention – perhaps its distinctive shape, its size, colour, position in the landscape or that it was associated with a particular person. I recall two such trees from my childhood; one was a hollow old tree 'the dedack' – that is, the 'dead oak' – the other was 'the hangman's tree'. The two trees have long since gone, but the corner in the Oakham Road near Dudley, where the 'hangman's tree' stood, was always known locally by that name. This does, however, give one a fascinating first-hand experience of how readily such names arise. So let's look at a few names of this latter type. **Rattery** (Devon) commemorates a 'red tree' that once grew nearby, while the Shropshire hamlet of **Faintree** recalls an unusual 'variegated tree' (*'fāg'* – many-coloured'). The possible identities of these trees must be left to the expert deductions of our botanist friends. The origin of the village name **Hallatrow** (Somerset) centres on a perceived 'holy tree' (*'hālig-trēow'*) and **Oswestry**, the town in Shropshire, can recall 'St Oswald's tree' – perhaps in reality a tall wooden cross. **Wrangle**, a locality on the Lincolnshire coast, not far south of Skegness, may recall a 'crooked tree' (*'wrang'* – wrong, bent). It might be interesting to speculate on the types of trees these would have been.

Some trees were more valuable for their yield of autumn nuts than for their wood. Some of the villages that recount this useful food source in their names are **Nurstead** (Kent – there is a Walnut Wood nearby), **Nutfield** (Surrey),

Nutbourne (Sussex), **Nutford** (Dorset), **Nuthall** (Nottinghamshire), **Nuthamp-stead** (Hertfordshire), **Nutley** (Hampshire) and **Nutwell** (Devon). Doubtless, some of the early villages named after the hazel and beech trees mentioned in the table earlier made good domestic use of their crops of nuts too.

Moving down the arboreal scale a step, we soon find that some shrubs and bushes have also earned a mention in place-names. Sometimes it will have been for their berries that they have been remembered and sometimes there will be other causes for note. **Bushey** (Hertfordshire) describes a location beside a prominent thicket. Its listing in Domesday (1086) is *Bissei,* after the Old English word *'bysce'* – a bush. *'Græfa'* meant a thicket of brushwood, which was always a useful fuel for the cottage hearths and the word has found its way into place-names: **Graveley** (Cambridgeshire and Hertfordshire), **Gravenhunger** (Shropshire – 'brushwood slope') and **Gravenhurst** (Bedfordshire) well illustrate this and all are recorded in Domesday (1086). However, the Old English word for a twig, *'hrīs',* also servēd to describe many an undergrowth of brushwood and we see this word in **Risborough** (Buckinghamshire), **Ryston** (Norfolk) and **Ruswarp** (Yorkshire – 'brushwood-strewn silt'). **Speke** (Lancashire) and **Spreyton** (Devon) offer yet other twiggy patches of ground (*'spræc'*), from which we have derived our words 'spray' and 'sprig'. Bracken is still a common sight as undergrowth in woodland and on hillsides and would have been a useful source of kindling for the hearths of the serfs and commoners since time immemorial. **Bracken** (Yorkshire) and **Brackenborough** (Lincolnshire) must have been close to good supplies of this rampant, though combustible fern.

London's **Wormwood Scrubs** is notorious nowadays for its association with a prison, but it was formerly a large area of scrubland, as befits its name (*'scrybb'* – undergrowth) and was known in the late 12th century as *Wermeholte,* which clearly referred to the exisitence of reptiles, probably snakes, that were known to dwell in its extensive brushbood undergrowth. There are other woody areas in England with this descriptive name too: **Scrubs** (Buckinghamshire) and **The Scrubs** (Wiltshire, Essex and Gloucestershire).

Late summer berries were a much appreciated source of sweetness when added to foods, for honey was the only other means of sweetening and this delicacy was not readily available to many of the poorer villagers. Three villages that have berry names are **Baydon** (Wiltshire, *'bēger'* – berry), **Barmoor** (Northumberland, possibly referring to the cranberry) and **Imberhorne** (Sussex, *'hindberige'* – raspberry). Hips too, were welcomed into the cooking pots of the simple dwellings. Their fleshy parts provided a sweetish nutty flavour in the stews and pottage commonly prepared and no doubt were always a welcome supplement to the salted meat and beans. **Ebbsfleet** (Kent), **Hepworth** (Suffolk), **Shipton** (Yorkshire – recorded as *Epton* in Domesday) and **Heapham** (Lincolnshire) all remind us of the mediæval proximity of these places to useful sources of hips.

Herbs and flowers in place-names

As an almost wholly agricultural society, the country-dwelling English of the 8th and 9th centuries were well versed in the values and properties of the wild plants that filled the woods and covered the heaths, valleys, meadows and wastes around their settlements. Foodstuffs, seasonings, medicines, aromatic herbs and dyes were all to be found and were gathered in season. Even poisonous plants were well-known and could be avoided. Children would be taught early on what to gather and what to avoid. Vegetable matter that would not be used immediately would be dried and stored for later use. As we have discovered in the previous section on tree names, we should not now be surprised to find that the names of many other more modest plants have found their way into our place-names. I will not be able to include quite all of them, but a look at some of the herbs that were eagerly collected as seasonings, flavourings or supplements for the cooking pot might be a good place to begin, together with the place-names that they have generated:

Herb	Old English	Place-names
Burdock	*clæte*	**Clatford** (Wilts), **Clothall** (Herts), **Cleatham** (Lincs)
Dill	*dile*	**Dilham** (Norfolk), **Dilworth** (Lancs), **Dulwich** (Surrey)
Garlic	*hramsa*	**Ramsey** (Essex), **Ramsden** (Oxon), **Ramsholt** (Suffolk)
Gentian	*meargealla*	**Marldon** (Devon), **Marlborough** (Wilts), **Marwell** (Devon)
Hemp	*henep*	**Hempstead** (Norfolk), **Hempholme** (Yorks)
Marjoram	*felte*	**Feltwell** (Norfolk)
Mint	*minte*	**Minety** (Wilts), **Minstead** (Hants), **Minterne** (Dorset)
Saffron	*croh*	**Croydon** (Surrey), **Crofton** (Lincs), **Crafton** (Bucks)
Sweet Gale	*gagel*	**Gailey** (Staffs), **Galton** (Dorset), **Galsworthy** (Devon)

If place-names deriving from herbs seem somewhat surprising to us today, perhaps I should balance them with some other, more substantial foodstuffs that might well have accompanied the herbs into the peasants' cauldrons. Orach was a spinach-like leaf, much appreciated for its nourishing qualities. Its Old English name, *'melde'*, has given us the Suffolk village name **Milden**. Peas and beans were grown in many a cottage plot, though the results were smaller and less sweet than today's varieties, but nevertheless, there are place-names associated with each: **Peasemore** (Berkshire) and **Pishill** (Oxfordshire) recall the pea, while **Banstead** (Surrey) and **Beanley** (Northumberland) are two villages whose origins lie in the cultivation of beans. Barley and Rye were corn-crops grown by farmers, but a handful of seeds of either would thicken the daily pottage to make a satisfying and filling meal. Settlements near to rye fields included **Ryton** (Durham), **Ruyton** (Shropshire) and **Rayleigh** (Essex), though **Rye** in Sussex does not recall the crop, but means 'at the island' (*'atter īeg'* – see page 56 for more information on *'atter'*). **Barlow** (Derbyshire), **Bearl** (Northumberland) and **Barley** (Lancashire) have their origins in their proximity to northern barley farms.

Few people today will have heard of 'smallage', but it is the old name for wild celery – a plant valued by our first millennium ancestors for its distinctive flavour. Even this has made an impression on our place-names – **Marcham** (Oxfordshire) and **Marchwood** (Hampshire) have their origins in the Old English word for this plant, *'mẹrece'*. One of our commonest vegetables, the leek, was also well-known in its early form and was grown in the cottage patch or was gleaned in its season. Domesday (1086) records the villages of **Lackford** (Suffolk), **Latton** (Wiltshire) and **Laughton** (Leicestershire), all of which trace their ancestries back to the word *'lēac'* – the leek. One might think therefore, that there can be no doubt about the origin of the town name **Leek** in Staffordshire, but it really has no connection with the vegetable, deriving instead from an Old Norse word thought to be *'lækr'*, meaning to dribble or leak and must have described a nearby brook or spring.

Two other useful green leaves in the early Englishmen's diet were those of a crude lettuce (*'leahtroc'*) and of watercress (*'cærse'*). These two plants' names have also crept into our place-names. **Laughterton** (Lincolnshire) and **Leighterton** (Gloucestershire) extol the humble lettuce, while **Kearsley** (Lancashire), **Kershope** (Cumbria), **Creswell** (Derbyshire) and **Creslow** (Buckinghamshire) are four of many places that owe their names to watercress. In 13th century England, cress was also known as *'billers'* and this word has produced the place-name **Bilbrook** (Staffordshire – 'the stream where cress grows'). It may have occurred to the reader that the place-names **Laughton** and **Laughterton**, just mentioned, are too similar in form to have different meanings. However, this is another instance where looking back at the earliest records must be our guide.

The earliest record of **Laughton** is in Domesday (1086) as *'Lachestone'* – clearly a written rendering of the spoken word *'lēac'*, while a charter of the year AD 680 shows **Laughterton** as *'Leugttricdun'* (probably *'Leagttricdun'* – the scribe has mistaken the written 'a' for a 'u'), which still clearly refers to the word for lettuce, *'leahtroc'*.

As well as providing food and seasoning for the simple daily fare of the common folk and for the wealthier tiers of society, the plant kingdom was almost the only source of medicines and treatments for everyone's ills. In fact, we still associate one sense of the word 'herb' with curative virtues and modern medicine recognises the restorative value of many plant extractions. Bacterial infections of both the stomach and of skin lacerations were very common and experience had taught that certain herbs could be used effectively according to the symptoms. I have counted at least ten herbs which were commonly used, mostly for treating stomach disorders and from which we have inherited a few interesting place-names:

Herb	Ailment	Old English	Place-names
Bog myrtle	Stomach, fever, liver	*gagel*	**Gailey** (Staffs), **Galton** (Dorset)
Comfrey	Sprains, broken bones	*gealloc*	**Galsham** (Devon)
Camomile	Stomach, skin abrasions	*mægþa**	**Maghull** (Lancs)
Dock	Stings, rashes, itches	*docce*	**Docking** (Norfolk), **Docklow** (Hereford)
Feverfew	Fevers, colds	*mægþa**	**Mayfield** (Sussex), **Mayford** (Surrey)
Germander	Stomach	*cymed*	**Kingcombe** (Dorset)
Gentian	Stomach	*meargella*	**Marldon** (Devon)
Hoarhound	Coughs, wheezes	*hārahūna*	**Arundel** (Sussex), **Hound** (Hants)
Pennyroyal	Stomach	*dwostle*	**Desborough** (Bucks)
Rue	Stomach	*rūde*	**Roudham** (Norfolk), **Rudyard** (Staffs)

*þ is thorn, the old 'th' sound.

There were undoubtedly many other potions and 'cures' and of course, all herbal knowledge was a matter of tradition and the potency and efficacy of these treatments had been determined by ancient trial and error. Almost every villager could point out the wild plants which were edible and those which were poisonous and children must have received early strict guidance. Comfrey (see table), for example, was known to have unpleasant gastric effects if swallowed, but its external application to help the recovery of strained muscles and fractured bones was widely practised. Henbane (*'hennebelle' and 'beolene'*) and other nightshades (*'nihtscada'*), hemlock (*'hymlīc'*), yew berries (*'īwbęrige'*) and foxglove (*'foxesglofe'*) were well-known as sources of poison and were carefully avoided. It is, however, interesting that henbane is the probable origin of the Worcestershire place-name **Belbroughton** ('farm at the brook where henbane *–beolene –* grows').

Various colours could be extracted from the leaves, stems or roots of certain plants for the purpose of dyeing cloth and colouring the skin, the commonest colours being saffron (yellow), madder (red), woad (blue) and gentian (violet). Places whose names originate in saffron and gentian have already been mentioned in the tables above, but the madder plant has given us **Matterdale** (Cumbria) and **Mayfield** (Staffordshire), while woad can boast several, including **Odell** (Bedfordshire), **Waddon** (Dorset) and **Wadborough** (Worcestershire).

We are left now with a miscellaneous group of wild plants which have somehow managed to infiltrate our place-names. Mallows, marigolds, waterlilies and ragged robin are pleasant on the eye and have little more than decoration to offer us today. They were recognised, however and named by our forbears and may have had other merits now forgotten. The mallow (*'hocc'*) must have been a prominent sight in the nearby meadows and woods to have given its name to the Norfolk villages of **Hockham** and **Hockwold**, which, by the time of Domesday (1086), were well established settlements. The marigold (*'golde'*) too, has been a prolific sight, for a number of places have their names rooted in its cheerful displays: **Goldhanger** (Essex – 'slope where marigolds grow'), **Goltho** (Lincoln-shire – 'enclosure where marigolds grew'), **Gowdall** (Yorkshire – 'corner where marigolds were found') and even **Rudheath** (Cheshire – *'rud'* seems to have been a later alternative name for the flower).

The inoffensive little flower of the ragged robin, or cuckoo flower (*'bulot'*), appears in **Boultham** (Lincolnshire) and the Domesday entry (1086) for **Bulford** (Wiltshire - *Bultisford*) shows that it too, has come from the flower name. Water-lilies always make a pleasing sight and share their Old English name with the dock – *'docce'*. Taking into account its location, **Dogdyke** (Lincolnshire) possibly celebrates more the waterlily than the dock.

The ivy (Old English, *'ifig'*) has bequeathed us several varied place-names, only two of which give us a clear hint at their origins: **Ivybridge** (Devon – the ivy-covered bridge – crossing the River Erme) and **Ivychurch** (Kent – the church being St George's, no doubt). The others are well disguised: **Evelith** (Shropshire – '*ifig-hliþ*' – ivy slope), **Haytor** (Devon – '*ifig-torr*' – ivy rock), **Tividale** (Staffordshire – '*ifig-dæl*' – ivy valley) and **Tudeley** (Kent – '*ifede-lēah*' – ivy-covered clearing).

The nettle ('*nꞓtel*'), an unlovely and irritating occupant of ditches and undergrowth, has also made its impression in the names **Nettlebed** (Oxfordshire), **Nettlestead** (Kent) and **Nettlecombe** (Dorset,) among others.

Clover ('*clæfre*'), a persistent weed, but liked by sheep and cows, plainly shows itself in **Claverley** (Shropshire), **Claverdon** (Warwickshire) and **Clavering** (Essex).

A useful thistle-like plant is the teasel ('*tæsel*'), which makes a single appearance in the Shropshire village of **Tasley**. The teasel was a particularly useful plant in the weaver's cottage, where the combing of wool (teasing) was being done, or for the raising of the nap of woven cloth to create a soft texture.

There are other instances of specific plants appearing in our place-names – mistletoe (**Mistley** in Essex), privet (**Privett** in Hampshire), thistles (**Thistleton** in Lancashirē), thorn bushes (**Thearne** in Yorkshire) and even the primitive lichen manages an unassuming mention in **Ragley Hall** (Warwickshire – '*ragu*').

To balance the specific with the unspecific, I might add to our list the villages of **Wedacre** (Lancashire) and **Wortley** (neaī Barnsley in Yorkshire). The first is from '*wēod-æcer*', meaning simply a weedy field, while the second is '*wyrt-lēah*' – a vegetable clearing.

Reeds and rushes made an important contribution to everyday life by providing easily renewable floor coverings in the poor cottages, thatch for roofs and wicks for simple lamps. It is perhaps appropriate that their value is reflected in the names of some settlements which arose near to areas in which there was a good reed supply. Of the several dozen place-names that derive from reeds and rushes and most of which show one of the '*reed*', '*red*', '*rush*' and '*rish*' elements, here are some unusual ones that do not contain these syllables: **Thaxted** (Essex, '*þæc*' – thatch), **Lever** (Lancashire, '*læfer*' – bulrush), **Beeston** (Bedfordshire, '*bēos*' – a reed) and **Bunwell** (Norfolk, '*bune*' – a rush).

We are nearing the end of this perusal of ancient English flora and the place-names that have arisen from them and of which I have mentioned over two hundred and twenty. However, I have left an obvious one until last last – the ubiquitous grass (Old English, '*gærs*'). That something as familiar as grass should earn a place in the place-name index is a little surprising, though perhaps we momentarily overlook its essential qualities as fodder. Nevertheless, it has generated a good number of names, most of which are located in the northern counties. Here are some of them:

Place-name	County	Earliest spelling	Meaning
Garsdale	Yorkshire	*Garsedale* (AD 1241)	'*Gærs-dæl*' – grassy valley
Garsdon	Wiltshire	*Gersdune* (AD 701)	'*Gærs-dūn*' – grassy hill
Garsington	Oxfordshire	*Gersedune* (AD 1086)	'*Gærsen-dūn*' – grassy hill
Grasmere	Cumbria	*Ceresmere* (AD 1203)	'*Gres-mere*' – lake with grassy banks
Grassendale	Lancashire	*Gresyndale* (13th cent)	'*Gærsen-dæl*' – grassy pasture
Grassington	Yorkshire	*Ghersintone* (AD 1086)	'*Gresing-tūn*' – grazing farm
Greaseborough	Yorkshire	*Gersebroc* (AD 1086)	'*Gærs-brŏc*' – grassy brook

It is clear from Old English word, '*gærs*', why the first three place-names in the table begin with '*Gars-*' instead of the expected '*Gras-*'. However, the later Old Norse word '*gres*' may be responsible for the slightly altered spelling of the others.

WILD MAMMALS IN PLACE-NAMES

More so, it seems, than their Roman predecessors, the New Englishmen of the 6th-9th centuries were keenly observant and inventive when it came to identifying and labelling the scenery around them. Most of the features of the countryside (and of each other) would soon have received a descriptive nickname. Such an entirely natural process was a useful aide to locating where a man could be found when at work in the fields or where to look for a particular herb or animal. When it came to labelling each other, as they did without dread of anything more than a possible scowl in response, they were unwittingly setting the foundations for the adoption of true surnames a few centuries later. Surname formation based on nicknames could not happen today in the 21st century: imagine the uproar there would be if someone were called 'crookleg', 'tub' or even 'sharpnose'!

The wild creatures and their habitats that were observed were numerous and most species we know today were recognised by name, with many individual members of a species also named. It is, however, a fact that a few animals known to Englishmen fifty generations ago, have since disappeared from England. The wolf, wild cat and wild boar are three that come immediately to mind. Wolves were still to be found in England until the early 14th century and wild boars were hunted in the south of the country as late as the first decade of the 18th century. The beaver too, had been long gone until very recently and the possible presence of bears during the Anglo-Saxon period is suggested by at least one place-name, **Barmer** (Norfolk), for a document of 1202 records the name as *Beremere* ('*bera-mere*' – bear-lake or bear-pool, though there is no body of water there today).

It is, I think, amazing and fascinating, to find that place-names can be found which reflect about twenty species of wild mammals, nearly forty types of bird, half a dozen varieties of insect and a handful of fish, together with two or three others outside these categories. It surely emphasises the acute awareness, shown by the early English, of the abundance of the countryside's fauna.

The easiest and clearest way to summarise the mammals' and birds' contribution to our place-names is by listing them in tables. Here are the mammals and some of the place-names their names have produced:

Wild mammal	Old English	Place-names
Badger	*brocc*	**Broxbourne** (Herts), **Brockhall** (Northants)
Beaver	*beofer*	**Beverstone** (Glos), **Beversbrook** (Wilts), **Bevercotes** (Notts)
Boar	*bār, eofor*	**Barwell** (Leics), **Everley** (Yorks), **Yaverland** (Isle of Wight)
Cat	*catt*	**Cattal** (Yorks), **Catfield** (Norfolk), **Ketley** (Shropshire)
Deer, doe, buck	*dēor, dā, bucc*	**Dearham** (Cumb), **Daccombe** (Devon), **Buckden** (Yorks)
Fox	*fox*	**Foxwist** (Ches), **Foxham** (Wilts), **Foxearth** (Essex)
Hare	*hara*	**Harden** (Yorks), **Harley** (Shrop), **Harewood** (Hereford)
Hart, hind	*heort, hind*	**Harton**(Durham), **Hindlip** (Worcs), **Hertford** (Herts)
Hedgehog	*igil*	**Ilmer** (Bucks)
Marten (weasel)	*mearþ**	**Martham** (Norfolk), **Marley** (Yorks), **Marefield** (Leics)
Mouse	*mūs*	**Moseley** (Worcs), **Musbury** (Devon), **Mowsley** (Leics)
Mole	*wand*	**Wansford** (Yorks)

Otter	*otor*	**Ottringham** (Yorks), **Otterham** (Corn), **Ottershaw** (Surrey)
Roe deer	*rā*	**Rodden** (Somerset), **Reigate** (Surrey), **Rowland** (Derbys)
Rat	*ræt*	**Rettendon** (Essex)
Stag	*stagga*	**Stagenhoe** (Herts)
Seal	*seolh*	**Selsey** (Sussex)
Wolf	*wulf*	**Wolvey** (Warwicks), **Wolsty** (Cumbria), **Ulley** (Yorks)

* '*þ*', the mediæval letter 'thorn', has the 'th' sound.

Rather surprisingly, the village of **Badger** in Shropshire has nothing to do with the shy, striped mammal, but is associated with a person. It is *'Bægi's shore'*, as can be deduced from its Domesday (1086) entry, *Beghesovre*. The village stands adjacent to several pools and is beside the winding River Worfe.

There are no domesticated animals shown in the table – I will introduce sheep, cows, horses, pigs, dogs and so forth later. It is interesting, though, to see the number of ways in which that stalwart of the mediæval hunting scene, the deer, in its various forms, is recorded: there are indeed eight words. It was clearly of fundamental importance to the society of the time and would remain so for centuries to come. On the other hand, the hedgehog, rat and seal seem to have had little significance in the early mind – understandably so as they could contribute little or nothing to the diet or welfare of the common folk, though one wonders whether boiled seal flesh had ever found its way into the stomachs of a few dwellers on the Sussex coast.

BIRDS

Bird names from the Old English form by far the largest contribution of the countryside fauna to place-names. The generic words 'bird', 'fowl', 'cock' and 'hen' themselves have given us a large number of place-names, not to mention surnames (mostly nicknames after distinctive bird-like physical characteristics such as a sharp nose, sparrow-like legs, a bright eye or twitching movements). Wild birds would always be a welcome addition to the Englishman's diet and the village birdcatchers (*'fuglere'*) were skilled in trapping them. The usual Old English word for a songbird was *'fugol'* (a clear relative of the German *'vogel'* and predecessor of the later English *'fowl'*), but the word that eventually became favoured was '*bridd*', which originally meant a chick. '*Fugol*' is the origin of the first element in the names **Foulness** (Essex) and **Fulmer** (Buckinghamshire), though once again, we must be careful here, since a similar word, '*fūl*', meant 'putrid or stinking' and has given rise to some places that might easily be mistaken for a reference to birds – **Fulbeck** (Lincolnshire – dirty stream), **Fulwood** (Lancashire – foul wood).

The Englishman's odd tendency to exchange letters within some spoken words soon turned '*bridd*' into our current word 'bird'. We can also see this curious mannerism in the surnames Crisp and Cripps, Samson and Sansom among others and in the place-name elements Thorp and Thropp. **Birdbrook** (Essex) speaks plainly for itself, though we are left to guess what sort of birds they were. The stream may have been the village spring or the nearby River Stour. **Bridgemere** (Cheshire), despite the appearance of the word, is actually a transformation of *Briddismere* (from a document of 1208), meaning 'a pool where birds were found' – there is still a good-sized pool (Doddington Pool) at the nearby Doddington Hall.

Other general words for larger birds like wild ducks and geese, were '*cocc*' and '*henn*', giving rise to the place-names **Cocklaw** (Northumberland – 'hill of the birds'), **Cogdean** (Dorset), **Henhurst** (Kent – 'bird wood') and **Henmarsh** (Gloucestershire).

As with the mammals earlier, it will be clearer and more informative to place the specific names of wild birds into a table:

Wild birds	Old English	Place-names
Blackbird	ōsle	**Ewesley** (Northumberland), **Nostell** (Yorks)
Bittern	pūr, bymera	**Purleigh** (Essex), **Bemerton** (Wilts)
Bluetit	hīce-māse	**Hykeham** (Lincs)
Buzzard	wrecan?	**Wroxton** (Oxfordshire), **Wroxham** (Norfolk)
Cuckoo	gēac	**Gokewell** (Lincs), **Yagden** (Surrey), **Yaxham** (Norfolk)
Crow	craw	**Crawley** (Sussex), **Cranage** (Ches), **Cranoe** (Leics)
Crane	cran	**Cranford** (Middx), **Carnforth** (Lancs), **Conksbury** (Derby)
Duck	dūc, ęned	**Doughton** (Glos), **Duckinfield** (Ches), **Enmore** (Som),
Dove	dūfe?	**Duffield** (Derbys), **Dufton** (Cumbria)
Eagle	earn	**Arley** (Warwicks), **Earnley** (Sussex), **Yarlet** (Staffs)

Finch	*finc*	**Finchale** (Durham), **Finchley** (Middx), **Finkley** (Hants)
Goose	*gōs*	**Gosfield** (Essex), **Goswick** (Northumb), **Gosford** (Devon)
Hawk	*hafoc*	**Hawkedon** (Suffolk), **Hauxwell** (Yorks), **Hawkinge** (Kent)
Heron	*hrāgra*	**Rawreth** (Essex)
Jackdaw	*cā*	**Cawood** (Yorks), **Cabourne** (Lincs), **Kigbeare** (Devon)
Kite	*glida, cȳta, putta?*	**Gleadless** (Yorks), **Kidbrooke** (Kent), **Putley** (Hereford)
Lark	*lāwerce*	**Larkbeare** (Devon), **Laverstock** (Wilts), **Laverton** (Som)
Owl	*ūf*	**Oldcotes** (Notts), **Ulgham** (Northumb), **Ousden** (Suffolk)
Peacock	*pāwa*	**Peamore** (Devon)
Pigeon	*culfre*	**Cullercoats** (Northumberland)
Plover	*gīfete?*	**Iffley** (Oxon), **Tivetshall** (Norfolk)
Raven	*hræfn*	**Ravenfield** (Yorks), **Renscombe** (Devon), **Rainow** (Ches)
Rook	*hrōc*	**Rookhope** (Durham), **Rockley** (Wilts), **Roxwell** (Essex)
Shrike	*scrīc*	**Shrigley** (Cheshire)
Snipe	*snīte*	**Snitterfield** (Warwicks), **Snydale** (Yorks)
Sparrow	*dunnoc? sugga*	**Dunnockshaw** (Lancs), **Suckley** (Worcs), **Sugwas** (Heref)
Stork	*storc*	**Storrington** (Sussex)
Swan	*Iɇlfetu, swan*	**Eldmire** (Yorks), **Elvetham** (Hants), **Swanage** (Dorset)
Swallow	*swealwe*	**Swalcliffe** (Oxon), **Swalwell** (Durham)
Thrush	*þryscele**	**Thrushleton** (Devon),
Woodpecker	*fina, speoht?*	**Finstock** (Oxon), **Finborough** (Suff), **Spetisbury** (Dorset)
Woodcock	*hrucge?*	**Rugley** (Northumberland)

*þ is the obsolete letter 'thorn', pronounced 'th'.

Several of the Old English words in the table are followed by question-marks because of some uncertainty about the meanings of the words concerned. We do not know all of the Anglo-Saxon vocabulary used twelve hundred years ago of course and sometimes it is necessary to make informed assumptions from the context of a word in contemporary documents.

A few of the birds listed are a little unfamiliar to us today – the bittern, shrike and stork are rarely seen, while the crane, a wading visitor, may sometimes have been decribed in the same terms as the heron. The falcon is probably behind the name **Faulkbourne** in Essex, but, although this village appears in Domesday (1086) as *Falcheburna*, the word 'falcon' is of Old French origin. There are several more bird-names that appear in our place-names, but they belong to the next era and therefore to another chapter.

The Anglo-Saxons did not name every variety of bird within each species, as we do today – for instance, '*lāwerce*' was a descriptive name for all birds of the lark family, while finches too, were all called '*finc*'. Ducks were usually referred to as '*ęned*', regardless of species. Even so, it is still quite surprising that the New English had named so many varieties of bird.

As with the village of **Badger** (Shropshire), mentioned earlier, some place-names which seem to shout their meanings clearly can be amusingly misleading. **Eagle** (Lincolnshire) actually means 'oak wood', as we can see from its 1086 entry in Domesday (*Aclei*). **Owlpen** (Gloucestershire) and **Swallow** (Lincolnshire) also tease us. **Owlpen** is '*Olla*'s enclosure' and **Swallow** derives from '*swillan*', which means 'to splash' and must have referred to the rapid or noisy flow of the nearby brook.

There are some bird-names, surprisingly, which do not seem to have found their way into place-names – the wren ('*wrænna*'), robin ('*ruddoc*'), linnet ('*linete*') and magpie ('*agu*') are four of them.

Reptiles and amphibians

Frogs, toads and newts were probably the most familiar members of this group, as indeed they will be today, with grass snakes and perhaps the occasional adder coming next. There are, therefore, not many contributions to expect to our place-names from them. However, those names that have come down to us are interesting and are worth a short section to themselves.

The Anglo-Saxons used several words for frogs and toads – '*frosc*' and '*ȳce*' usually referred to the frog, while '*pade*' and '*tādige*' were toad names. Another word, '*poce*', may have meant frog too, but it is uncertain. It seems though, that only a vague distinction may have been generally made between the frog and the toad – and the names seemed to be interchangeable much of the time. Several place-names will illustrate these origins: **Frostenden** (Suffolk), **Froxfield** (Wiltshire) are derivatives of *'frosc'*, while, unfortunately, there seem to be no surviving names that are based on *'ȳce'*. **Padfield** (Derbyshire) and **Podimore** (Somerset) are derived from *'pade'* and **Tadmarton** (Oxfordshire) and **Tathwell** (Lincolnshire) originate in the word *'tādige'*. **Polebrook**, a village in Northamptonshire, may have its roots in the uncertain *'poce'*.

Adders were well recognised and called *'næddre'*, giving us our modern word. A place which was specifically named after the adder is **Netherfield** in Sussex, as can be deduced from its entry in Domesday (1086) – *Nedrefelle*. A useful Old English word for reptiles in general, without specifying what was indicated, was *'wyrm'*, from which we have our word 'worm'. This could mean a snake, an earthworm, a newt, a mythical serpent or even a legendary dragon. The word has, however, generated a number of place-names – **Warmley** (Gloucestershire), **Worminghall** (Oxfordshire), **Wormley** (Hertfordshire) as well as **Wormwood Scrubs** mentioned in the section on trees earlier in this chapter.

The early documentation for some of these last place-names is a little ambiguous, in that a fairly common personal name for a man was *Wyrma* (sometimes shortened to *Wyrm* and perhaps a rather disparaging nickname from his appearance or demeanour). In the case of **Wormsley** in Herefordshire, there is no doubt that the original recorded name in Domesday (1086), *Wermeslai*, includes the genitive *'-es-'* and must refer to the meadow of a man called *Wyrma*.

Fish

Fish were always a useful addition to the diets of any household and the proximity of a good river might ensure a supply of edible fish. Weirs, as explained in Chapter Three, became a useful means of hoarding fish for the land holder's personal use, but the taking of the creatures by stealthy peasants was always widespread. River fish included gudgeon, pike, trout and eels, though only a few of these have earned a mention in our place-names. I have listed only five in the table below, though there may be others whose names have become obscured or lost in the many centuries since their emergence.

The word 'fish' itself is responsible for a number of names – **Fishlake** (Yorkshire), meaning 'fish stream' and **Fishbourne** (Sussex) must have been a good source of fish for the local peasantry. At **Fishwick** (Lancashire) we would probably have found fish being sold that had been caught in the nearby **River**

Ribble, while at **Fisherwick** (Staffordshire) lived the fish catcher himself, harvesting his catches from the **River Tame**, no doubt.

Fish name	Old English	Place-name
Eel	*æl*	**Ely** (Cambs), **Auburn** (Yorks), **Almer** (Dorset)
Gudgeon	*blæge*	**Blandford** (Dorset)
Minnow	*pinc?*	**Pinchbeck** (Lincolnshire)
Pike	*pīc*	**Pickburn** (Yorks), **Pickmere** (Ches)
Trout	*foran? scēota*	**Fornham** (Suffolk), **Shottesbrook** (Berks)

Again, there are words here (*'pinc'* and *'foran'*) of which we cannot be certain and about which we can only make informed guesses from their occurrences in other contexts.

Insects etc

Of all the insects that could have influenced our place-names, it might not surprise the reader at all to know that the honey-bee (*'bēo'*) is the most prolific. This fact must reflect the value placed on the insect for its ability to manufacture honey (*'hunig'*), a prized sweetening commodity and from which that delightfully refreshing and ancient alcoholic liquor, mead (*'medu'*), was fermented. So valued was mead, that the English town-dwellers established mead-houses (*'medu-ærn'*) where men gathered to drink (*'medu drynce'*). *'Medu gāl'* meant 'to be excited with mead' and if one went further still, *'medu wērig'* described the happy state of drunkenness. How little times have changed it seems! Anyway, here is a selection of bee-related place-names:

Place-name	Meaning
Beal (Northumberland)	Bee-hill (*'bēo-hyll'*)
Beauworth (Hampshire)	Bee-farm (*'bēo-wyrð'*)*
Beeford (Yorkshire)	Bee-ford (*'bēo-ford'*)
Beeleigh (Essex)	Bee-wood (*'bēo-lēah'*)
Beoley (Worcestershire)	Bee-wood (*'bēo-lēah'*)
Beobridge (Shropshire)	Bee-bridge (*'bēo-brycg'*)
Bewick (Northumberland)	Bee-farm (*'bēo-wīc'*)

* *ð* is the soft 'th' sound

Honey-bees were not the only variety of bee recognised by our distant forebears. Bumble-bees (or humble-bees) were well observed too and were

given the name *'dora'*, which has found its solitary way into the Buckinghamshire village of **Dorney** (meaning 'bumble-bee island'). This village is indeed
on an island between the **Jubilee River** and its looping tributary, **Cress Brook**.
Interestingly, the location of **Empshott** in Hampshire must have been worth
remembering at an early moment in its history, for the name is derived from the
Old English word for a swarm of bees, *'imbe'*, paired with *'scēat'*, a strip of land.

In Chapters One and Three I mentioned that annual plague of cattle, the
gadfly, often nowadays called the warblefly and a few of the place-names it has
produced. This insect and its irritating habits may seem an unlikely source of
place-names, but we must not forget that simple location names often preceded
the settlement names we know today – **Beaford** (Devon – 'ford where gadflies
– *'bēaw'* – were found'), as mentioned in the section *'Watercourses'* in Chapter
Three, obviously first referred to a river crossing-place near to which a village
subsequently grew up and assumed the ford's descriptive name. The same
process will have applied to **Brisley** (Norfolk) – a clearing or wood infested with
gadflies (*'brīosa'*). **Braiseworth**, also in Suffolk, may have acquired its colonies
of gadflies later, since the *'-worth'* element refers to a homestead, which must
have come first. The gadfly sometimes also gave rise the surname Breese (or
Breeze), leaving us to wonder just what feature of a man could have evoked such
a nickname.

I have also touched on gnats and midges in Chapters One and Two, but
they belong firmly here in the Anglo-Saxon period of place-name formation.
Pyecombe (Sussex) was clearly originally a valley notable for its seasonal clouds
of gnats (*'pīe'*), from which the current village later took its name. **Midgley**
(Yorkshire) and **Midgehall** (Wiltshire) both recall their associations with infes-
tations of those summer biters – the midges.

Butterflies and moths, common sights though they must have been, have not
lent their names to places, unfortunately, perhaps because of the length of the
words – *'butorflēoge'* and *'nihtbutorflēoge'* (that is, 'night butterfly'), though we
can still easily read our modern words in the two Old English names. Beetles of
some kind, however, have found a modest home in the name **Wigley** (Derbyshire and Hampshire and perhaps the Shropshire one too), for this contains
the word *'wicga'*, a general word for beetles. As for caterpillars – the answer is
probably also yes, they too appear in place-names. **Embleton** in Northumberland and in Cumbria are the only homes I can trace that might be assigned to an
Anglo-Saxon caterpillar. The names' origins lie in the word *'emel'*, which appears
in very early records of both places. The Durham village with the identical name
of **Embleton**, however, is revealed in an 1190 document to be *Elmedene* and

therefore must have its origin in the name of the elm tree – 'elm-valley'. The alternative spelling of 'ymel' (for 'emel' – a caterpillar), seemed to have been applied to the corn-weevil in some northern places, though the source of the place-name **Hamsterley** (Durham) was probably 'hamstra', a weevil or maggot.

Finally, the spider; not an insect of course, but, for convenience, we will place it in this section. It is suggested that **Warkleigh** (Devon) and **Warkworth** (Northamptonshire) may have their origins in either the words 'wæferce' (spider) or 'wæfregang' (spider's web). Professor Ekwall[1] seems doubtful, however, although Professor Mills[2] thinks **Warkleigh** does have the spider connection.

Three miscellaneous creatures in place-names

I couldn't allow crabs, leeches and snails to escape our scrutiny for, although they are perhaps not the most endearing of nature's creations (to man at least), if they have a contribution to make to our story of place-names, then they shall have their moment of exposure.

The Cheshire hamlet of **Crabwall** seems to have 'crabba' as its core word, which was Old English for 'a crab'. Since the hamlet is only about three miles north of Chester and a long way from the coast, it would seem that in this case 'crabba' may have referred to crayfish rather than crabs, particularly as there are, even today, more than a couple of dozen small pools to be found near to the settlement.

Leeches must occupy one of the least lovable positions in the human psyche, yet their ancient medical value in the letting of human blood must, if appropriate, qualify them for a place in our place-name history. It is interesting to note that the Old English word for both a leech and a physician was 'læce', so that anyone consulting a physician was likely to have leech treatment prescribed almost as a matter of course. Two places which derive their names from 'læce' are **Lesbury** (Northumberland) and **Lexham** (Norfolk). **Lesbury** is on the **River Aln** and **Lexham** is on the **River Nar**, so any still pools at their margins may have been well supplied with leeches, with the physician who made use of them perhaps living nearby. Adjacent to **Lexham** is **Litcham**, which looks persuasively similar, especially when one looks at the early recorded forms of the place-names: *Lechesbiri* (AD 1190), *Leceham* (AD 1086) and *Lecham* (AD 1086). Professor Ekwall, however, inclines to the opinion that **Litcham** probably

---

1. Eilert Ekwall, *Concise Oxford Dictionary of English Place-names*. Oxford University Press 1960 Ed.

2. A.D. Mills, *Dictionary of British Place Names*. Oxford University Press 2003 Ed.

arises from *'lycce'* – an enclosure. I think there may be an argument here for the leech too.

PEOPLE

By the end of the 8th century, the Anglo-Saxons could be said to have become the English. King Ælfred (later called 'The Great') was a respected king of Wessex and later styled in official charters as 'King of the English', though there were seven major kingdoms in England by this time (Wessex, Mercia, Northumbria, Essex, East Anglia, Sussex and Kent), each with its own ruler. Ælfred was the strongest and most visionary ruler in England at the time and his approach to kingship and the leadership of his people in the south and west set in motion the process which would truly unite England under a single monarch in the following century. The country was by now largely Christian and paganism, though not extinct, had become a secondary pastoral phenomenon.   -

The English at this time were still farmers and hamlet-dwellers and had little taste for living in larger settlements, but as markets slowly became established, often at a convenient junction of cross-country tracks as they passed close to hamlets, or near to a river crossing, a settlement might begin to grow. As the 9th century gave way to the 10th century, so the steady growth of some villages into something like small 'townships' was becoming evident. People who lived in neighbouring districts could come to the markets and exchange the goods they had gathered, grown or made, for goods or services they required in return. The peasant who lived in a cottage near to where teasels grew, could gather a sack full and bring them to market in a village where there was a family of weavers who made cloth and who would use the teasel heads to comb the nap. In return, the 'seller' might be handed a length or two of coarse cloth to take home to be turned into clothes. Thus a regular demand-and-supply arrangement could easily be established. Similarly, a valley dweller might bring along the pelts of perhaps twenty hares to exchange for a pair of strong leather shoes from the village shoesmith. And so a community would begin to grow and function as a small co-operative unit – the nucleus of a future town.

The market would eventually become an important social, as well as a commercial focus of a community and this was significant enough for the early English to name the sites of some such places: **Chipstead** (Kent and Surrey – *'cēapstēde'*, place with a market), **Kepwick** (Yorkshire – *'cēap-wīc'*, hamlet with a market) and **Chipping** (Lancashire – *'cēaping'*, market village). Many places can be found in our roadmaps which have Chipping as their first element.

The regular bearer of the teasel heads just mentioned might easily be nicknamed *'Tæsel'* by the weaver, while the leather-worker might know the hare-catcher as *'Hara'*. To his customers, the clothmaker might readily attract the nickname, *'Wębba'* and the shoemaker, *'Scōh'*. There must have been hundreds, if not thousands of possible nicknames, flattering and derogatory, applied to friends and to acquaintances, but which vanished with their bearers. Other than such transient and casual nicknaming, there was no need for anything resembling a surname in the modern sense. However, everyone had a personal (or 'given') name of course (as distinct from a nickname) and it is these that frequently appear in place-names, though often in some modified form, since they were usually recorded from direct vernacular speech by a scribe, who had to do his best to write down what he had heard as accurately as he could. It is from these birth names that we have inherited an important group of place-names and which form group *(iiia)* in my list of place-name groups in the Introduction (see page 5). Although by the 10th century, English society had been officially Christian for over two hundred years, there remained an inevitable and significant pagan memory and the place-names in this group will include a few names of those bygone, though not forgotten, pagan deities.

Since the society of the New English was almost wholly male orientated, it is only to be expected that the great majority of personal names which have generated place-names will be those of men. However, women's names do form a small, but interesting cluster within the main group. Unless there is a charter or some other surviving document which mentions a person by name and gives other information, the place-name is the only memorial to a long forgotten individual. Having said that, however, which of us, even in our modern era of painfully extreme public vanity, would shrink from having a place named in our memory?

One of the easiest ways of identifying a place in the locality was to call it after its owner or after the person who lived there. We do it today. Near to where I lived as a boy were three farms. Our parents always knew where to find us because we would tell them whose meadows we would be in or whose cowsheds we would be cleaning out – just the mention of the farmer's name would be enough. Fields, meadows, woods, enclosures, farms, homesteads, pools, hills, valleys, streams and so on – they often would attract a personal name as their first element. The very first name-entry in Professor Ekwall's great Dictionary is one such, **Abberley** (Worcestershire). Domesday's record (1086) shows that this was the clearing or meadow belonging to *Ēadbeald* (a name meaning 'prosperity-bold'). Halfway through the Dictionary we find **Levenshulme** (Lancashire). This means 'the island (or dry ground) of *Lēofwine*' ('beloved–friend'). Further on in the Ekwall book there is **Siefton** (Shropshire) which is interesting for the reason that it derives from a woman's name, *Sigegifu* ('victory-gift') and refers to 'the village or homestead of *Sigegifu*'.

If the definitions of some of these personal names ('prosperity-bold', 'victory-gift') seem a little strange to us, it is because of a naming tradition of the times which took one element from the father's name and combined it with another from the mother's name. The intention was not necessarily to make perfect sense, but to form a name-bond between the parents and the child – a rather pleasant idea. We occasionally see this same process today – a mother whose name is Kay and a father whose name is Leigh might call their new daughter Kayleigh. Other possibilities could be Eve + Lynn = Evelyn, Mary + Ian = Marian, Lee + Anne = Leanne and Joe + Anne = Joanne. The following table lists some of the Old English personal name elements:

Common first elements	Meaning	Common second elements	Meaning
Ælf-	elf	-eald	old
Æthel-	noble	-gifu	gift
Beorht-	bright	-hild	war
Ēad-	prosperity	-mund	guardian
Frith-	peace	-ræd	council
Gōd-	good	-ric	ruler
Lēof-	beloved	-stan	stone
Sig-	victory	-weard	protector
Wulf-	wolf	-wig	warrior
		-wine	friend
		-wulf	wolf

There were many other name elements of course, but those above are some of the more commonly seen in Old English personal names. There will be many combinations possible, only a few of which will seem to make acceptable sense to our minds: *Æthelrǣd*, *Ēadric*, *Godwine* and *Wulfstan* are perfectly possible and are recorded. When a first element is combined with one of the many local feature suffixes such as '-tūn', '-wīc', '-wiell' or '-cot', the number of possibilities becomes huge. As examples, I might quote the place-names **Atterton** (Leicestershire, '*Æthelred's tūn*' – 'dwelling of *Ethelred*'), **Adwell** (Oxfordshire, '*Ēadda's wiell*' – '*Eadda's* spring'), **Godwick** (Norfolk, '*Gōda's wīc*' – 'the settlement of *Gōda*') and **Woolscott** (Warwickshire, '*Wulfsige's cot*' – 'cottage of *Wulfsige*').

A glance through Domesday (1086) will reveal a large number of ancient place-names which incorporate many other personal names of men. *Beonna, Ceatta, Dryhtla, Gyssa, Lulla, Peden, Sibba, Stūt, Thuri* and *Werca* are some of the men's names that crop up. These men had been, of course, leaders of their communites or of their extended families occupying a small settlement, or were landowners on whose lands were several hamlets or farms. Women, however, were less often in charge of such holdings, though rather more so than was thought to be the case by historians not very long ago. It was perfectly possible for a widow to inherit her dead husband's property and manage it for the rest of her active life or until she found another husband. I would like to celebrate the female side of this topic by listing fifteen women's names and their associated place-names that have come down so many centuries carrying the memory of their original bearers to us. As was the general custom, only a single personal name was given at birth and any nicknames acquired during their lives would have died with their bearers. Their names are unlike any of our modern personal names. It is, however, an intriguing thought that there may be people living today who are descended from some of these women. The places named after the women shown in the table are all first documented in Domesday (1086) or before.

Woman's name	Place-name, date and meaning	Location
Æþelswiþ*	**Elson** (AD 948, *Æþelswiþ's* dwelling)	Hampshire
Ælfwynn	**Elvington** (AD 1086, *Ælfwynn's* dwelling)	Yorkshire
Aldgȳþ*	**Audley** (AD 1086, *Aldgȳþ's* clearing)	Staffordshire
Bucge	**Bognor** (AD 680, landing place of *Bucge*)	Sussex
Burghild	**Bucklebury** (AD 1086, *Burghild's* fort)	Berkshire
Ēadgifu	**Eddington** (AD 984, *Ēadgifu's* dwelling)	Berkshire
Hēahburg	**Habberley** (AD 1086, *Hēahburg's* clearing)	Worcestershire
Hereburg	**Harbury** (AD 1002, *Hereburg's* manor)	Warwickshire
Hūnburg	**Hubberholme** (AD 1086, *Hūnburg's* meadow)	Yorkshire
Cynehild	**Kenilworth** (AD 1086, *Cynehild's* homestead)	Warwickshire
Lēoftæt	**Leftwich** (AD 1086, *Lēoftæt's* home)	Cheshire
Ricola	**Rickling** (AD 1086, Queen *Ricola's* people)	Essex
Wǣrburg	**Warbleton** (AD 1086, *Wǣrburg's* dwelling)	Sussex
Wilflǣd	**Willington** (AD 1086, *Wilflǣd's* village)	Cheshire
Wulfþrȳþ*	**Wolterton** (AD 1086, *Wulfþrȳþ's* dwelling)	Norfolk

* þ, the obsolete letter 'thorn', has the 'th' sound.

Interestingly, **Womenswold** (Kent, AD 824) does not refer to women at all, but to the forest location of the family of a man probably called *Wīmel*. However, **Whenby** (Yorkshire, AD 1086) actually does mean 'village of the women'!

Having looked at some of the individuals, we can now turn to some of the groups of people. Family groups and historic clans were geographically very stable, living and farming together or within a short distance of each other and this began to be reflected in the structure of many of the place-names that came to be associated with them.

One of the most familiar patterns found in English place-names is illustrated in the names **Adlington** (Cheshire), **Billingham** (Durham) and **Kislingbury** (Northamptonshire). Each of these names has three elements, the central one being '-*ing*-'. This short syllable is an abbreviation of the Old English suffix '-*inga*' or its plural '-*ingas*', which signified 'the family or people of...' Hence **Adlington** refers to the settlement (the '*tūn*') of *Ēadwulf's* people, **Billingham** was 'the village of the *Billingas*' (a family or tribe) and **Kislingbury** meant 'the stronghold of *Cysela's* folk.' The final syllable can be one of many: **Theddingworth** (Leicestershire – 'the homestead of *þēoda's* people'), **Sunninghill** (Berkshire – 'the hill of the followers of *Sunna*'), **Bassingfield** (Nottinghamshire – 'the lands of *Bassa's* people) and of course, the person's name will be incorporated into the first element of each word. As always though, we must not make assumptions – **Wormingford** (Essex) seems to fit nicely into our pattern, but the Domesday scribe (1086) records the name of the village as *Widermondefort*, thus intimating that the personal name referred to is *Wiþermund* and not his people. **Norrington** (Wilitshire) too, tries to deceive us, for an early record (1212) shows that it is *Northintone* – that is, '*norþ in tūne*' ('north end of the village'). Domesday is always a valuable first reference.

HUMAN ACTIVITIES

For the whole of the five hundred years of the Anglo-Saxon period – and long after that – the majority of undertakings of the populace were centred around the demands of agriculture. Cattle farming, sheep and pig rearing and the growing of crops accounted for the bulk of human occupation throughout England.

Within this sphere were the herdsmen of various animals, ploughmen, birdscarers and, when the time came, reapers and threshers. Most men would be able to turn their hands to all of these jobs when the need arose. Within the later, bigger settlements one would also expect to find some specialists: metal-smiths, a blacksmith, weavers, leather workers, a miller, wood-workers, potters and, in those parts of the country where metal ores were accessible, the occasional smelter.

In addition to these were the churchmen and monks, sellers of goods and small groups of militia, amongst others. As some settlements gradually developed into small townships during the 9th and 10th centuries, further specialist occupations evolved and a basic local administration began to become necessary.

Since farming, in its many aspects, was the major occupation of the English, we should perhaps begin by examining the influence it has had on English place-name formation.

ANIMAL HUSBANDRY

The study of English place-names, whose origins lie in the Anglo-Saxon era, reveals that hardly anything has changed – all of the animals we expect to find on today's farms were reared on farms twelve hundred years ago. Although the general word for a farm was *'feormehām'*, a farm is still usually implied when we see the suffix *'-wick'*, as in **Bulwick** (Northamptonshire – *'bula-wīc'*, a bull-rearing farm), **Cowick** (Essex – *'cū-wīc'*, a cow farm), **Goswick** (Northumberland – *'gōs-wīc'*, a farm where geese were kept) and **Scopwick** (Lincolnshire – *'scēap-wīc'*, a sheep farm). There are, however, many other references to domesticated animals that indicate that they belonged to a nearby farm. Here is a list of them:

Animal	Place-name	Old English	Meaning
Bulls	**Fazeley** (Staffs)	*fearr-lēah*	clearing used for bulls
Calves	**Calver** (Derbys)	*calf-ofer*	slope where calves grazed
Cows	**Quy** (Cambs)	*cū-ēg*	cow island
Ewes	**Ewanrigg** (Cumbria)	*eowena-hrycg*	Ridge where ewes grazed
Goats	**Gateley** (Norfolk)	*gāt-lēah*	goat pasture
Heffers	**Strickland** (Cumbria)	*styric-land*	young bullock enclosure
Hens	**Hinwick** (Beds)	*henn-wīc*	hen farm
Horses	**Stadhampton** (Oxon)	*stōd-ham (-tūn)*	horse enclosure
Kids	**Tixall** (Staffs)	*ticca-hahl*	enclosure for kids
Lambs	**Lamberhurst** (Kent)	*lamb-hyrst*	hill where lambs graze
Oxen	**Oxhey** (Herts)	*oxa-hæg*	pen for oxen
Pigs	**Swindon** (Wilts)	*swīn-dūn*	hill where pigs were kept

Rams	**Rampton** (Cambs)	*ramm-tūn*	enclosure for rams
Sheep	**Notton** (Yorks)	*hnoc-tūn*	sheep farm
Stallions	**Hinxworth** (Herts)	*hengest-worþ**	enclosure for stallions

* '*þ*' is the obsolete letter 'thorn', pronounced 'th'.

There are many other place-names associated with these animals than the fifteen examples I have listed here. Sheep and cows, especially, have generated a large number of place-names, but the first column of the list does emphasise that early English farmers were progressive in their attitudes to livestock breeding, with half a dozen sorts of meat and two sources of milk, together with eggs, most for the cooking pots of the villagers, but some for sale at market. In addition, there would be the fleeces, hides, bones, gut and feathers to press into use. The oxen provided the ploughing power and the horses the specialist overland transport – and sometimes the sport, as in **Follifoot** (Yorkshire), a place that recalls the ancient love of horse racing and of horse fighting, although the earliest records of the village are from the 12th century.

Always on the lookout for contradictions and teases, I can't resist pointing out three place-names relevant here, that fall squarely into these categories: **Cowm** (Lancashire), **Ewesley** (Northumberland) and **Oxted** (Surrey). These certainly look as though they are telling us about cows, ewes and oxen, but it's a bluff: **Cowm** is really '*cumb*', the ancient Briton's word for a valley, **Ewesley** is an unexpected transformation of '*ōsle-lēah*', meaning 'blackbird wood' and **Oxted** is a contraction of '*āc-stede*' – 'the place where oak-trees grew'.

Apart from the animals specified by name in the table above, **Natton** (Gloucestershire) and **Neatham** (Hampshire) commemorate cattle herds in general, for their names originate in the word '*nēat*', meaning simply 'cattle'.

I have already mentioned the value our distant ancestors placed on honey ('*hunig*'), for there was little else than summer fruits and berries to provide a pleasing sweetness to appreciative palates in all ranks of society. As a consequence of their worth, some farmers went to considerable trouble to maintain collections of hives on their land so that honey could be harvested after the flowering season. **Beauworth** (Hampshire), in spite of appearances, recalls this activity, for it is '*bēo-wyrð*' – bee-farm. **Honington** (Warwickshire) and **Hunnington** (Worcestershire) also speak of important honey farms, while the banks or meadows of the Gate Inn Brook, flowing through **Honeybourne** (Worcestershire – 'honey-stream'), seem to have been a local source of honey worth remarking.

However, honey was not the only desirable product of the bee-farmer's endeavours: beeswax was the other prized commodity and was collected and sold for ointments, medicines and later for candles. If **Bickerton** (Cheshire) commemorated the bee-keepers, **Waxholme** (Yorkshire) and **Wexham** (Buckinghamshire) honour the memories of their local wax gatherers.

Holwick (Durham) seems to recall a dairy-farm located in a hollow (*'hol'*), though **Butterwick** (Durham), as can be seen from its name, was regarded as a specifically butter-making establishment. **Butterlaw** (Northumberland) and **Bitterley** (Shropshire) also emphasise the local sources of good butter. The other useful product of the dairy-farm is of course, cheese (*'cīese'*) and this is remembered in several place-names: **Keswick** (Cumbria), **Chiswick** (London), **Cheswardine** (Shropshire) and **Cheswick** (Northumberland).

Feeding the cattle which produced the milk for the butter and cheese a good diet was of major importance to the quality and **Filton** (*'filiþe-tūn'*) in Gloucestershire must have specialised in this aspect, for it means 'hay-farm'.

Many farms and homesteads will have had shelters for their animals against both the weather and predators, including thieves and there is a surprising number of records of such structures lurking in some of our place-names.

The barn is probably the first name that comes to mind when we think of a farm and this is recalled in a few of our place-names: **Barnes** (Surrey – *'berern'*, a barn) is specific in its meaning.

The cowshed is another familiar farm building and has retained a strong memory in **Byram** (Yorkshire), **Burdon** (Durham), **Berden** (Essex), **Cowarne** (Herefordshire), and **Skiplam** (Yorkshire). The first three originate in the Old English (and still current) word *'bȳre'* – a cowshed, while **Cowarne** also contains the word for a storehouse, *'ærn'*. **Skiplam**, however, is a later, Scandinavianised version of the original place-name *Scipnum* – a cattle fold. Bulls were given shelter from the elements in **Bulcote** (Nottinghamshire) and sheep in **Sapcote** (Leicestershire – *'scēap-cot'*). In the place-name **Binchester** (Durham), we have an interesting case of turning a local, very old and redundant Roman fortification (*'ceaster'*) to good use as a secure cattle shelter (*'binn'* – a manger). Fascinatingly, this village lies beside a Roman road with the remains of the actual Roman fort still at hand.

Happily, the herdsman himself was not forgotten, for his shelter has given names to the villages of **Hurcot** (Somerset – *'hierde-cot'*), **Shields** (Durham – *'scield'*) and **Lockerley** (Hampshire – *'loca-lēah'*).

Pigs would need shelter nearer to the farmstead itself and their protection was the *'hlōse'*, which has given rise to the names **Loose** (Kent), **Loosley** (Buckinghamshire), **Loseley** (Surrey) and **Liscombe** (Somerset – 'valley with a pigsty').

The swineherd's dwelling is thoughtfully remembered in the Derbyshire name **Swanwick** (*'swān-wīc'*). Having reared the pigs, thick bacon was a much enjoyed meat and could be smoked over the cottage fires for storing until the coming of the cold weather. **Flitcham** (*'flicce'* – bacon) in Norfolk was a local site where good sides of bacon – flitches – were produced.

Apart from the villages named after unspecified shelters, such as **Hove** (Sussex), **Hulcote** (Northamptonshire) and **Lawshall** (Suffolk – *'hlāw-gesella'*, a hillside shelter), the only other shelter we are likely to encounter that survives in place-names is one for geese and is to be found in the place-name **Goscote** (Staffordshire).

Fish-keeping must, I think, come under the heading of animal husbandry too. I discussed the importance of fish and the usual means of farming them in the section on Weirs in Chapter Three, so here I will just mention a few villages whose names have associations with fish-keeping occupations. **Brockweir** in Gloucestershire is located against one of the most famous earthwork boundaries in England – Offa's Dyke (constructed in the late 8th century) – and at a point where the **River Wye** is joined by a brook, giving the village its name – 'the weir at the brook'. **Wareham** (Dorset), straddling the **River Piddle** and the **River Frome**, together with **Warham** (Herefordshire) on the **River Wye**, recall once workable fish weirs, though there is none present today. **Yarwell** (Northamptonshire, *'gear wiell'* – a weir spring) is close by the **River Nene** which probably fed a pool where the fish were harvested.

Thus we have the familiar domestic livestock whose multiple values to the early English society lay in their meat, milk, eggs, hides, fleeces, feathers or great physical strength.

I have already mentioned that horses were trained for racing and fighting, but possession of a horse by a member of the peasant classes was most unlikely; such a luxury was for the wealthier landowners. I must now emphasise that horses were of great worth as war-mounts and as hunting mounts for the ruling classes, as well as mounts for messengers. Horses could also be working pack animals, though donkeys and oxen were more commonly used. The horse is recognised in the large number of place-names that are derived from the Old English *'hors'* (and its variation *'hross'*), which was the familiar domesticated animal and from the *'hengest'* – the stallion. *'Stōd'* – a stud of breeding horses – has given rise to a number of place-names. **Horseheath** (Cambridgeshire), **Hursley** (Hampshire) and **Horsenden** (Buckinghamshire) illustrate the first group, while **Rosley** (Cumbria) exemplifies the variation, *'hross'*. The stud of horses can be seen in **Stodmarsh** (Kent), **Stody** (Norfolk) and **Stoodleigh** (Devon).

Dogs ('*hundes*') that were tamed and trained for hunting are remembered in the place-name **Hunton** (Hampshire), while the huntsmen themselves lived at **Hunston** (Suffolk) and **Hunton** (Kent). Significant hunting grounds are recalled in **Huntercombe** (Oxfordshire – 'huntsman's valley'), **Huntley** (Gloucestershire – 'huntsman's wood') and **Huntington** (Cheshire – 'hunting hill'). There are, however, very few place-names based on the Old English word for the dog, '*dogga*'. **Dogbury** in Dorset is one of the few. A curious memory of the dog is to be found in **Hounsditch** (Middlesex, 13th century) which appears to refer to a ditch or pit into which dead dogs were thrown – a rather unappealing progenitor of the place-name!

So here we can leave the domesticated animals and their attendants and turn our focus on the farm land itself, which has much to tell us about the other aspects of early mediæval land use.

The farm holdings

Farmers were not the only holders of agricultural lands; members of the ruling classes too, owned great estates which were managed on their behalves by lesser tenants and on whose lands were scattered small villages and isolated dwellings.

Some of these estates were descriptively remembered in the names of settlements near the halls at which the nobility would be permanently resident or, if the lands belonged to the monarch, at which the kings or queens would lodge during their tours of the realm. **Conistone**, beside the **River Wharfe** in Yorkshire (recorded in Domesday as *Cunestune*) seems to be a Scandinavianised version of an older place, *Cyningestūn* – 'the king's estate'. **Kenton** (Northumberland) and **Kineton** (Gloucestershire) too, are memorials to ancient royal manors, for they each signified the '*cyne-tūn*' – 'the king's residence'.

Sometimes, the estate was remembered as belonging to, or the favourite quarters of, the queen. **Quinton** (Warwickshire) is one such place and in AD 848 is recorded as *Quentone* – 'the queen's manor'. The Domesday commissioners (1086) also noted three other queens' estates: **Queniborough** and **Quenby** (both in Leicestershire) and **Quainton** in Buckinghamshire.

The Norwich suburb of **Earlham** (Norfolk) and the village of **Arlington** in Sussex remind us that these settlements once stood on the estate of an earl.

The lands around the farms would vary in their landscape according to their locations. Most lowland farms would have streams and meadow settings with enclosures for animals and fields for grazing or for ploughing and crop growing.

Upland farming varied according to whether sheep were the principal herds, in which case the shepherds would tend their flocks on the hills and rougher terrains, or whether cattle could be reared on the lower slopes. In this latter case, enclosures with stone walls would be maintained and the animals would have to be moved around as the grass became exhausted and from season to season – the lower, 'home' pastures kept for the winter. Crops such as rye, wheat, barley and oats were commonly cultivated in the lowlands and ploughing, reaping, threshing, winnowing and milling would be the regular tasks necessary to maintain the operation of the farm. All of these aspects – the geographical and the occupational – are well represented in our place-names.

Pastures and grazing land in general reveal themselves in place-names such as **Danehill** (Sussex – 'hillside pasture'), **Denmead** (Hampshire – 'meadow pasture') and **Gresham** (Norfolk – 'grazing land'). In some places, a field might well be distinguished by its size, which would sometimes be expressed in our familiar acres and sometimes in 'hides'. A hide was a taxable stretch of land, of no definite area, but deemed sufficient for supporting a family. **Halnaker** (Sussex, *'healf-æcer'* – 'half acre') is an example of the former measure and **Fifield** (Oxfordshire – 'five-hides field') is an example of the latter. **Tinhead** (Wiltshire) and **Stokeinteignhead** (that is, Stoke-in-Teign-head, Devon) both mean 'ten-hides'. **Halsnead** (Lancashire), however, is less definite, for it is *'healf-snæd'* – 'a half measure of ground'.

We can visualise the nature of the fields around an arable estate from the place-names that have survived the centuries: there were the important well-established ploughed lands; then the fallow lands at rest for a season; next the newly cultivated ground and last, the waste – scrubby ground at the edges of the of the farmland and yet to be cleared. There are still English place-names that recall each of these states of cultivation: **Eartham** (Sussex) must have been settled near to significant ploughed land; fallow land is commemorated in **Fallowdon** (Northumberland) and newly cultivated land appears in the names **Falinge** (Lancashire), **Felling** (Durham) and **Newland** (Gloucestershire). **Weaste**, now part of the city of Salford (Lancashire), was once uncultivated or common ground. Apart from these distinctly farmland stretches, there would be the woodlands and perhaps even a patch of marsh or heath under the stewardship of the farmer.

I have mentioned animal enclosures from time to time. These vital livestock pounds – which our American friends will know as 'corrals' – could consist of a paddock-sized area enclosed by a hedge, a woven hurdle fence or, if stone were near at hand, especially in the hillier districts of the Cotswolds or Fells of

Cumbria, could be strongly constructed of stone in order to prevent the animals from straying and to keep out foxes and wolves. The words for an enclosure, *'hæg'* and *'hege'* crop up in the place-names **Hay** (Herefordshire) and **Hayes** (Middlesex), as well as in the second syllable of **Pleshey** (Essex) and meaning an 'interwoven fence', **Woodhay** (Berkshire and Hampshire, 'enclosure in a wood') and as the first element in **Haywards Heath** (Sussex).

CROPS

On the whole and compared with the range of vegetable varieties available to a modern farmer, the early English farmer was rather limited in his scope, though he undoubtedly made the most of what he had.

There is evidence in our place-names for the cultivation of barley, beans, flax, hops, oats, rye and spelt (an early variety of wheat) and there will have been the occasional patch of peas, orach (a spinach-like leaf), onions, leaks, celery and lentils too, though onions and lentils seem not to have entered into our place-names (see Herbs and Flowers earlier in this chapter).

We know too, that some soft fruits were harvested from small orchards in some localities – gooseberries, blackcurrents, quinces, medlars, damsons and greengages – as well as apples and pears. Although recognisable, most of these fruits would be unlike our modern varieties which have been selectively bred over several centuries. In addition, cottagers often cultivated their own vegetables in their cottage patch, producing welcome supplements to their usual fare. Potatoes and tomatoes were of course, unknown.

A very common place-name in the present context is **Barton**. It is found alone in at least ten English counties, as well as in many compounds like **Barton Stacey** (Hampshire), **Middle Barton** (Oxfordshire) and **Barton-under-Needwood** (Staffordshire). In all of these places its origin is the Old English *'bere-tūn'* – a barley farm. For several centuries barley (*'beren'*) was the important basis of flour used to make a coarse bread and when the barley seeds were roasted, it was known to produce a malt which could be fermented into barley-beer. Wheat (*'hwæte'*) too, became important for the improved nature of its flour and consequently a better quality bread. Its impact is recorded in many lowland place-names, including **Wheatley** (Oxfordshire), **Wheatacre** (Norfolk), **Whaddon** (Buckinghamshire) and **Wheddon** (Somerset).

Rye (*'ryge'*) is a barley-like cereal that was also cultivated. Because it will tolerate poorer soil and cold temperatures better than barley and wheat, it was often grown as an alternative, though its flour was inferior to that of wheat, but, like barley, the roasted seeds could be fermented into a slightly alcoholic ale. Rye must have seemed an important crop since there are place-names derived from its name. I have already listed a few of them earlier in this chapter in the section *Herbs and Flowers,* but it's appropriate to add one or two more here: **Raydon** and **Reydon** (both in Suffolk), **Ryhall** (Rutland) and **Ryarsh** (Kent, *'ryge-ersc'* – a rye-stubble field) all testify to the importance of the crop.

The last of the cereal crops of the period to mention is the oat. Like rye, oats were regarded largely as a supplementary crop and provided a coarse-grain flour which would readily thicken the daily stews into a more substantial gruel. **Oteley** in Shropshire has the right sound and indeed comes from *'āte'*, the Old English word for oat. Other places having their names rooted in the oat come to us via the Old Scandinavian word *'hafra'* and we will meet them in the next chapter.

Having grown the cereals, the ripened seed pods had to be separated from the husk and stalks. This called for the process of threshing – a manual beating of the stalks and heads, often carried out on the hard earth floor of a barn. However, **Threshfield** (Yorkshire) seems to indicate that it was a custom in that locality to carry out the operation on open land.

By the 9th century, hops (*'hymele'*) were known in parts of England and were beginning to be grown for the slightly bitter flavour their flower heads would impart to stews and fermented drink. However, their widespread use in brewing lay several centuries in the future. A few place-names that remind us of the early English hop growing have survived the centuries: **Himbleton** (Worcestershire) is first recorded in AD 816 and its early spelling, *Hymeltun*, shows its direct connection to the hop plant. **Humbleton** (Yorkshire) and **Himley** (Staffordshire) also proclaim their early associations with local hop growing.

Beans and peas would be grown as a useful addition to the humble cottage cooking pot and to mix with animal feed no doubt and I have mentioned some place-names associated with them in the earlier section *Herbs and Flowers.* **Benacre** (Suffolk) and **Bendish** (Hertfordshire) are two other villages that have inherited their names from *'bēan'* – a bean. **Posenhall** (Shropshire), from *'pise'*, a pea, can serve as our farewell to the edible vegetables.

One final useful crop worth a mention was flax (*'līnen'*), used for producing linen fibres for spinning into cloth and for its oil (linseed oil). It is probable that **Linton** in Cambridgeshire has its origins in the nearby cultivation of flax, since its recording in a document of AD 970 is *Lintune*. The hamlets of **Old Lindley** (Yorkshire) and **Linley** (Shropshire) also attest to the fields of flax on adjacent farms, but **Flaxton** (Yorkshire) has evolved from the alternative word for the plant, *'fleax'*.

Occupations in and around the towns

For about three hundred years after the first Anglo-Saxon settlers arrived on British soil, the abandoned Roman towns were shunned in favour of rural farm-steads and small agricultural settlements and many fell into ruin. With the es-tablishment of small centres of specialisation – leather-working in one village, wood-working in a neighbouring village, weaving in another and so forth – a basic 'township' could easily be established by bringing craftsmen together. By the time of King Ælfred the Great (reigned 871 – 899) many such settlements had evolved and had acquired defensive embankments and walls with entrance gates, carefully manned to regulate outsider access into the communities. These self-supporting towns were given the old name *'burhs'*, a word which is the precursor of our 'boroughs' and detectable in many place-names by the suffix *'-bury'* – **Oldbury**, **Newbury**, **Highbury**, **Bradbury**, **Ledbury** and many more. Within these larger settlements began to congregate small groups of tradesmen: one street might have a couple of leather tanners; nearby we might see a col-lection of weavers' workshops and further on, an alley with two or three shoe-makers' houses. We can discover a wide range of occupational and recreational activities which have left their marks on the area in which they were practised. Most towns will still have memories of ancient tradesmen in their street names: Baker Street, Shoe Lane, Fisher Row, Cornmarket Street, Butchers Row, Smith Lane, Cooper Place – the reader will probably be able to add to the list from his or her own locality.

Craft workers

This aspect of human occupation is one from which the English later acquired a great many of their surnames: Smith and its compounds like Goldsmith, Naismith ('nail-' or 'knife-smith') and Sixsmith ('sickle-smith'), Glaser, Potter, Twiner, Weaver, Tiler, Glazer and very many more. So we owe a double debt to the later first-millennium settlers for providing the foundations for English place-names and a host of surnames of their descendants.

Within this branch of creative activity we can find workers in various metals (iron, copper, tin, gold and silver), glass makers, potters, shingle (wooden tile) makers, shoemakers, stone-masons and carpenters, among others. The goldsmith (*'gold-smið'*) would be a well respected member of the community and from one ancient Somerset title-deed we note a workplace named *Goldsmiðecote* ('cottage or workplace of the goldsmith'), now identified as **Golsoncott**, a hamlet about eight miles south-east of Minehead. The goldmith's expertise would of course, extend to silver, copper and any other bright metal, as well as incorporating gemstones into his work, according to his commission. The blacksmith, too, was a considerable artisan whose wide ranging expertise could fashion delicate knives, robust swords, plough shares, a dozen other tools, horse gear and nails exactly fitted for their purposes. One of the most famous place-names in this context is London's **Hammersmith**, once an outlying village, where a notable smithy or two were to be found. **Smeaton** (Yorkshire), **Smeetham** (Essex) and **Smethwick** (Staffordshire) easily give away their origins as workplaces of smiths – probably blacksmiths. Items that any ironsmith could readily turn out were the iron hoops that held the wooden sections of a barrel together (the barrel maker was known as the cooper). If a man were well known for making these iron hoops, he might well be called the 'hooper' and **Hopperton** in Yorkshire reminds us of one such nearby specialist.

Glass (*'glæs'*) was a fairly rare commodity in the 9th and 10th centuries. Glass windows were affordable only by the wealthy and by well-supported churches and abbeys. Glass vessels too were an expensive luxury, but glass beads were not uncommon and jewellery incorporating glass was well known and is found in excavations of Anglo-Saxon burials among the grave goods. The local glass maker has given his craft-name to **Glascote** ('the glass-maker's cottage') in Staffordshire.

There was always a demand for clay pots for storage and cooking and potters would be constantly at work with their clay and kilns. **Potterne** (Wiltshire) was the *'pott-ærn'* – the potter's house and **Potterton** (Yorkshire) was 'the potters' *tūn* or village'), where one, or perhaps several, potters had their workshops.

The shoemaker was the specialist in fashioning shoes from leathers from the tanner. Usually the leather was soft and would wear quickly, but, with care, shoes could be re-stitched or repaired several times by a patient housewife. *'Sūtere'* was the Old English word, borrowed from the Latin *'sutor'*, for a shoemaker and the Domesday scribe records in 1086 the location of a settlement, *Sutrebi* in Lincolnshire, now spelt **Sutterby**, but retaining the characteristic Danish suffix '-*by*', of which we shall see more in the next chapter.

That universally adaptable resource, wood, had dozens of applications of course, as it still has today and woodworking craftsmen were never out of employment. Their general name was '*wyrhta*', from which we have our suffix '-*wright*', which later became attached to a first element that specified the man's skill – wheelwright, cartwright, boatwright, arkwright, ploughwright and much later, playwright. Several places recall the wright's location and craft: **Rigbolt** (Lincolnshire – 'the wright's dwelling') and **Wrightington** (Lancashire – 'the village of the wrights') are two examples. **Aldoth** (Cumbria – 'old lath') is slightly unusual in that it may refer to a tool of the wright – his lathe – or to the planks or laths ('*laððe*') of wood he produced.

Outside some of the settlements skilled men could be found at work in various heavily manual occupations – in quarries where the rock was at the surface, in shallow pits clawing coal from the ground or extracting iron ore. Living an isolated life in the woods or in a woodland clearing would be found the occasional charcoal burner.

The stone hewers were important for extracting the rock for the making of building blocks, millstones and querns and their tasks are remembered in the names **Stonegrave** (Yorkshire) and **Biddulph** (Staffordshire – '*bū-delfan*', the dwelling at the diggings). Quarrying is a principal factor in the place-names **Quarley** (Hampshire), **Quarndon** (Derbyshire) and **Quarr** (Isle of Wight). The sites of ancient ore quarries have left us with two relevant Lancashire place-names: **Orrell** and **Orgreave** and there are still open-cast pits to be seen at **Orgreave**. At the other end of England, **Orsett** in Essex also recalls the extraction of iron ore, or 'bog-ore', as it was sometimes called.

A related, but rarely heard of and rather unexpected, industry in England is to be found in the village names **Pitchford** (Shropshire) and **Pitchcott** (Buckinghamshire). Perhaps the reader can guess which natural deposit is being recalled in these two names. In fact, it is bitumen, which oozed from a geological fissure in the ground nearby and was a recognised useful waterproofing material. I believe there still may be a viable pitch well in the grounds of Pitchford Hall.

It had always been evident to the early English that the earth was a storehouse of a great deal of valuable substance and many a thinking man must have wondered what else the great Mother could provide. In Chapter One, I referred to salt-making in Staffordshire and Cheshire as being a well established activity. As a preservative of meats and fish, salting was second only to smoking and in this respect the mineral was a valuable resource to the village dwellers. Cheshire was an important district for saline springs and salt-boiling has given us the name of **Wallerscote** (Cheshire), which is believed to have arisen from an ancient local dialect word ('*waller*' – a salt boiler) for this occupation. **Seasalter**

(Kent) is a little more obvious and the prefix '-*Sal*' is again suggestive of salt-making in the names **Saltram** (Devon) and **Salcott** (Essex) – in these three cases from sea water.

Soap making is perhaps a task we give little thought to, especially when we are taught that personal hygiene was of relatively small importance to our distant ancestors. However, soap-like substances have been known from great antiquity and also that the ashes of some plants, notably bracken, when boiled with fats or the oils pressed from seeds, will set when cool, into a slimy, rather soapy deposit, which will remove grime from almost any surface and has the advantage that it is fairly soluble in water. Just a couple of place-names remain, in four counties, that recall the soap-maker's occupation: **Sapiston** (Suffolk) and **Sapperton** (Derbyshire, Lincolnshire and Gloucestershire) and all are recorded in Domesday (1086), which means that they too, were well established villages by the mid-11th century.

I have mentioned the weaving craft once or twice, but an associated aspect of this occupation is rarely mentioned – that of fulling. Newly woven cloth, whether of linen (flax) or of wool, was rather coarse and stiff and required softening in order that it could be tailored into simple clothing. The 'fuller' was the worker who carried out this process by laying the woven sheets in running water and trampling the cloth until it was supple. He was also called the 'walker' in some areas, though folk in the south-west of England preferred the word 'tucker'. These three occupational words are the origins of the three surnames Fuller, Walker and Tucker. Two place-names which indicate the presence of these workers are **Walkern** in Hertfordshire and **Tuckerton** in Somerset. Nearby rivers and streams would have provided the necessary running water. **Fullerton** (Hampshire) looks as though it belongs here, but its Domesday entry (1086) (*Fugelerestune*) shows that it derives its name from the 'birdcatchers' dwelling' (*'fugolere'* – a birdcatcher).

Just a small group remains to be mentioned in this section on the craftworkers. The first, a trader who hawked his modest wares around the neighbourhoods was called a 'chapman' (*'cēapmann'*) and he undoubtedly performed a useful service for villagers, who would be alerted by his cries. Domesday (1086) records the village of **Coppingford** (now in Cambridgeshire), as *Copemaneforde* – the ford near which the chapmen traded. **Capernwray** in Lancashire also refers to a 'chapmen's corner', though this place-name derives from Scandinavian words and is first recorded in the mid-13th century.

The hamlet of **Harcourt** (Shropshire) recalls a hawker of a different kind – the man whose calling was to train his master's hunting birds, the falcons. The name originates in the Old English *'hafocere'* – a falconer.

Watermills were set beside streams, or else channels from adjacent rivers were diverted to turn the grinding stones so that flour could be produced for the kitchens of the community leader. Mills were therefore landmark buildings in many districts and have given rise to many place-names as memorials to their value. **Milborne** (Dorset – *Muleburne*, 'mill stream') has an early record (AD 939) and **Milcote** (Warwickshire – *Mulecote*, 'mill cottage'), an even earlier one (AD 710). **Mileham** (Norfolk – *Muleham*, 'homestead with a mill'), gets its first mention in Domesday (1086).

There are many **Prestons** *('prēost-tūn')* in England and most will refer to the house of the priest (*'prēost'*) – the teacher, advisor and comforter to everyone in the district, particularly, it appears, the poorest of the poor, who are remembered in **Lattiford** (Somerset), a name that originates in the word *'loddere'* – a beggar.

Finally, there are two places that bring forward the king's chief law officer in each district, the sheriff (that is, the 'shire-reeve'). His status meant that his house would be grander than those of the commoners and this man's office is recalled in the place-names **Screveton** (Nottinghamshire) and **Shurton** (Somerset).

Worship and superstition

The earliest Anglo-Saxon settlers practised a form of 'paganism' whereby a multitude of deities were held to have the potential to influence every aspect of human existence and who could respond favourably to acts of worship and adulation. Earth, water, fire, weather, thunder, harvest, war, health, retribution, fate and many other states and singularities were ardently believed to be regulated by and under the control of the supernatural realm.

In addition to the supreme deities, there were believed to be lesser beings, such as elves and sprites, some of which could assume the protection of individuals or households and would remain appeased and quietly co-operative as long as appropriate offerings were maintained from those under their guardianship. Conversely, dwarfs, goblins, giants, dragons and demons were also acknowledged and were believed always to be ready to perform mischief and harm given the opportunity.

Amazingly, relics of the principal ancient deities remain with us to this day in our daily lives, for the days of our week celebrate four of them – *Tiw* (*'Tīwesdæg'* – Tuesday), *Woden* (*'Wōdnesdæg'* – Wednesday), *Thunor* (*'þunresdæg'* –

Thursday) and the goddess *Frige* (*'Frīgedæg'* – Friday). Saturday ('Saturn's day') is a relic of the Roman occupation, while the ancient and continuing mystic acknowledgment of the sun and moon are, of course, remembered in Sunday and Monday. However, it is not quite so widely known that some of our place-names also reflect those more mystical, pagan times. *Tiw*, one of several battle gods, has found a comfortable home in the place-names **Tewin** (Hertford-shire), **Twiscombe** (Devon), **Tuesnoad** (Kent), **Tuesley** (Surrey) and **Tysoe** (Warwickshire). *Woden*, one of the principal deities and an almost universal superintendent of death, retribution, the hunt, wisdom, magic and more, still has, unsurprisingly, lent his powerful name to a number of places, among which are **Wansdyke** (an earthwork running between Wiltshire and Somerset), **Wednesfield** and **Wedensbury** (both in Staffordshire), **Wensley** and **Wensley-dale** (both in Derbyshire), and **Woodnesborough** (Kent). The inhabitants of **Thundersley** (Essex), **Thundridge** (Hertfordshire) and **Thursley** (Surrey) will be comforted by the thought that they are all under the protection of *Thunor* (*Thor*) and his thunderbolts. *Frige*, a goddess of love, fertility and perhaps wisdom, makes a plain statement in **Fridaythorpe** (Yorkshire), but only shy appearances in the three Hampshire villages of **Froyle** (probably *'Frige's-hyll'*), **Frobury** (*'Frige-byrig'*) and **Freefolk** (*'Frige's people'*).

Following St Augustine's papal-inspired mission to England in AD 597 and the subsequent conversion to Christianity of King Æthelberht of Kent, Chris-tianity's firm advance throughout the next two centuries gradually pushed the pagan ideas and rituals of native Englishmen into the background, though by no means obliterated them, for the old ways, as always, are stubbornly averse to change. This can be seen in a group of surviving and well distributed place-names that recall places of the persisting non-Christian ceremony – **Weoley Castle** (Birmingham – *'wēoh'*, an idol temple or shrine), **Weyhill** (Hampshire – *'wēoh-hyll'*), **Wyville** (Lincolnshire – *'wēoh-wella'*, the stream at a heathen shrine) and **Wysall** (Nottinghamshire – *'wēoh-hōh'*, a shrine on a hillside spur). Even today, twelve hundred years later, a species of paganism is pursued by small groups.

Superstitions die hard and anyway, they are curiously exciting, especially when woven into story-telling – hair-raising experiences, weird phenomena and wild imagination can create memorable impressions in the minds of one's audience. The simple, pastoral Englishman of the later centuries of the first millennium had no doubts about the reality of supernatural beings that inhab-ited the woodlands, streams, caves and anywhere that was dark. Perhaps it is not altogether surprising then, that places with eerie local reputations earned descriptive names that have persisted down the centuries. This is fortunate for us as modern students of the early English, since it gives us a valuable insight into the minds and thinking of our distant forebears. So, let's see what remains in our place-names of the mystical side of pre-Conquest England. Beginning with those rather less fearsome entities, the fairies, sprites and goblins, which were often associated with pools and streams: the place-name **Puckeridge** (Hertfordshire – '*púca-hrycg*', a bank frequented by goblins) displays immediate hints of Shakespeare's mischievous fairy Puck, in his play 'A Midsummer Night's Dream'. This village lies very close to the **River Ribb**, where, no doubt, the goblins were also to be encountered. **Purbrook** (Hampshire) takes its name from the neighbouring brook – '*púca-bróc*' (the goblin brook). **Shobrooke** (Devon) recalls the '*scucca*' – a sprite or goblin that probably frequented the adjacent stream called Shobrook. **Scugdale**, a rather lonely valley in Yorkshire, must also have been haunted by the '*scucca*', this time emerging from Scugdale Beck which flows down the valley. The same root is to be found in the villages **Shocklach** (Cheshire), **Shugborough** (Staffordshire) and **Shuckburgh** (Warwickshire) and, as one would by now expect, each has a nearby stream.

So much for the smaller apparitions – one can only hope that the modern residents of these six neighbourhoods will continue to sleep easily at night once the spooky history of their localities has been pointed out to them, if they didn't know it already!

Giants and demons seem to have evoked similar mental images in the minds of our ancestors; each was believed to have been of superhuman size and strength. A handful of place-names may still conjure the monsters from their slumbers (if we know the right words and say them in the right tones of course!). An ancient ford across the **River Stiffkey** at the village of **Thursford** (Norfolk) must have borne the attentions of a mediæval giant or demon, for the name is '*þyrs-ford*' – 'ford frequented by a demon'. 'The Lake' in the parkland of Tusmore House in Oxfordshire, the site of the mediæval village of **Tusmore**, once had the reputation of being haunted by demons, for its name derives from '*þyrs-mere*' – 'the demon lake'. **Shincliffe** (Durham), however, may feel it is let off lightly in the supernatural stakes – its neighbouring hill was possessed only by a phantom ('*scinn*' – a spectre).

Finally, we come to the least believable of mythical creatures, the dragon. A few places were believed to be terrorised by such creatures and its name, '*draca*', has survived, but only very tenuously, in four minor districts: **Drakelow** (Derbyshire and Worcestershire), **Drakedale** (Yorkshire) and **Drake Hill** (Surrey).

MEETING PLACES

All communities, no matter how small, tend to look to, or appoint, a spokesman and leader, on whom is conferred a degree of authority for decision making. This was as true in the latter half of the first millennium AD, as it is today. For such occasions, agreed assembly places are important. In ancient times, these may simply have been in the open, on a nearby prominent hillock, in a clearing in a wood, at the junction of local trackways or at a local landmark such as at a river crossing or beneath a great rock, under a prominent oak tree or beside a spring. Eventually, a wooden building may have been erected on the customary site as protection against the weather and where a blazing fire could form a comfortable centre-piece. These small, but important centres of civic activity would inevitably give rise to place-names and we have plenty of surviving evidence of them throughout the country. **Mottisfont** (Hampshire) recalls a meeting place beside a spring and at **Mottistone** (Isle of Wight), the assembly was held at a great stone on the hill. The gathering point at **Mutford** (Suffolk) was beside a shallow river crossing, probably over the adjacent Hundred River. Each of these place-names has, at its core, the old word '*mōt*', meaning a discussion or council. **Runnymede** (Surrey), famous as the location of King John's signing of the *Magna Carta* in 1215, is '*rūniēg-mæd*' – 'council-island meadow'. Meetings were held in a glade at **Spetchley** (Worcestershire), for the name, '*spæc-lēah*', means the 'speech meadow', while only a few miles further north at **Stoulton**, near Worcester, was an ancient seat of justice – '*stōl-tūn*' – 'the place of the throne'. **Stoulton** was probably the meeting place of one of the shire courts, called the 'hundreds', at which the king's justices heard the pleas and arguments and from where justice was dispensed. Hampshire too, retains a recollection of an important ancient seat of justice in **Damerham**, a few miles north-east of Fordingbridge. The village's earliest record (AD 880) gives the name as *Domra Hamm*, meaning 'meeting place of the judges'.

And so we see that here we have the very beginnings of what we now know as the 'town hall', with its council chamber and even the humble origins of our magistrates' courts. However, there were meeting places with less serious purposes than these we have been looking at so far. Villagers from neighbouring communities would congregate at favourite locations for ceremonies, festivals, weddings, fairs, markets and, with great anticipation no doubt, for sports and games. These latter occasions encompassed many activities, including running, throwing, wrestling, sword play, swimming, tests of personal strength and horse racing. Naturally, betting and wagers were commonplace. '*Plega*' (pronounced 'pleya') was the general word for a game or sport and a player or sportsman was the *'plegere'* and *'plegmann'*, so the origins of our modern words, 'play' and 'player' are quite clear. Some places that illustrate the love of these early sporting gatherings are **Playford** (Suffolk), **Plealey** (Shropshire), **Plaxtol** (Kent) and **Plaistow** (Derbyshire, Essex and Sussex).

Perhaps allied to the games aspect are **Chilwell** (Nottinghamshire) and **Childwall** (Lancashire), each of which refers to streams where children would congregate, though we are left to guess at the amusements they enjoyed.

CRIME AND PUNISHMENT

If an allegation were found to be irrefutably proved against a defendant, sentence would be passed by the appointed justice. For the crimes regarded in those times as most serious, the options were three: a fine, mutilation or death. Imprisonment was not an option, however, for there were no prisons. The main offences for which a hearing before the king's sheriff was called were theft, damage to property (including arson), loss of life and treason against a lord or the king. Proven guilt of any of these could attract the capital penalty, unless the crime had been committed against a slave, in which case a fine might be levied. A sentence of death would customarily be by hanging, though beheading, disembowelling and drowning are known to have been carried out in some places. Other serious convictions, including that of murder, usually led to the imposition of a fine and compensation (*'wergild'* – 'man-value') paid by the felon to the victim's family. Inability or failure to pay the fine might well lead to the accused himself being condemned to a period of slavery.

If, however, a defendant vigorously maintained, on oath, his innocence, regardless of the evidence given against him, the king's justice might order 'trial by ordeal' – that is, placing the verdict in the hands of God. The accused was usually permitted to choose between 'ordeal by water' or 'ordeal by heat'. If 'ordeal by water' were chosen, he must first drink a goblet of holy water, brought to the scene by a supervising churchman, after which the defendant would be thrown into a river or pool. If he floated he would be declared to be guilty. If he sank, his innocence was assured (as long as he could be pulled out before he drowned!). In the event of 'ordeal by heat' being chosen, the accused man was usually permitted the option of plunging his bare arm into a cauldron of boiling water in order to lift out a stone, or he must seize a red hot bar of iron and walk with it for five paces (about nine feet). In either case, his raw wounds would be bound and if, after three days, the lesions were clean with no sign of infection or putrefaction, he was declared to be innocent. Otherwise, guilt was proclaimed and due sentence would be passed.

That hanging was the preferred and frequent means of execution is affirmed by the number of known pre-mediæval sites of gallows that have survived in our place-names. I have located seven definite hanging places and two that suggest drowning. Yorkshire seems to have several gallows' sites: **Galphay** (*'gealga-haga'*, the gallows enclosure), **Gawber** (*'gealga-beorg'*, gallows mound), **Wrelton** (*'wearg-hyll'*, outlaw hill) and **Deedle Hill** (*'dēad-hyll'*, deadman's hill). The latter is difficult to locate on road maps, but is mentioned by G.J.Copley in his 'English Place-names' (publ. David & Charles, 1971).

There is evidence that drownings were sometimes carried out in, or near, the Yorkshire village of **Wheldrake**, about seven miles south-east of York, for the name derives from *'cwięld-ric'* – death-stream. **Warnborough** (Hampshire) too, seems to have been a drowning site, if the name's origins are any guide, *'wearg-burna'* – the felon's stream.

Dethick (Derbyshire) was 'the death oak' – clearly a hangman's tree, but **Worgret** (Dorset) was *'wearg-rōd'* – 'the felon's cross' and perhaps suggests a site of crucifixion. **Wreighill** (Northumberland – *'wearg-hyll'*) is non-committal and simply means 'the hill where criminals were executed'.

Death and burial

By the 8th century, the Christian religion was dominating the burial practices of the English and the earlier cremation rituals had mostly disappeared. Corpses of the lowest classes were usually buried, lying east-west, in designated cemeteries, but higher ranking deaths would be treated very differently and on a grander scale, a prominent mound (*'hlæw'*) being thrown up over the grave, which would probably also contain belongings of the deceased, and sometimes marked with a great stone. Within some of the recently excavated mounds there have been found multiple burials, indicating the later opening of the chamber for the interment of the bodies of relatives and descendants of the initial occupant.

There are many references in English place-names to the burial sites of these higher ranking individuals, both because of their local status and because of the prominent nature of the barrow in the landscape, this latter revealing itself in the suffixes *'-low'*, *'-lowe'* or *'-loe'*, a modification of the Old English word *'hlæw'*, meaning a mound or hillock. Such place-names often refer directly to the identity of the buried person: **Atlow** (Derbyshire – *'Eatta's hlāw'*, burial mound of *Eatta*), **Cutteslowe** (Oxfordshire – *'Cūþen's hlāw'*) and **Bledisloe** (Gloucester-shire – *'Blīþe's hlāw'*).

Some place-names recalling burial mounds lack any reference to the deceased individual, however, probably because the location was a traditional burial site and there were several mounds close together: **Barrowden** (Rutland – *'beorg-dūn'*, hill with burial mounds), **Brainshaugh** (Northumberland – *'byrgen-halh'*, burial place) and **Brailsham** (Sussex – *'byrgen-hamm'*, burial enclosure).

A Final Miscellany

Inevitably, when considering such an encyclopædic contribution to a country's history as was made by the Anglo-Saxons, there will be some aspects which, through space limitations or by reason of their relatively minor importance, are likely to be discounted from the discussion. However, because of the fascination of the subject of the evolution of our place-names, I'd like to add this interesting miscellany as an epilogue, in which I will mention a few unusual structures, some place-names that refer to colours, compass directions and to end with, a small group of just plain interesting place-names.

Featherstone (Yorkshire and Staffordshire) is an unlikely twin of **Fourstones** (Northumberland), for both relate to a 'tetralith' – three standing stones capped by a roof stone, perhaps marking a burial site, an ancient ritual assembly point or simply a territorial boundary.

Colours in the form of dyes have cropped up already in this chapter (*Herbs and flowers*), but there are many concealed mentions of colours in our place-names: black, white, blue, gold, grey, greeñ, red and even variegated patterns are to be found, as well as simply 'dark', 'bright' and 'sparkling'. **Blakenhall** (Cheshire) is *'blæc-halh'* – a black place, though the reason for this is now obscure. Despite its appearance, **Wheatfield** (Oxfordshire) is 'white field', for its Domesday (1086) entry is *'Witefelle'* and the village lies at the foot of the range of chalk hills called The Chilterns. The colour blue is half-concealed in the village name **Blofield** (Norfolk), where it may have referred to a natural, local swathe of the woad plant, whose leaves were a well known source of a blue dye.

Guildford (Surrey) may think itself of special historic value, since its nāme arises from the old word for gold, *'gylden'*. However, the ford across the River Wey was simply a place where a striking annual profusion of golden marigolds was to be seen.

One would think that greyness is hardly worth remarking, but it does appear in our place-names. **Harewood** (Hampshire) looks as though it should refer to a wood where hares are found, but its early recorded spelling, *Harwode*, shows that its origin lies in *'hār'* – 'grey' and not in the expected *'hara'*, meaning a hare.

Green is a very familiar word in our place-names, usually referring to an area of common land in a settlement, when standing as a separate word, rather than the colour. Nevertheless, the colour has found its way almost undisguised into many place-names such as **Greenham** (Berkshire) and **Greenfield** (Bedfordshire), though it is disguised a little in **Grinton** (Yorkshire).

The colour red in place-names can derive its inspiration from several sources (other than as an abbreviated form of 'reed'). **Radwell** (Bedfordshire) is 'red spring' and **Rawmarsh** (Yorkshire) means 'red marsh', both names originating in the colour of the local sandstone geology.

The glimpse of the remains of a nearby mosaic Roman pavement may have been the reason for the naming of the Oxford village **Fawler**, for the name is from *'fāg-flōr'*, meaning 'colourful or variegated floor'. Although this village has a fairly late first record from the year 1205, it must have been established, at least as a homestead, long before that.

Although the four principal compass directions are very familiar to us in our place-names, both in doublets like **North Shields** and **South Shields** (Durham), **West Bromwich** (Staffordshire), **East Ham** (London) and as first elements of names – **Northwold** and **Southwold** (Suffolk), **Westerham** (Kent), **Easthope** (Shropshire), they occasionally hide themselves rather cleverly – **Ascot** (Berkshire), **Exton** (Hampshire) and **Owstwick** (Yorkshire) are really 'the eastern cottage', 'the east Saxons' place' and 'the eastern farm'. **Sudeley** (Gloucestershire) means 'the south meadow' and **Norwich** (Norfolk) is 'the north settlement'.

To end our little miscellany, let's take a glance at a dozen place-names that have an interesting look to them, but which give no clue at all as to their origins and meanings:

Place-name	County	Origin	Meaning
Adel	Yorkshire	*adela*	a foul place
Affpuddle	Dorset	*Æffa-pidele*	Æffa's estate on the River Piddle
Blubberhouses	Yorkshire	*bluber-hūsum*	dwellings near the bubbling stream
Havenstreet	Isle of Wight	*hæðen-stræt*	a street of the heathen
Honeychild	Kent	*Hūna-celde*	Hūna's spring

Mixon	Staffordshire	*mixen*	a dunghill
Mucking	Essex	*Mucca-ingas*	the dwellings of *Mucca's* people
Potto	Yorkshire	*pott-haugr*	a hill where pots were found
Ripe	Sussex	*rip*	a strip of harvest land
Wem	Shropshire	*wemm*	a polluted place
Wendy	Cambridgeshire	*windan*	a place at a river bend
Wetwang	Yorkshire	*wæt-wang*	a marshy field

At this point and after many pages in two whole chapters, it is time to draw a line under the conspicuous Anglo-Saxon contribution to the evolution of English place-names. Of course, the Anglo-Saxons (the original English) continued to dominate the country's fortunes until the advent of the Normans in the mid-11th century, but their influence became diluted by the appearance and settlement of new and determined incomers from the near continent during the later 9th century, who were to have their own distinctive effect on English place-names. However, it was through the Anglo-Saxons' thinking processes that England received most of its legacy of place-names and, as we have seen, these have proved enormously durable.

Chapter 5

NEW THREATS –
NORSEMEN AND DANES

THE ERA OF SOLE ANGLO-SAXON DOMINATION in England seemed to be at its peak in the closing years of the 8th century. What we call 'Old English' was the principal spoken language in all but the far south-west, Christianity was widely practised and the rulers of the various English kingdoms still enthusiastically fought each other from time to time. The first sign that a change to the *status quo* might be heralded was the fierce raid on the hallowed island of **Lindisfarne**, just off the coast of Northumbria, in AD 793 by a band of Danish marauders whom we know as 'Vikings' – a title adopted by some of the raiders themselves ('*vikingr*', meaning 'pirates'). The **Lindisfarne** monastery, founded nearly a century earlier by St Aidan, was sacked, its valuables plundered and the monks were killed, before the raiders withdrew to their Danish homeland. Coastal areas of Britain were to suffer further sporadic Viking raids over the coming decades, until the 860s saw a full-scale invasion by Danes in the east and Norsemen in the north. By the end of the 870s, the Danes had won control of the kingdoms of Northumbria, East Anglia and the territories in the east Midlands, while the Norsemen were beginning to dominate the north-west. Only the southern kingdom of Wessex held fast against the Vikings' western onslaught, until its king, Ælfred ('The Great') and the Danish leader Guthrum, signed a peace treaty which ceded to Danish rule the territory they already occupied in the north and east, Watling Street being the specified boundary between the two kingdoms. The territory under Danish control later became known as the Danelaw and accounted for about half the area of England (see figure 3, page 129). An increasingly uneasy relationship between the English Anglo-Saxons and the English Danes continued for the next one hundred and fifty years. Such was the tremendous impact of the Scandinavian invasion, that logical thinking would suggest that a large proportion of modern English people are surely descended from those Scandinavian occupiers of this large area of England.

Throughout the 10th and 11th centuries, Danish migration into the eastern districts increased, with the effect that more and more place-names of Danish origin were introduced as many entirely new settlements were established. Where existing English settlements were absorbed into the Danelaw regime, the new migrants tended to modify the existing English names simply by the addition of a Danish or Norse suffix. The Scandinavian legacy in our place-names can most easily be seen in these characteristic suffixes, the most familiar one being '-by'. Here are twelve of these suffixes as they appear in our place-names and which are typically found in the northern and north-eastern counties of England:

Suffix	Meaning	Example
-by	a settlement	**Haconby** (Lincs) – 'Hacum's settlement'
-garth	a passage, gap in the hills	**Aysgarth** (N.Yorks) – 'passage with oak trees'
-gill	a ravine	**Fothergill** (Cumb) – 'cattle fodder ravine'
-holm	an island, water meadow	**Baldwinholme** (Cumb) – 'Baldwin's meadow'
-keld	a spring	**Threlkeld** (Cumb) – 'spring of the peasants'
-kirk	a church, temple	**Ormskirk** (Lancs) – 'Orm's church'
-o(e)	a hill	**Clitheroe** (Lancs) – 'hill of the song thrush'
-scale	a shelter or hut	**Seascale** (Cumb) – 'shelter near the sea'
-thorp	a farm, hamlet	**Oglethorpe** (W. Yorks) – 'Odkell's farm'
-thwaite	a meadow, a clearing	**Crossthwaite** (Cumb) – 'clearing with a cross'
-toft	a homestead	**Eastoft** (Lincs) – 'farm near the ash trees'
-with	a wood	**Askwith** (W.Yorks) – 'ash tree wood'

The first element in the place-name is often a personal name, usually Scandinavian, but sometimes English, as illustrated in the first, fourth, sixth and ninth examples above and will usually recall the name of a local chief or leader of a settlement. It is not always easy to determine the exact spelling of the personal name in these place-name components because there are very often no other known documented mentions of the name, but nevertheless, these personal elements have given us a significant number of pre-mediæval personal names that we might otherwise not have known.

Having won control of half of England, the Scandinavians did not set about changing everything in sight, but gradually imposed their traditional ways on their new territories. The newcomers knew that they had to co-exist with the indigenous population in as mutually co-operative a way as could be achieved, though there was always a certain amount of dissention and friction between the two cultures. Existing place-names were spoken and written, when neces-sary, with modified spellings and sometimes with new Danish or Norse suffixes. New words for familiar features of the landscape – hills, ridges, slopes, valleys, bogs, bays, headlands and so forth were inevitably heard by the native English. Farms, dwellings, animal shelters, animals, trees and work practices – all had their Scandinavian equivalents of course. For several generations there will have existed dual names for everything in the Danelaw regions: an English word and a Scandinavian word, until a single expression predominated and eventually became the norm.

THE NATURAL LANDSCAPE – *UPLANDS AND VALLEYS*

As in previous chapters, we will begin by looking at the features of the natural landscape that will have attracted attention and therefore will have received descriptive Scandinavian names early on. The Norsemen and Swedes were well acquainted with mountainous terrain of course, though the Danes' homeland was much more like the English Midlands. The most impressive feature of any landscape is going to be a mountain and most of the English mountain-like scenery is in modern-day Cumbria (now incorporating the old counties of Westmorland, Cumberland with parts of Lancashire and Western Yorkshire) and it was this area which was to come under the occupation and influence of the Norsemen (Norwegians), whose word for a mountain, *'fjall'*, quickly found its way into names as the suffix *'-fell'*, as in **Scafell**, **Blackfell** and **Whinfell** and in doublets like **Carrock Fell**, **Cam Fell** and **Bowscale Fell**. Old Swedish and Old Norwegian often have similar words and in this case the Old Swedish word was the almost identical *'fjäll'*. The Danes, whose territory lay to the east of England and encompassed the East Midlands, had *'bjerg'* as their 'mountain'

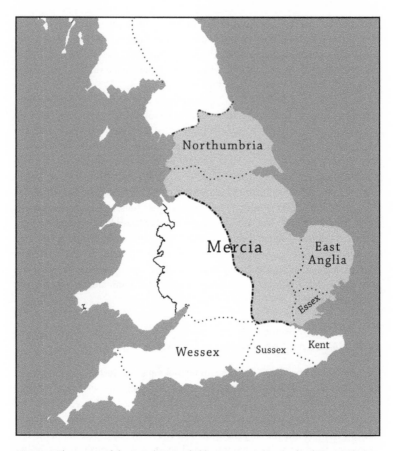

Figure 3 The extent of the Scandinavian-held territory at the death of King Ælfred in AD 899.

word. We can detect the presence of this word, in a rather camouflaged form, in **Barby** (Northamptonshire) and **Barrowby** (Lincolnshire), two places that were within the Danish sphere of influence and each meaning a settlement beside (or even on) a mountain or a hill. The Domesday entries (1086) of these two places confirm their origins: *Berchebi* and *Bergebi* respectively. Other 'hill' or 'upland' elements arising in place-names within Danelaw are shown in the table below:

Upland element	Meaning	Place-names
Banke	hillside or slope	**Firbank** (Cumb), **Ninebanks** (Northumb)
Brekka	slope, hill	**Scarisbrick** (Lancs), **Haverbrack** (Cumb)
Haugr	hill or mound	**Ulpha** (Cumb), **Huby** (Yorkshire)
Hryggr	ridge	**Ribby** (Lancs), **Grayrigg** (Cumbria)
Kambr	crest	**Combs** (Suffolk), **Cambo** (Northumb)
Hlið *	slope, hillside	**Lythe** (Yorkshire), **Litherland** (Lancs)
Hofuð *	headland	**Escowbeck** (Lancs), **Whitehaven** (Cumb)
Hváll, holl	rounded hill	**Whale** (Cumbria), **Falsgrave** (Yorkshire)
Skialf	ledge	**Raskelf** (Yorkshire), **Ranskill** (Notts)

* 'ð' is a defunct letter ('thorn') having the soft 'th' sound.

The Old Norse word *'nes'*, a headland, is also a familiar suffix, but it can be indistinguishable in its origin from the Old English *'ness'*, also meaning a promontory, in such place-names as **Ness** in Cheshire, **Furness** (*'Fuð-nes'* – *Fuð's* headland) in Lancashire and **Skegness** (*Skeggi's* headland) in Lincolnshire and many others, though their northerly locations would perhaps lean more towards a Norse origin. A tongue of high ground or even a prominent headland was occasionally described as *'oddr'* and this has found its way into **Greenodd** (Lancashire – green headland), which is indeed situated opposite such a green elbow of land which pushes out into the estuary of the **River Leven**.

Crags, rocky outcrops and mountain passes will be familiar to everyone who climbs the Cumbrian Fells and we find Scandinavian words for these natural features in many place-names: *'sker'*, *'hallr'* and *'steinn'*. **Ravenscar** (Yorkshire – 'rock of the ravens') and **Skerton** (Lancashire – 'settlement at the rocky place') incorporate the first of the three, while **Hallam** (Yorkshire) may hold the second, though it is often impossible to separate the Norse *'hallr'* from the Old English *'heall'*, meaning a nook or corner, even in the earliest records. The Old Danish word *'steinn'* is the source of the Yorkshire place-names **Staincross** and **Stanwick** and is also present in **Stenwith** and **Stainfield** (both in Lincolnshire). There are many other similar place-names having *'Stain-'* or *'Stan-'* as a first element and which refer to stone or rock, but the Old English word *'stān'* also meant stone and, as I have mentioned, we cannot easily be certain which gave rise to the place-name.

A useful passage or gap through the hills was sure to be a feature remarked upon and we find the word *'skarð'* (pronounced *'scarth'*) does good service in names like **Lintzgarth** (Durham – 'passage through the hills'), **Scartho** (Lincoln-shire – 'gap in the hill') and **Scarcliff** (Derbyshire – 'gash in the rockface'). The word *'Leið'* (probably pronounced *'leyth'*) too, indicated a track through the hills in northern lands and **Laithbutts** (Lancashire and Yorkshire) recalls this.

As we have seen in earlier chapters, valleys are to be found in various forms, though shallow and deep valleys are probably likely to be most often remarked upon and there is an appropriate group of descriptive Old Scandinavian words that often crops up in valley-related place-names: *'slakki'*, *'gil'*, *'geil'*, *'dal'* (Old Danish) and *'dalr'* (Old Norse). *'Slakki'*, a 'shallow valley', is the origin of the three Cumbrian names: **Slack**, **Hazelslack** ('valley of hazel trees') and **Withers-lack** ('wooded valley') and perhaps also the Lancashire village of **Hainslack**.

The words *'gil'* and *'geil'* are probably regional variations of each other and seem to have originally referred to a narrow ravine. *'Gill'* is illustrated by **Gayles** (Yorkshire), which is located on a rising hillside down which flows Priest Gill and **Reagill** (Cumbria), meaning 'valley of the foxes'. Neither place, however, is situated near a deep gorge.

It can easily be seen that *'dal'* and *'dalr'* are closely related to the English word 'dale' and are the sources of a profusion of place-names within the Danelaw regions. **Rosedale** (Yorkshire) and **Rosgill** (Cumbria) are good illustrations of Old Norse words present in both syllables of each name – *'hross-dalr'* and *'hross-gil'*, each meaning 'valley where horses were kept'.

WATER – *SPRINGS, STREAMS, RIVERS*

The Danes and other Scandinavians were restless warriors and, despite the westward spread of their occupation of 9th century England, their leaders were always keen to take on the powerful kingdom of Mercia in central England, ruled in the late-9th century by King Ælfred (died 899). The families and dependants of the Viking warriors were installed and settled in hundreds of localities throughout the east and north-east of England, sometimes in newly established Danish communities, having seized stretches of useful land from the native inhabitants and sometimes as gate-crashers of existing Anglo-Saxon settlements.

The indigenous populations must have lived in constant fear of these assertive and demanding intruders. The new language (Danish in the east and north-east and Norse in the north and north-west) would soon become a familiar sound to the local English and inevitably each race would adopt some of the other's words for everyday things, so that their hesitant efforts at communication would gradually become a little less awkward. Because of the ultimate supremecy of the newcomers, the incorporation of their words into the geography of their territories was to be of major significance by the end of the 1st millennium AD. We have already seen some of the Scandinavian adoptions in the previous section regarding the hills and valleys. Now we will examine the Viking contribution to water-related names.

In Chapter Three I pinpointed nearly a dozen natural water features to which the Anglo-Saxons had applied distinct names. The Scandinavians too, were quick to re-name such systems they had discovered in their new English localities. The most obvious of these will have been the rivers, streams, springs and brooks which are so commonly seen across all parts of the countryside, but especially in the eastern districts which came under the Danes' subjugation. '*Flod*' and '*ström*' (in which we can see the antecedents of our own words 'flood' and 'stream') and '*vatn*' were all used as river or stream words, but it is the Old Norse '*kelda*' that has provided a rather distinctive collection of river-related place-names from this group: **Threlkeld** (Cumbria – 'stream of the serfs'), **Kellet** (Lancashire – 'slope with a spring'), **Kelleth** (Cumbria) and **Trinkeld** (Cumbria).

There is clearly an ancient kinship between the Old Scandinavian '*kelda*' and the Old English '*celde*' (a spring), which has also made a very occasional appearance in southern place-names such as in the Kentish names **Bapchild** (*Bacca's* stream) and **Honeychild** (*Hūna's* stream). '*Ström*' is in fact an almost universal word within the Scandinavian and Germanic languages to which of course, the Old English word '*strēam*' belongs. However, there are very few place-names which incorporate the word. **Bournstream** (Gloucestershire) is one which re-emphasises the Old English '*burn*' with the old Norse '*ström*', each word having the same meaning.

Other Scandinavian water-words which appeared in place-names were '*bekkr*' and '*lǽkr*', each meaning a brook. The first is very familiar to us in the English place-name element '*-beck*', in such names as **Gosbeck** (Suffolk – 'goose stream'), **Holbeck** (Nottinghamshire – 'stream rising in a hollow'), **Skirbeck** (Lincolnshire – 'sparkling brook') and in **Beckermet** (Cumbria – 'junction of streams' – that is, the Kirk Beck and Black Beck). In this latter place-name we also have the derivative of the word '*mōt*', meaning 'a meeting' – in this case where two streams meet. This word is also present in **Beckermonds** (Yorkshire) which is at the confluence of the **River Wharfe**, **Green Field Beck** and **Oughtershaw Beck**.

Both **Leek** (Staffordshire) and **Leake** (Lincolnshire) probably have their origins in the Old Scandinavian word '*lǽkr*', though as with '*kelda*' and '*celde*' above, there is an equivalent Old English word, *'læcc'* which might be the source. Unusually, it is not possible to decide on the origins from the two Domesday entries, *Leche* and *Lec*, respectively. In these cases we have to remember that King William the First's hard-pressed clerks, bilingual though many of them must have been, had to do their best to record the strange sounds regional voices were pronouncing.

The mouth of a river, *'mynni'*, is recalled in a few place-names. In the name **Minsmere** (Suffolk), the Scandinavian element is combined with the Old English *'mere'* – a lake, while in **Stalmine** (Lancashire), it's first syllable partner is the Old English *'stall'*, meaning 'an outflow'.

Some of the other natural developments on the running water theme are worth mentioning. **Skelwith** (Cumbria) is a village bestriding the **River Brathay**. The point in the village at which the modern road (A593) crosses the river was very likely a ford in the 10th century and close by is Skelwith Force, a spectacular and roaring waterfall. The ford and the waterfall are ultimately responsible for the village's name – *'skjallr-vað'*, meaning 'ford beside the roaring water'. The same origin ('loud, roaring') can be assigned to **Skell Beck** which flows through Ripon in Yorkshire.

The hamlet of **Fossdale** (Yorkshire) lies close to two 'forces', **Cotter Force** and **Hardraw Force**. The word 'force', in the sense of a waterfall or a roaring torrent of water, derives from the Old Norse *'fors'* and **Forcett** (Yorkshire) may also have referred to a torrent in a nearby stretch of **Forcett Beck**.

Sites of local features near, or in, the bend of a river are found in some place-names and in the northern and eastern districts very often derive from the similar Old Danish or Old Norse words *'krōk'* and *'krókr'*. The names **Crook** (Durham and Cumbria), **Crookhouse** (Northumberland) and **Crookes** (Yorkshire) are all near to winding rivers and recall this particular river feature.

Caldbeck (Cumbria) and **Caldwell** (Yorkshire) tell of water found to be uncomfortably, or refreshingly, cold (Old Norse, *'kaldr'*) and refer to the nearby streams **Cald Beck** and **Caldwell Beck**, no doubt. Again, we see two words, *'kaldr'* and our modern word 'cold' (Old English *'ceald'*), that must have a common ancestor.

I have already mentioned fords in relation to the Old Norse word *'vað'*. This can be seen in place-names, in a transformed state, as the suffix '-with', but is possibly also present in some place-names ending in '-way' and even '-worth', which make exact definitions confusing. **Brawith** (Yorkshire – 'broad ford', across the **River Leven**) and **Sandwith** (Cumbria – 'sandy ford', perhaps across Rottington Beck or its small tributary) are unambiguous, as are **Wassand**

(Yorkshire – 'ford near sandbanks') and **Wath** (Yorkshire – 'ford', probably across the **River Nidd**). **Watford** (Northamptonshire) rather amusingly, emphasises its nature in both Old Norse *and* Old English and means 'ford-ford'.

LAKES, POOLS, BAYS, CREEKS

The Old Norse '*vatn*' could sometimes mean a lake, as well as simply 'water', in the same way that we imply a lake in the Cumbrian names **Elterwater**, **Derwent Water** and **Wastwater**. **Watendlath** and **Wasdale** (both in Cumbria) incorporate the same Old Norse word '*vatn*' as their first syllables. **Watendlath** has a small adjacent lake (Watendlath Tarn) and **Wasdale Hall** is located at the southern tip of **Wastwater**. **Wasdale Fell**, however, has only several fast flowing becks and a waterfall and is several miles from **Wastwater**.

Having just mentioned the word 'tarn', which first cropped up in Chapter One and in more detail in Chapter Three, perhaps I should say that it is derived from the Old Norse word '*tjorn*', originally meaning a lake without tributaries. There are many small mountain lakes and pools known as 'tarns' in Cumbria, though most do have a surface stream running to or from them. There are not many single-word place-names that incorporate the element 'tarn', unless it stands alone, as in **Blea Tarn** (Cumbria – dark water). However, the hamlet of **Tarnbrook** (Lancashire) lies on a beck called Tarnbrook Wyre, which feeds a nearby reservoir. **The Tarns, Tarns** and **Low Tarns** (all in Cumbria) are clustered around a pool called **Tarns Dub** ('*dubb*' is thought to be a forgotten Old English word for a pool). **Tarnside** (Cumbria) is a delightfully located hamlet beside **Martin Tarn**.

An interesting Old Danish word for a pool is '*flask*' and this too, has found its way into a few of our place-names – **Flass** (Cumbria) is still close by a boggy area called **Heckgill Mire**, although the nearest pool is half a mile away; nor is there now a pool at **Flash** in Staffordshire, though this village name also originates in the Old Danish word.

Seafaring nations though they were, the Scandinavians left behind surprisingly few contributions to English place-names which recall seaside locations. An Old Scandinavian word for the sea was '*sáer*' (which could also do service for an inland lake) and, because of their locations, this may be the source of names like **Seamer** (Yorkshire), **Semer** (Suffolk) and **Seathwaite** (Cumbria). The first of these, **Seamer** (Yorkshire), has no lake or pool, but is close to the sea, while **Semer** (Suffolk) does possess a minute pool (Semer Mere), fed by the **River**

Brett. There is a small tarn, named after the village of **Seathwaite** (Cumbria), about four miles to the north-east, whose stream, Tarn Beck, links the village to the tarn.

Coastal features too, are rarely found in place-names derived from Old Scandinavian words. '*Vik*', a bay, cove or creek was one feature, however, that has given us a few names. **Blowick** (Cumbria) is sited on the notched southern margin of **Ullswater** (Cumbria), and was probably '*blár-vík*' – 'dark cove or creek'; **Lowick** (Cumbria) is at the point where the **River Crake** joins two small streams and derives its name from the Old Swedish '*lauf-vík*' ('leafy creek'). It has been thought that **Wigtoft** in Lincolnshire might also have the root of its first element in the word '*vík*' (a bay), but its location is several miles from the coast, though of course, this is fenland and the occupying Danes may have used the word '*vik*' simply to refer to a surrounding marsh or a natural water course. The village is still surrounded by numerous 'drains' and water channels. Its earliest record too (written as *Wiketoft* in the year 1212), gives some support to the origin.

Islands and banks

The old Scandinavian languages have given us one of our most familiar and characteristic northern place-name elements – '*holm(e)*'. The word is similar in all of the Old Scandinavian languages and usually referred to a piece of dry ground rising a little above a generally wet environment – that of a marsh or perhaps an extensive water meadow. The names **Willow Holme** (Cumberland) and **Holme Nook** (Derbyshire) certainly have a comfortable and pleasing sound to them and each place may once have been something of a low island. The name **Holme** itself is to be found in Lincolnshire, Cambridgeshire, Nottinghamshire, Cumbria, Yorkshire and has even reached as far south as Bedfordshire. In each case the settlement is low-lying and is today nearly surrounded by watercourses, thus still deserving its ancient descriptive island name. Its variation, **Hulme** is to be found in Lancashire and Staffordshire. In compound place-names, '*-holme*' usually occurs as a second element, as in **Almholme** (Yorkshire – 'elm island'), **Keldholme** (Yorkshire – 'island with a spring'), **Levenshulme** (Lancashire – '*Lēofwine's* island') and **Kettleshulme** (Cheshire – '*Ketil's* island').

A complicating factor in the oral evolution of '*-holme*', is that it is easily made to sound like '*-ham*'. Thus some place-names ending in '*-holme*', are in fact well disguised versions of '*-ham*'. **Hubberholme** (Yorkshire) is recorded in

Domesday (1086) as *Huburgheham*, that is, 'dwelling belonging to the woman *Hūnburg*' and **Dunholme** (Lincolnshire) occurs in Domesday as *Duneham,* meaning '*Dunna's* village'. **Barholm** (Lincolnshire) too, is deceptive, for its earliest notation is *Bercaham* – 'enclosure on a hill'.

Sandbanks were a noticeable feature in some places and could form shifting islands. **Meols** (Cheshire) is an example of a simple derivative of the Old Norse word '*melr*', meaning a sand bank or dune. It lies on a sandy North-East coast. **Ambleside** (Cumbria, '*á-melr-sætr*' – 'river sandbank shelter') lies at the confluence of **Rydal Beck**, **Stock Ghyll** and **Scandale Beck** at the northernmost point of Windermere lake. **Cartmel** (Cumbria) also refers to a sandy situation beside the interestingly named **River Eea**. **Rathmell** (Yorkshire, '*rauðr-melr*' – red sandbank) lies at the junction of the River Ribble and its tributary, Rathmell Beck, and on an area of sandy ground.

The Old Norse '*ey*', an island, is so similar to the Old English word '*iēg*' in pronunciation and in early spellings, that it is impossible to tell whether such place-names as **Ealand** (Northumberland), **Eland** (Lincolnshire) or **Nayland** (Suffolk) have arisen from the Old Scandinavian or Anglo-Saxon words.

WETLANDS – MARSHES, BOGS, SWAMPS, MUD

There is a surprising number of words in English which refer to unpleasantly waterlogged ground – bog, swamp, marsh, mire, quagmire, fen, morass, slough, wetland and (in the north), moss. I have already mentioned a number of these in Chapter Three, since they originate in the Old English of the Anglo-Saxons.

However, Scandinavian occupiers of the east and north of England brought their own words and grafted them into the emerging English language. The simplest of their words in this context was '*vátr*', a word that looks suspiciously like our word 'water' and indeed it has the same Germanic origin as our own word. It meant simply 'wet' and is present in both the Yorkshire place-name **Watton** ('wet hill' – although there is actually only a slight rise in the nearby terrain) and the Cumbrian **Waitby** ('wet homestead' – though it is located rather high amongst surrounding hills).

A truly marshy area would have acquired the noun '*kjarr*', which gave rise later to the largely forgotten English word '*kerr*', also meaning a marsh or fen. We can see this Old Norse element in **Aldercar** (Derbyshire – 'marsh amongst the alders') and **Redcar** (Yorkshire – 'reedy marsh'). Although **Blacker** (Yorkshire – 'black marsh') and **Bicker** (Lincolnshire – 'village near the marsh') may reflect either a Norse or an English origin, their meanings were indicative of marshy terrain.

As is so often the case in place-names, an Old English word and an Old Scandinavian word are very similar and will have the same root: '*mos*' and '*mire*' in Old English and '*mosi*' and '*mȳrr*' in Old Scandinavian conform to this pattern and all mean a bog or swampy ground. Because of their similarity, it is not easy to say from the earliest recorded sources whether the origins of a place-name will lie in the English or the Scandinavian languages.

However, northern English place-names have a better than average chance of Scandinavian origins: **Mosser** and **Mozergh** (both in Cumbria – *Moserg* – 'shelter in a marsh') and **Moss** (Cumbria – *Mosse* – 'swamp'), together with **Wragmire** (Cumbria).

In some north-country places, bad weather could reduce pastureland to a boggy morass, which would have been unsuitable for grazing cattle. Such terrain was called '*snap*' and is enshrined in the Yorkshire place-name **Snape** and in Lancashire's **Blacksnape**.

Muddy places were often singled out with the word '*saurr*', which appears in the names of two villages called **Sawrey** (Cumbria). These villages lie between Lake Windermere and Esthwaite Water, with **Wilfin Beck** flowing between them, so it is perhaps not surprising that the ground could have been prone to muddiness or worse, at times. Several places called **Sowerby** ('*saurr-by*') are also located near to rivers and must have become boggy periodically to have earned their descriptive names. **Sosgill** (Cumbria – '*saurr-skáli*' – 'huts on boggy ground') too, is situated near to marshy ground called Leady Moss and with springs and streams in every quarter. Another Scandinavian mud-word, that makes a very occasional appearance in place-names, is '*leirr*' and is to be seen in the name **Layerthorpe**, a district of the city of York.

FLORA – *TREES*

The landscape of England in the centuries of Danish and Norse occupation was considerably more wooded than we are used to seeing in our present century. However, wood was a most versatile material and, as has always been the case, was in constant demand for building purposes and was, of course, a vital domestic fuel. Woodland, though a common sight, nevertheless attracted descriptive names, often related to the predominant species of tree to be found there or a particular bird or animal which frequented the locality.

A general Scandinavian word for a wooded area was '*viðr*' (pronounced '*vithr*') and this tends to show itself in place-names that have evolved the suffix '*-with*', as in **Blawith** (Cumbria – 'black forest'), **Menwith** (Yorkshire – 'common wood') and **Tockwith** (Yorkshire – '*Tocca's* wood'). '*Skógr*' too, was commonly used for a stretch of woodland and is the nucleus of the names **Scorborough** and **Skewsby** (both in Yorkshire) and is well hidden in **Swinscoe** (Staffordshire).

Lound (Lincolnshire, Nottinghamshire, Suffolk), **Lund** (Yorkshire) and **Lunt** (Lancashire) all exemplify the specific feature of a grove or copse, which were described by the Old Norse word '*lundr*'. This also forms the second element in **Snelland** (Lincolnshire) and **Toseland** (Cambridgeshire). On the other hand, there must have been something particular about **Aintree** (Lancashire), for it meant 'one tree' ('*eintré*').

Clearings in woods could often be the result of human activity – erecting dwellings, animal shelters, clearing areas for cultivation or cutting wood for fuel. Such an opening was a '*þveit*' (pronounced approximately 'thvait') and is a very common place-name suffix in the form of '*-thwaite*', of which there are very many examples, such as **Langthwaite** (Lancashire – 'long clearing'), **Husthwaite** (Cumbria – 'house in a clearing') and **Radmanthwaite** (Nottinghamshire – 'clearing with a reedy pool'). There is also a number of villages named simply **Thwaite** (Suffolk, Durham, Yorkshire, Cumbria), all within the Danelaw regions, as we should expect.

The oak has always provided the best wood for most structural purposes – its outstanding strength, solid durability and weather-proof qualities have always been well-known and appreciated. '*Eik*' is the Old Norse word for our most characteristic tree and there is no shortage of Scandinavian-derived place-names celebrating its presence, though the variety of forms of the original word is quite striking – there are six variations of '*eik*' in this list:

Place-name	Location	Meaning
Aigburth	Lancashire	Oak hill
Aikber	Yorkshire	Hill of oaks
Aiskew	Yorkshire	Oak wood
Aikton	Cumbria	Farmstead by the oaks
Eyke	Suffolk	The oak
Greenoak	Yorkshire	The green oak
Aysgarth	Yorkshire	Passage through the oaks

That other stalwart of the English countryside, the ash too ('*askr*' and '*eski*'), is a frequent element in place-names of the Danelaw districts – perhaps, if a count were to be made, the ash tree would feature even more frequently than the oak:

Place-name	Location	Meaning
Askern	Yorkshire	Corner where ashes grow
Askham	Nottinghamshire	Homestead near the ashes
Askrigg	Yorkshire	Ash tree ridge
Askwith	Yorkshire	Ash wood
Eastoft	Lincolnshire	Ash tree farmstead
Eske	Yorkshire	The ash trees
Escrick	Yorkshire	Ashes at the bend

Not quite as many Old Scandinavian tree-names seem to have survived as have those from the Anglo-Saxon. For example, the willow was *'pil'*, the pear was *'pære'* and *'haga'* was hawthorn. It may just be possible that the Durham place-name **Hawthorn**, first recorded in 1115 as *Hagathorn*, originated in this latter word. However, here is a tabulated list of the ones which we do know have come down to us in our place-names:

Tree name	Old Scandinavian	Place-names
Alder	*elri*	**Ellerbeck** (Yorkshire), **Ellershaw** (Cumbria)
Apple	*epli*	**Appleby** (Cumbria), **Eppleby** (Yorks)
Birch	*birki*	**Briscoe** (Yorks), **Birkdale** (Lancs), **Birkenside** (Yorks)
Blackthorn (sloe)	*slāh*	**Slaithwaite** (Yorks), **Sloley** (Norfolk)
Elm	*almr*	**Almholme** (Yorkshire)
Hazel	*hasl* & *hesli*	**Hasland** (Derbyshire), **Hazelslack** (Cumbria)
Lime	*lind*	**Linby** (Notts), **Lindal** (Cumbria), **Linthwaite** (Yorks)
Yew	*ýr*	**River Ive** (Cumbria)

Other shrubs and plants

Thorn bushes of various sorts could all be described as *'Thyrnir'* (pronounced roughly *'thornir'*) and **Thurnscoe** (Yorkshire), **Thrimby** (Cumbria) and **Thurnby** (Leicestershire) each incorporate the element in their names. A bush in general was called *'buskr'*, which has crept into **Busky Dale** (Yorkshire – 'a bushy valley').

Brushwood was frequently seen forming dense undergrowth in copses and woods and '*storð*' ('storth') and '*hris*' were the brushwood words in Old Norse. However, the closely related word '*hrīs*' was also the Old English word for brushwood and, as we have seen so often in this chapter, it is usually impossible to distinguish their origins in northern or eastern place-names, though **Riseholme** (Lincolnshire –'brushwood island') and **Risby** (Lincolnshire – 'settlement amongst brushwood') are likely candidates for Scandinavian origins because of their locations and the two characteristic Scandinavian suffixes. **Storrs** (Cumbria and Yorkshire) and **Storth** (Cumbria) are, however, distinct examples of a '*storð*' origin.

Grassland might be thought of too little significance to warrant a special allusion in place-names, but Old Norse has not neglected it, for Domesday (1086) reveals that **Grassthorpe** (Nottinghamshire – 'farm on the grassland') and **Gresgarth** (Lancashire – 'grassy enclosure') are derived from the Old Norse '*gres*'. Again, the Old English word ('*gærs*') is similar and is easily confused with the Scandinavian in early records. An unusual inclusion into this grassy discussion is '*fit*', meaning a grassy riverside. This Old Norse word is to be found in a few small places: **Lambfoot** (Cumbria – '*lange-fit*' – long meadow) and **East Keswick Fitts** (Yorkshire, lying beside the River Wharf, north of Leeds).

Sedge, a coarse, grass-like plant, often favouring poorer soils or wetlands, has been remembered in several place-names based on two Old Norse words for the plant, '*sef*' and '*storr*'. **Sefton** (Lancashire – 'settlement near the sedges') and **Seathwaite** (Cumbria – 'sedge clearing') illustrate the first, while **Stargill** (Cumbria –'sedge ravine') and **Starbeck** (Yorkshire – 'stream through the sedge'), though the latter does not seem to have been recorded before 1817.

Heather ('*heiðr*') is quietly concealed in a few north-country names such as the **Hatfields** in Yorkshire and Nottinghamshire. The early records of the two **Hatfields** in Essex and Hertfordshire also recall heather, but their origins lie in the Old English word for a heath, '*hæþ*', which is not far removed from a heather origin.

Fauna – *Mammals*

As we would expect, we have inherited a number of Scandinavian names of common early mediæval mammals in our place-names. I have already mentioned the domesticated horse ('*hross*') in the earlier section of this chapter, '*Uplands and valleys*', together with a couple of place-names derived from this word. Here, however, I will list some of the wild animals recognised by the occupying Scandinavians and incorporated into local names.

Wild animal	Old Norse word	Place-names
Boar	*goltr*	**Galtres Forest** (Yorks)
Fox	*refr*	**Reagill** (Cumbria)
Roe deer	*rā*	**Raskelf** (Yorks), **Rayhead** (Yorks), **Rowland** (Derbys)
Stag (hart)	*hjortr*	**Hartwith** (Yorkshire), **Harter Fell** (Cumbria)
Wolf	*ulfr*	**Owlands** (Yorkshire), **Ullock** (Cumbria)
Wildcat	*kati*	**Catterall** (Lancashire)

There would probably have been more names of wild mammals than I have listed here, but there seems to be no trace of other survivors in our place-names.

Very few other forms of wildlife are recorded in their Scandinavian forms in our place-names. Some creatures have very similar names to their Old English counterparts – Scandinavian *'mygg'*, *'frosk'* and *'bie'* are cognate with Old English *'mycg'*, *'forsc'* and *'bēo'*, meaning gnat, frog and bee – and may have played a part, especially in the northern English districts, in some of the place-names featuring these creatures mentioned in Chapter Four dealing with the Anglo-Saxons.

I will end this section by mentioning a couple of instances of 'fish' and 'snake'. **Fiskerton** (Lincolnshire) has the Old Norse word *'fisk'* (a fish) as its first element and meant 'the dwelling of the fisherman', while **Ormside** (Cumbria) may be the only example of a place-name that incorporates *'ormr'* in its probable reference to a snake. **Fiskerton** stands on the River Witham and was within the Danish influence, while the two **Ormsides** are located within the Old Norse districts.

BIRDS

As with the fauna names I listed in Chapter Four when discussing the Anglo-Saxon contribution to our place-names, Scandinavian names of birds also form the largest fauna group. Wild birds will have contributed to the diet of Danes and Norsemen as much as to that of neighbouring Englishmen and a skilful Norse birdcatcher was called the *'fuglefængeren'*. The word for a bird was very similar in all of the Scandinavian and Germanic languages – *'fugl'* (Old Danish and Old Norse), *'fågel'* (Old Swedish) and *'fugol'* (Old English). One of the Domesday (1086) entries for **Fowlmere** (Cambridgeshire) is *Fuglemære*, which suggests a possible Danish first element, coupled with the English '*mere*' – a lake or pool.

Songbirds feature only rarely in place-names, the majority of descriptions being of the larger, more impressive and less melodic species such as the hawks and members of the crow family. The cuckoo is one of the few songsters whose names have endured into modern times.

In the following table I have listed most of the birds whose Scandinavian names can be shown to be the probable origins of the related place-names.

Bird	Old Scandinavian	Place-names
Buzzard	*vrák*	**Wraxall** (Dorset), **Wroxham** (Norfolk)
Crake (crow)	*krákr*	**Cracoe** (Yorks), **Crackpot** (Yorks), **Crakemarsh** (Staffs)
Crane	*trani*	**Tranmere** (Cheshire), **Tranmoor** (Yorkshire)
Cuckoo	*gaukr*	**Gauxholme** (Yorkshire), **Gawthorpe** (Yorkshire)
Hawk	*haukr*	**Hawkhill** (Northumb), **Hawkwell** (Northumb)
Jackdaw	*kā*	**Kaber** (Cumbria), **Cabourn** (Lincolnshire)
Owl	*ugla*	**Ugglebarnby** (Yorkshire)
Raven	*hrafn*	**Ranskill** (Notts), **Ravenstonedale** (Cumbria)
Puffin	*lundi*	**Lundy Island** (Devon)
Sandpiper	*ló*	**Lucker** (Northumberland)
Swan	*elptr*	**Elterwater** (Cumbria)
Woodpecker	*spætte*	**Spexhall** (Suffolk)

Farming – *Animal husbandry*

Two of the most attractive features of first millennium England were its stable, temperate climate and rich agricultural lowlands. These assets proved a constant attraction to foreign invaders. The Saxons and the Danes (in their Viking guise) became expert agriculturalists and used the lowlands to great advantage over several centuries, in the end co-existing in a racially divided England until the middle of the 11th century. By the end of the first millennium there would have been little difference in the farming techniques and village life between the English in the south and west and the Scandinavians in the north and east. Domesticated animal husbandry and crop cultivation must have seemed very much the same to a traveller moving between the regions.

The typical name for a farmstead was '*þorp*' ('thorp'), which usually occurs as a second element in a great many place-names, mostly in the east and north-east ('Danelaw') regions, but only rarely in the Norse-settled areas of the north-west. The first element is often the name of the landholder, as in **Freethorpe** (Norfolk – 'farmstead of the man *Frǣthi*'), **Friesthorpe** (Lincolnshire – 'farm belonging to the Frisians') and **Wrenthorpe** (Yorkshire – 'farm of the woman *Wifrūn*'), but it could also be a location word – **Milnthorpe** (Cumbria – 'farm with a mill') and **Wothorpe** (Northamptonshire – 'farm near a thicket'). **Thorpe** itself occurs alone in at least seven counties in the Danelaw and even once in Surrey. A curious and characteristic English trick with some words, as we have seen before, was to exchange two of the inner letters: in this case,*'thorp'* becomes *'throp'* and this too appears in some place-names – **Dunthrop** (Oxfordshire – 'farm of the man *Dunna*') and **Southrop** (Gloucestershire – 'southern farmstead').

An alternative word for a dwelling house with farm outbuildings attached was *'bū'* and we catch a rare glimpse of this word in **Bewaldeth** (Cumbria – 'homestead of the woman *Aldgȳþ*') and **Barnbow** (Yorkshire – *'Biarni's* homestead').

A structure we naturally associate with the farm is its barn (*'hlaða'*), a useful storage building and the importance placed on this convenience is reflected in a group of place-names with this word as their core – **Latham** (Yorkshire), **Laytham** (Yorkshire), and **Silloth** (Cumbria – 'barn near the sea') are three of them.

Boundaries between agricultural holdings or even between tribal districts could be conveniently denoted by natural features like rivers, ditches or hills, but where no such convenient natural element existed, a series of posts might be erected. This means of separating areas of land was called a *'rá'* and dwellings or hamlets close by a boundary marker might incorporate it into their names – **Raby** (Cheshire), **Roby** (Lancashire) and **Raughton** (Cumbria – 'boundary stream') do just that. Another word for a prominent pole was *'stong'*, which, when it appears in a place-name, may have referred to a nearby boundary marker: **Stanghow** (Yorkshire), **Garstang** (Lancashire). In some places piles of rocks or stones may also have served as convenient indicators of territorial limits. Several words were in use for such a feature – *'horgr'*, *'hreysi'* and *'varða'*, though the first often had the more specific meaning of an altar, while *'hreysi'* sometimes meant a cairn, marking the grave of someone. *'Hreysi'* is the source of **Harras** (Cumbria) and may mean a boundary point or the site of a cairn, as indeed may **Roseacre** (Lancashire). *'Varða'* is the origin of **Warboys** (Cambridgeshire) and **Warcop** (Cumbria) and, although a tower of stones was undoubtedly created, the original purpose of each may have been more as a beacon site than as a boundary point.

Where lands under different ownership came together, perhaps at a stream, a hedge or at some other marker, a general word was *'mōt'* and would usually indicate a people's meeting place too. The place-name **Landmoth** (Yorkshire) illustrates this exactly, for it is shown in Domesday (1086) as *Landemot*, a rendering of the Old Scandinavian *'landamōt'*, meaning 'meeting of lands'. **Beckermet** (Cumbria – 'meeting of streams') incorporates the same word.

As I have emphasised on a number of occasions, there are many similarities between the Old English and Scandinavian languages, leading to uncertainty in the exact origin of many place-names. An example in the present section of domesticated animals is the respective words for 'cow' – *'cū'* in Old English, *'ku'* in Norse and *'ko'* in Danish. 'Duck' is another instance – *'ened'*, *'and'* and *'and'* are the corresponding words. As before, a table will display some of the place-names and their origins with clarity.

Animal	Old Scandinavian	Place-names
Bull	*boli*	**Bowness** (Cumbria), **Bulby** (Lincolnshire)
Foal	*foli*	**Fowberry** (Northumberland)
Goat	*geit, hafr*	**Gatesgill** (Cumbria), **Haverigg** (Cumbria)
Horse	*hross*	**Rosthwaite** (Cumbria), **Rosgill** (Yorkshire)
Pig	*griss*	**Grisedale** (Cumbria), **Grizebeck** (Cumbria)

A word borrowed from the Irish, during the period of the Norse occupation of the east of Ireland before their assault on England in the early 9th century, is *'kapall'*, which meant a horse, or more likely a 'nag', or packhorse. This word may be present in **Capplerigg**, just west of Kendal in Cumbria.

Perhaps surprisingly, animal shelters have also become incorporated into some our place-names. There are several Scandinavian words involved here and perhaps the one most commonly occurring was *'erg'*, meaning a shelter located on a hill-pasture. This can be found, in a rather camouflaged form, in the first syllables of **Argam, Arram** and **Eryholme** (all three in Yorkshire) and in the second syllables of **Winder** (Cumbria) and **Medlar** (Lancashire). *'Sætr'* too, seemed to mean a hill refuge: **Satterthwaite** and **Setmurthy** (both in Cumbria) and **Yarlside** (Lancashire) exemplify this. A more general word for a haven against the weather was *'skáli'*, which might often have implied a shepherd's hut or other human shelter. **Scales** (Cumbria), **Scole** (Norfolk) and **Scholes** (Yorkshire) are variations on the original word, while it appears as the second element in both **Brinscall** (Lancashire) and **Winskill** (Cumbria).

A common word for a byre or cowshed was '*būð*' (pronounced 'booth' and is the source of our modern word). This word is the generator of a surprising number of place-names, including **Bootham** (Yorkshire), **Boothby** (Lincolnshire) and **Bouth** (Cumbria). The Scandinavian word is also clearly similar to the Old English '*botl*', meaning a dwelling house or building and is the source of the name **Bolton**.

Pastures for enclosing grazing animals had various names applied to them: '*hagi*', '*hegning*', '*spenning*' and '*garðr*' are some and have provided us with **Haigh** (Lancashire), **Haining** (Northumberland), **Spennithorne** (Yorkshire) and **Arkengarthdale** (Yorkshire) respectively.

CROPS

Staple crop cultivation was divided into two components – those for human consumption and those for animal fodder. Unpredictably wet or dry weather in the growing season could lead to catastrophic harvest failures and potential starvation of both humans and cattle. The staple human foods were based on familiar cereal crops, together with beans, peas, leeks, cabbage and other minor additions where possible, while animal fodder relied on good grass, hay, clover and oats.

We would reasonably expect some of the more common names of crops to have found their way into place-names and indeed this is the case. However, not all crop words have survived in our place-names, but I have listed in the following table six that can be proved to be the origins of some names of places.

Crop	Old Scandinavian	Place-names
Barley	*bygg*	**Biglands** (Cumbria), **Bigrigg** (Cumbria)
Flax	*lín*	**Linethwaite** (Cumbria)
Hay	*hey*	**Heathwaite** (Yorkshire), **Haythwaite** (Durham)
Leek	*laukr*	**Lawkland** (Yorkshire), **Loughrigg** (Cumbria)
Oat	*hafri*	**Haverthwaite** (Cumbria), **Haverholme** (Lincolnshire)
Rye	*rugr*	**Roughton** (Lincs), **Rowrah** (Cumbria), **Ruckcroft** (Cumbria)

Quite a few Old English crop names are similar in their spellings to their Old Scandinavian counterparts and it might be an interesting aside to compare some of them in a list –

Crop	Old Scandinavian	Old English
Bean	*bønne*	bēan
Cabbage (kale)	*kål*	cāl, cawl
Clover	*kløvr*	*clæfre*
Cress	*karse*	*cærse*
Grass	*gras*	gærs
Wheat	*hvete*	*hwæte*

It is once again clear that English has a close historical relationship with the Scandinavian languages.

People

By the 870s, Guthrum had risen to become the most powerful leader of the Danes in England and saw himself as the Danish king, eclipsing all other chieftains. Ambitious to be master of the whole country, he led many battles against the English who were under the command of Ælfred, King of Wessex and whose predominant position as military planner and battle strategist had caused him to be regarded as the King of the English. For a while it seemed that Guthrum's forces would eventually win the upper hand, for he led his armies to a series of victories over King Ælfred's men. However, ultimate triumph was to be Ælfred's: Guthrum's forces were entirely routed at the Battle of Edington in the year 878. However, there was no hope of driving the Danes out of England altogether, desirable though this idea must have been to King Ælfred and other lesser English rulers, so a treaty (known as The Treaty of Wedmore) was subsequently drawn up between the two leaders. This confined Guthrum and his compatriots to the eastern territories of England, which were known henceforward as the Danelaw. Surprisingly, Guthrum quickly converted to Christianity and adopted the Anglo-Saxon name of Æthelstan, probably as an assurance to his English subjects and to King Ælfred in particular, of his good will and intentions. He seems to have remained true to his word and ruled his half of England effectively and with authority until his death in AD 890.

There are numerous place-names celebrating a connection with Danish kingship (*'konungr'*), usually beginning with the typical element *'Coning-'* or *'Conis-'*. **Coningsby** (Lincolnshire – *'kunungsbȳr'*) means 'the king's estate' and must have been firmly connected with Danish kings, for it is located in the centre of the Danish-held territory and is acknowledged in Domesday (*Cunin-*

gesbi, 1086) as a well established settlement. **Conington** (Cambridgeshire), **Conisholme** (Lincolnshire) and **Conisborough** (Yorkshire) are also typical references to the king's lands. **Coneysthorpe** (Yorkshire) and **Cunscough** (Lancashire – '*kunungs-skógr*' - 'the king's wood') are a little less obvious in their royal connections.

At the other end of the social scale from the king was the serf ('*þræll*'), who owned little and worked hard to maintain a basic existence. He too, is recalled in a few place-names for various reasons: **Thirlby** (Yorkshire – 'place of the serfs') and **Threlkeld** (Cumbria – 'spring of the serfs').

Between the extreme stations of king and peasant, our place-names help us to detect a few other ranks: the '*holdr*' – a yeoman and usually a prosperous landholder, has given us **Holderness** (Yorkshire) and the '*leysingr*' – a freedman, that is, one who has been freed from the service a person of higher rank – shows itself in **Lazenby** (Yorkshire). An unfree tenant, on the other hand ('*bóndi*'), is remembered in **Bonby** (Lincolnshire). A '*drengr*' was a general servant and the word appears in both **Dringhouses** (Yorkshire) and **Drointon** (Staffordshire). Finally in the ranking, a house-boy, or knave ('*knapi*'), has his moment of modest limelight in the place-name **Knapton** (Norfolk).

Two members of the wider community, who probably provided a useful service, are enshrined in the place-names **Farmanby** (Yorkshire – '*farmann*', an itinerant seller of goods) and **Copmanthorpe** (Yorkshire – '*kaupmaðr*', a merchant), while an outcast or maybe a criminal, the '*vargr*', was probably a less than welcome drifter, but has somehow managed to wheedle his title into the place-name **Wragholme** (Lincolnshire) and is a possible source of our word 'vagrant'.

Carlinghow (Yorkshire) must have had a sinister, if not eerie aura about it, for the origin of the name is the Old Norse '*kerling*', meaning a hag or witch and it may have been the meeting place of such weird local women.

SETTLEMENTS

If there is one identifier that most people remember about the Danish settlements in the eastern regions of England, it is the give-away suffix '-*by*', found in so many of our place-names. The original '*bý*' was a word meaning a farmstead or even a cluster of dwellings that could amount to a small village. It has not survived as an independent name, although **Aby** (Lincolnshire – 'settlement near a stream') comes quite close. It only rarely occurs as a first syllable in place-names, though **Bicker** (Lincolnshire) and **Byker** (Northumberland) each suggest a 'village at the marsh' – '*bȳ-kiarr*'. There are hundreds of Scandinavian-derived place-names in England having the suffix '*-by*' and the reader is sure to be able to name a few without much pondering. The first elements in most of them are very often personal names hailing the leader or head man of that community or household. Women's names occur much more rarely in the '*-by*' place-name index. However, one woman is to be found celebrated in the Yorkshire village name of **Rudby** ('*Rudda's* homestead'), which lies about ten miles south of Stockton-on-Tees.

The personal names we will come across in these places are usually of Scandinavian form, though there will be the occasional English (and later, even Norman) personal names to be found. Examples of Scandinavian male personal names as first elements are frequent, for example **Amotherby** (Yorkshire – 'place of *Eymundr*'), **Ormesby** (Norfolk – '*Orm's* homestead') and **Claxby** (Lincolnshire – 'farmstead of *Klakkr*'). Other than his name, there is usually nothing else known about him and the place-name remains his only, though durable, memorial.

When not recalling a person, the prefix would be descriptive of a local feature, as in **Grasby** (Lincolnshire – 'settlement on stony ground') or **Beeby** (Leicestershire – 'place where bees were kept'), or else simply descriptive of the village itself – **Mickleby** (Yorkshire – 'large village') and **Normanby** (Lincolnshire – 'village of the Northmen').

Settlements were mostly composed of dwellings which, to our modern eyes, would seem no more than crudely built huts or even hovels, though the Old Norse word for them, '*hūs*', reminds us of our word 'house' and, unlikely though it may seem, this rather ordinary word has given rise to a number of place-names; for example, **Howsham** (Lincolnshire), **Husthwaite** (Yorkshire – 'land with a dwelling') and **Loftus** (Yorkshire – 'house with an upper floor'), this last pattern of dwelling being unusual thus drawing forth a reference in the locality.

Some of the larger villages often had a customary meeting place ('*þing*' – pronounced '*thing*') where tribal gatherings could be arranged, questions debated and decisions taken and sometimes justice dispensed. The place may have been a barn-like building or a specially built hall and is remembered in the place-names **Thingwall** (Cheshire) and **Thingoe** (Suffolk).

Beyond the body of the village may have stood a few plots of land rather larger than those belonging to the cottagers themselves and on each of which stood the dwelling of the holder. Such a smallholding would often be called a '*toft*' and we will see this as a suffix in many place-names, usually preceded, as we might expect, by the owner's name – **Lowestoft** (Suffolk – 'holding of *Hloðvér*), **Wibtoft** (Leicestershire – *'Vibbe's* plot') and **Sibbertoft** (Northamptonshire – '*toft* of *Sigbiorn*'). There are several examples of the word **Toft** itself (in Cambridgeshire and Lincolnshire among others) and a few instances where the word is the first syllable of a name – **Toftwood** (Norfolk) and **Toftshaw** (Yorkshire), in both of which examples the word is partnered with an Old English element: '*-wood*' (*'wudu'* – a woodland) and *'-shaw'* (*'scaga'* – a copse or thicket).

A building associated with many a settlement was the church – a wooden or stone structure – and its importance is signified in the number of place-names that are derived from the Old Scandinavian word *'kirkja'*, which can feature both as a first or last element of the name. **Kirkby** and **Kirby** are very obviously Scandinavian examples and both are common place-names in many Danelaw districts, either standing alone or as a doublet or even a triplet – **Kirby Bedon** (Norfolk), **Kirkby-in-Ashfield** (Nottinghamshire).

Things can be complicated, however, by the similarity in pronunciation to the Old English word for a church, *'cirice'*. This word is the origin of some place-names that have since become 'Scandinavianised' and have been modified, either in response to the pressure of Nordic linguistics or perhaps to make them look more remarkable. **Kirkdale** and **Kirkham** (both in Lancashire) are probable examples of this, for in Domesday (1086), **Kirkdale** is recorded as *Chirchedele*, while in a Lancashire charter of 1094, **Kirkham** is shown as *Chercheham* – each clearly having its root in the Anglo-Saxon word *'cirice'* rather than in the Scandinavian *'kirkja'*.

Local felons – *'vargr'* (in which we can see an early echo of the word 'vagrant') – might, on conviction, meet their ends by execution, which was carried out by hanging at designated places where a prominent tree was to be found, or at a place, often on a mound outside the village boundary, where a gallows could be erected. **Galby** (Leicestershire) is a very likely spot where a gallows stood, for its entry in Domesday (1086) is *Galbi*, suggesting an origin in the Old Scandinavian word *'galgi'* – a gallows. **Galligill** (Cumbria) too, has the same origin.

Roads and streets in the predominantly Scandinavian districts were referred to by the Old Norse word *'gata'*, from which we have inherited many north-country street names – Stricklandgate in Kendal, Shaddongate in Carlisle (both in Cumbria) and Kirkgate in Settle (Yorkshire) for example. The word itself is the origin of a number of place-names too – **Harrogate** (Yorkshire, *'horgr-gata'* – road to the cairn), **Framwellgate** (Durham – road to the rushing spring).

Settlements' locations were frequently near to rivers or streams in order to ensure a reliable water supply for grazing animals as well as for human use.

Crossings had to be manageable in all weathers and if the river were too deep or too fast-flowing for a ford to traverse the current, then a bridge of some sort would be the only remaining option. In some remote situations, all that would be needed would be a simple wooden span wide enough for a single file of animals to pass from one meadow pasture to another.

Such structures were easy to maintain and could be repaired quickly when the need arose. However, a dry and safe passage across an area of marsh was also desirable in some lowland places and this really only amounted to a causeway, often made up of layers of brushwood, an effective and easily renewable local resource. **Bracebridge** (Lincolnshire – 'bridge of twigs') may have been an example of this latter technique.

The more substantial bridges were a noteworthy feature of a local scene and in many cases these have earned a mention in our place-names, if only in the form of a town's Bridge Street, of which there are many examples. The Old Scandinavian '*bryggia*' is usually distinguishable from the Old English '*brycg*' in place-name origins by the appearance of the '*brig*' or '*brug*' elements in the earliest written examples of a name. **Brighouse** (Yorkshire) and **Brigsteer** (Cumbria) are recorded as *Brighuses* and *Brigster* respectively, in their mid-13th century records, thus supporting their Norse origins. **Felbrigg** (Norfolk – 'plank bridge') too, reveals its Scandinavian roots in its Domesday entry (1086), *Felebruge*.

In places where a river was wide and deep enough, a landing place – '*stoð*' (pronounced approximately '*sterth*') – was often constructed, where cargoes could be put ashore. This shows itself in the two Lancashire place-names **Toxteth** and **Croxteth** and in the Lincolnshire village of **Burton Stather**.

A NORSE MISCELLANY

We are approaching the end of our examination of the Old Scandinavian contribution to English place-names, but before we leave, I think it is worth mentioning a group of words – mostly adjectives, though not all – each of which has influenced the formation of some of our place-names. The easiest way to present these is, as often, within a table, which will show the original word, its meaning and some examples of the place-name that it has generated. So here are eleven of them:

Old Scandinavian	Meaning	Place-names
austr	east	**Austwick** (Yorkshire – east farm)
blár	dark or blue	**Blaby** (Leicestershire – farm of the dark man)
botn	valley bottom	**Starbotton** (Yorks – valley where stakes were got)
breiðr*	wide	**Braithwaite** (Cumbria – broad clearing)
grár	grey	**Graythwaite** (Cumbria – grey meadow clearing)
hvitr	white	**Whitby** (Yorkshire – white village)
kringla	ring or circle	**Cringleford** (Norfolk – ford near the round hill)
meðal	middle	**Melton** (East Yorkshire – middle village)
mikill	large	**Micklethwaite** (Cumbria – large clearing)
rauðr*	red	**Rauceby** (Lincs – village of *Rauð**, the red man)
vestr	west	**Westerfield** (Suffolk – western field)

* 'ð' is the mediæval letter 'thorn', pronounced 'th'.

At the close of our study of the 'Viking' influence on English place-names, we have seen that their contribution has been enormous and second only to that of the Anglo-Saxons. In this chapter, we have encountered a great many words of Old Norse, Danish and Swedish origins which have been absorbed into our English place-names and many of which still sound familiar to us. We have also seen that the great majority of these places are located in the counties of Suffolk, Norfolk, Lincolnshire, Northumberland, Cumbria and Lancashire, with significant contributions from Leicestershire, Durham, Derbyshire, Shropshire and Cambridgeshire. These are largely the regions which bore the weight of Scandinavian occupation, though for only the relatively short period of little more than two hundred years. Yet the Scandinavian impact was to be far-reaching on our place-names, as we have seen. Another discovery has been that there was a close connection between early English and the Old Scandinavian languages, with so many similar words indicating a common ancient Continental source. And we should not forget that a proportion of the modern English population will have early mediæval Scandinavian ancestry.

Chapter 6

THE LAST INVASION –
NORMANS, 1066

BEGINNING IN THE EARLY 10TH CENTURY, the kingdom which lay in the east and north of England, known as the Danelaw (see map *figure 3*, page 129), was gradually retaken by the English King Edward the Elder and his successors and England became a unified kingdom once more. The Danes were naturally much aggrieved at this turn of events and from the early 980s, unleashed a series of retaliatory raids with increasing determination in the southern and south-western counties until, in 1013, the Danish King Sweyn was eventually able to proclaim himself King of England. His son, Cnut (known later as Canute), eventually earned for himself the distinction of becoming King of England, Norway and Denmark. However, the Danish succession to the English crown was once more broken when, in 1042, the Anglo-Saxon Edward (later called 'The Confessor'), son of King Æthelred, 'The Unready', became King of England. Thus the English crown returned to the stewardship of an Anglo-Saxon monarch, though one with strong French connections, for Edward had spent many years living in France during Cnut's rule. Soon after the death of Edward's father in 1016, his mother, Emma of Normandy, had married the new Danish King of England, Cnut and it was on the death, in 1042, of Harthacanute, the son of Cnut and Emma, that Edward became king.

William, Duke of Normandy, and probably a second cousin of Edward, maintained that Edward had promised him succession to the English throne, but on King Edward's death in January 1066, the Duke was enraged to learn that Harold Godwinsson, Earl of Wessex, had been named as successor by the childless Edward as he lay on his deathbed. Thus it came about that England was subjected to yet another invasion: this time by the Norman French, whose leader was determined to subjugate the turbulent kingdom and ruthlessly bring it under a stern and resolute discipline.

As everyone knows, the unlucky King Harold, who had reigned for only nine months in 1066, was killed near Hastings in October of that year while defending his throne and his kingdom from the Norman expropriator. On learning of Harold's death in October 1066, a council was quickly assembled of the highest ranking English noblemen (the *Witenagemot*), who proceeded to elect to the vacant English throne Edgar (the Ætheling), the 15-year-old grandson of King Edmund II (Ironside), who had briefly reigned in 1016 and on whose death in that year, England had once again come under Danish rule in the figure of Cnut (Canute). However, the boy was not crowned and the victorious Duke William proclaimed himself King of England. He was himself crowned on Christmas Day 1066. England and all its great assets – the realm, its wealth, its literature, arts, scholarship and philosophy – all would now fall into the hands of the French.

King William confiscated almost all land held by English barons, earls and others, with only two compliant Englishmen retaining their holdings by 1085. He then divided the country into three unequal parts: the tenancy of half of the kingdom was distributed in the form of 'fiefs', or grants, between his faithful Norman supporters, the tenancy of one quarter was handed to the Church and the remaining quarter the King retained as his own personal domain. Whether residing in England, or in his native Normandy (for William spent a great deal of his time in France), the king ruled his new kingdom with a ruthless brutality, especially in the north, where resistance remained obstinate and vigorous.

In 1085, there arose a new threat from an old adversary, Denmark, whose ruler, Cnut IV, regarded the English throne as rightfully belonging to him by descent. This potential threat to King William's English crown was probably a significant motive for what would come to be regarded as William's greatest administrative achievement. At the end of the year 1085 he commissioned the compiling of a great register of the all land holdings in the kingdom, their principal tenants, their values, the number of ploughs and livestock held and the number of men at work on the land. From the information thus gathered King William could not only rate the fiscal value of his kingdom, but he was in a strong position to assess his military capability, should the Danish threat materialise into war.

The results of the great survey, once assembled into interpretive form, would become forever known as *Domesday* of course and is an invaluable source of Mediæval English place-name information. Unfortunately, only a few personal names are mentioned – mostly of the more important tenants – the rest of the population was simply counted. Astonishingly, the survey was completed within a year and was subsequently assembled into two bound volumes, *Great Domesday* and *Little Domesday*. Regrettably, for historians, the cities of **London** and **Winchester** and some other towns were omitted, as well as the northern-most shires, which were at the time still in rebellion against the Norman-born king.

For modern historians, the *Domesday* information is a goldmine in very many respects. For us, as place-name enthusiasts, it records the village names as the commissioners' French-speaking scribes (many of them undoubtedly bi-lingual) heard them spoken a thousand years ago and who did their best to put into writing the sounds that the often aging and toothless peasants uttered. Although there is no doubt that *Domesday* is the foremost treasure trove of documentary evidence that we possess, another valuable source of names, both of people and of places, is the *Anglo-Saxon Chronicle*. This is a series of copies of histories begun in the later 9th century, possibly at the instruction of King Ælfred the Great and maintained by monks in several monasteries across the country, who entered brief reports of political, military and ecclesiastical events for each year. The earliest version begins, retrospectively, with the year 60BC and ends in the year AD1154. It too, is a remarkable document.

The radical social and political changes that were to result from William's victory would re-shape and steer English society for centuries to come and one might well think that after so decisive a conquest, there would also have been, as a consequence, a major French influence on both surnames and place-names. The surprising fact is that the real effect was rather small – indeed, very much less than that of either the Anglo-Saxons or the Scandinavians, though considerably more than that of the Romans over six hundred years before.

Most English place-names of course had already been formed by this time and the Normans, unlike their predecessors, established relatively few new settlements, but commandeered numerous existing manors, estates and great halls, simply re-naming many of them, thus also conferring a new, or modified, name onto the neighbouring village. This, in part, discloses what was to be perhaps the most significant Norman influence on English place-names – that of form and configuration. Very often the original village name was retained but, in order to stamp a personal ownership on a place, a second name might be added. Sometimes it would be the new Norman occupier's family name, or else a descriptive title would be added by the King's new tenant. There are hundreds of examples across England of place-names displaying the mediæval tenant's personal addition (sometimes referred to as an 'affix'), turning them into impressive looking (and sounding) double-barrelled names. Here are twelve examples of this process taken from nine counties throughout the length of England:

Place-name	Tenant[1]	Recorded[1]
Ashby Folville (Leics)	The Folleville family (of Calvados)	1233
Bentley Pauncefote (Worcs)	Richard Panzeuot (Old Fr. – 'round belly')	1185
Crowmarsh Gifford (Oxon)	Walter Gifard (Old Fr. – 'bloated')	1086
Hinton Waldrist (Berks)	Thomas de St Walerico (of Somme)	1192
Marston Moretaine (Beds)	The Moretaine family (of Normandy)	1229
Newton Ferrers (Devon)	William de Ferers (of Normandy)	1242
Newton Harcourt (Leics)	Richard de Harcourt (of Normandy)	1240
Roding Berners (Essex)	The Berners family (of Normandy)	1086
Seaton Delaval (Northumb)	The De la Val family (of Normandy)	1270
Theydon Garnon (Essex)	Radulfus Gernun (Old Fr. – 'moustache')	1200
Sutton Courtenay (Berks)	Reginald de Curtenai (of Loire)	1161
Wharram Percy (E.Yorks)	William de Perci (of Calvados)	1177

Nine of these place-names refer to the Norman towns of origin of the tenant family concerned. However, I have included three in the list – numbers (ii), (iii) and (x) – which, though they still include the family names, give us no clue as the families' Norman places of origin. I have therefore given the meaning of the name instead – each of which is clearly a nickname, possibly of the landholder himself, or else of a recent tenurial ancestor.

Not all double names of this type feature the family name as the *second* element, however. In the place-names **Mears Ashby** (Northamptonshire), **Meynell Langley** (Derbyshire) and **Walters Upton** (Shropshire), it is the *first* word of the doublet that signifies the family name and in the case of **Walters Upton**, rather unusually, it is not the family name, but the *personal* name of the holder of the manor, Walter Fitz-John, who was tenant of this manor during the latter part of the 11th century. In the case of **Aston Rogers** (Shropshire), the *personal* name of the tenant, Roger, rather than the family name, forms the *second* word of the doublet of the original village name, though there is no

1 Eilert Ekwall, Concise Oxford Dictionary of English Place-names. OUP 1960 Ed.

evidence of a Norman family ancestry here.

Thus it was that, at a stroke, King William made a single sweeping demonstration of his authority over the conquered English. By quickly removing almost all of the English land holders and replacing them with his Norman confederates, he ensured the Normans' continued allegiance and an embedded means of disciplining the native population. *Domesday* was thus soon looked upon as an incontrovertible authority, whose information was called upon and upheld in any dispute.

Having looked at a typical aspect of the 'Normanisation' process of existing English place-names – that of a French addition (the 'affix') – we can now turn to a different, and perhaps more expected, process. This is where a new name, of true Norman origin, was conferred upon a place. Sometimes it would entirely replace the existing English name and sometimes it would be created for a newly founded community where none had existed before. A newly built castle or manor might naturally acquire a Norman name, while the location and lands of a recently established monastery would have gained a characteristic French name. These new names were often of a flattering nature, frequently containing the words *'beau'* or *'belle'*, (or short forms of the words), adjectives meaning 'beautiful' and usually referring to the locality. Here is a group of such names:

Place-name	Meaning	First recorded[1]
Beachy Head (Sussex)	Beautiful headland	1279
Beamish (Durham)	Beautiful mansion	1251
Beaudesert (Warwickshire)	Beautiful wild place	1181
Beaulieu (Hants), **Bewdley** (Worcs)	Beautiful place	1300, 1275
Beaumanor (Leics)	Beautiful seat	1265
Beauvale (Nottinghamshire)	Beautiful valley	1414
Bearpark (Durham)	Beautiful retreat ('beau repaire')	1267
Belper (Derbyshire)	Beautiful refuge	1231
Belsize (Hertfordshire)	Beautiful location	1254
Belvoir (Leicestershire)	Beautiful view	1130

The dates of the first known recordings of the above places are rather late, for they will all be, by definition, post-Conquest (1066) and the establishment of such places by descendants of the original Norman landholders would continue for several generations.

1   Eilert Ekwall, Concise Oxford Dictionary of English Place-names. OUP 1960 Ed.

Mediæval France and Normandy in particular, was very firmly Christian and tolerated the worship of no other gods. Monasteries, created by the new wave of Norman ecclesiasts, as auxiliaries to their French parent establishments, have also provided us with a specific variety of French-derived place-names: **Grosmont** (Yorkshire – 'great hill') and **Beauchief** (Yorkshire – 'beautiful promontary'). As with so many others, these are transposed directly from their Norman locations. There are many mediæval sites of monastic remains throughout England – **Dieulacres** (Staffordshire – 'God increase'), **Grace Dieu** (Leicestershire – 'God's favour') and **Rievaulx** (Yorkshire – 'rye valley') are three with evocative names. **Jervaulx** (Yorkshire), however, is simply a rendering of 'Ure valley'. **Battle Abbey** (Sussex – *'La batailge'*), founded by King William the First, is a unique initial memorial to those killed in the Battle of Hastings (October 1066).

The Normans were assiduous church builders and erected small places of worship near to many villages, often on the site of a former wooden Anglo-Saxon structure, but rebuilt in stone. The church would frequently be dedicated to a particular saint, whose name would then come to be associated with the nearby village. Our road maps will disclose clusters of such village names in various districts – **Ormesby St Margaret**, **Ormesby St Michael**, **Burgh St Margaret** and **Moulton St Mary** is one of several groups in Norfolk and all four lie within a few miles of each other near Great Yarmouth. Suffolk too, has similar groups – **Ilketshall St Margaret**, **Ilketshall St Lawrence**, **Ilketshall St Andrew** are within three miles of each other and **St Peter South Elmham**, **St Margaret South Elmham**, **St James South Elmham**, **St Nicholas South Elmham**, **St Michael South Elmham** and **St Cross South Elmham** are separate villages which also lie within three miles or so of each other. Though not all members of such clusters will necessarily be of Norman origin, the groupings of saints' names attached to village names like those just mentioned are characteristic of the mediæval Norman naming process.

Not only were the Normans dedicated church builders, but they are probably best remembered for their diligence in the construction of castles. By the end of the 11th century and within only thirty years of the Hastings battle, the great Norman barons had built almost ninety castles throughout the kingdom. Initially, most of these were built of wood for the sake of urgency and only later were they converted into the great stone structures with which we are familiar today. Unlike some later 'castles', these were genuine fortresses intended to withstand and suppress the angry uprisings of the unruly regional English, still enraged by the tyrannical sovereignty of an interloping foreigner. A few of these great fortifications remain habitable today, while the ruins of many of the rest are still to be seen and marvelled at, across England.

The Latin word '*castellum*', meaning a fortress, had been adopted directly, as '*castel*', into Old Norman French and was subsequently brought into English. '*Castel*' soon proved to have many useful applications and began to be widely applied to ancient defences and hillforts, now recognised as Iron Age structures, such as at **Barbury Castle** (Wiltshire), **Maiden Castle** (Dorset) and **Maen Castle** (Cornwall).

Here is a list of some of the Norman-built castles which gave their names to, or took them from, a nearby contemporary English village:

Castle	County	Original holder	Date built
Alnwick Castle*	Northumberland	Gilbert de Tesson	c.1070
Barnard Castle	Durham	Guy de Baliol	c.1095
Corfe Castle	Dorset	King William the First	c.1070
Devizes Castle	Wiltshire	Osmund, Bishop of Salisbury	c.1080
Helmsley Castle	Yorkshire	Walter L'Espec	c.1120
Ludlow Castle	Shropshire	Roger de Lacy	c.1090
Pevensey Castle	Sussex	Robert, Count de Mortain	c.1100
Trematon Castle	Cornwall	Robert, Count de Mortain	c.1075
Totnes Castle	Devon	Judhæl of Totnes	c.1070
Winchester Castle	Hampshire	King William the First	c.1067

*Still a residence.

The ten places listed above represent only a small fraction of England's castles, the creation of which lie in the decades following the Norman invasion. There are of course, many place-name doublets in which the word 'castle' is the first word in the pair – **Castle Acre** (Norfolk – founded about 1090), **Castle Camps** (Cambridgeshire – founded in the Anglo-Saxon period) and **Castle Cary** (Somerset – founded in the early 12th century).

Many a 'castle' is such only in name, however, for manors were sometimes built on such a grand scale that their lords liked the idea of calling them 'castles'. In the case of **Castle Ashby** (Northamptonshire), its early 14th century owner, the Bishop of Coventry, simply modified and extended his mansion, adding impressive castle-like crenellations and turrets. **Auckland Castle** (Durham) too, was at first a manor house, converted in the late 12th century into a mock 'castle' and is still a Bishop's residence.

Just as there was a fashion for applying the word 'castle' to a mansion or a grand manor residence, so there developed a taste for making place-names 'all Frenchified', as the 16th century London antiquary William Camden puts it. Having become used to hearing the French suffix '-ville' in such place-names as **Langford Budville** (Somerset) and **Stoke Mandeville** (Buckinghamshire), many of which places came under the lordship of descendants of the Normans only in the 12th and 13th centuries, it became an easy verbal step for villagers to convert a name ending in the English '-feld' into one ending in the French '-ville'. Thus we find that **Clanville** (Hampshire) is recorded in a 1316 document as *Clanefelde* and **Morville** (Shropshire) is written in 1291 as *Momerefeld*. This shows that the adoption of the '-ville' form occurred quite late. Other places that have undergone the same transformation from '-feld(e)' to '-ville' are **Enville** (Staffordshire – after 1240) and **Turville** (Buckinghamshire – after 1176). In post-mediæval times, right up to the 20th century in fact, the '-ville' suffix was a much favoured element in the naming of newly established towns, as in **Ironville** (Derbyshire), built in the 1830s for the workers at a local iron works and **Bournville** (Warwickshire), a community in the Birmingham suburbs established by George Cadbury in 1879 for the workers at his chocolate factory. We see a huge proliferation of the '-ville' suffix as new towns were established in America as settlers pushed westwards during the 18th and 19th centuries. The next chapter will pursue the 'modern' theme much further.

Although Norman French was much further removed from Old English than were the Scandinavian languages, it was bound to make a few early inpressions on the spelling of place-names because of some typical English peculiarities of pronunciation, which the Normans found very awkward and unnatural. Even today, the man who lives in **Houghton** (East Yorkshire), when asked his address, if he is away from home, will have to spell it for his enquirer, for it could easily take the forms of **Horton** (Gloucestershire), **Haughton** (Cheshire) or **Hawton** (Nottinghamshire).

The government of King William's new realm was naturally based on procedures directed by French-speaking administrators, many of whom were necessarily bilingual. Nevertheless, changes to spellings were made for ease of both reading and pronunciation by the Norman clerks and many of these adjustments would prove to be permanent. **Nottingham** is an example. In the Domesday survey (1086), the commissioner's clerk listened carefully enough to the voices of his English informants to record the word more or less correctly as *Snotingeham* ('settlement of *Snot's* people' – *'snotor'* meant 'wise' and was clearly a personal and flattering nickname in this case) and the district as *Snotinge-hamscyre*, but the *'sn'* combination is unnatural and awkward for the French speaker and before long the initial letter 'S' had been dropped and thus it has remained. The same change occurred later in the case of **Trafford** in Lancashire. Originally named Stratford, the initial 'S' vanished, together with the central '-*t*-' which, preceding the letter '*f*', presented another stumbling block for the French tongue. *Struttorp* also lost its inital letter 'S' sometime after 1231, to become **Trusthorpe** (Lincolnshire – '*Strūt's* homestead').

Another uncomfortable pronunciation problem for the Normans concerned the occurrence of the letter '*r*' within some English words. This would frequently become an '*l*' in speech and therefore in script: the city of **Salisbury** (Wiltshire) is correctly recorded in Domesday (1086) as *Sarisberie*, but by the 13th century, its spelling had been slightly adjusted to suit Norman pronunciation. The village of *Pirelaie* (as recorded in Domesday, 1086) had been transformed into *Pilisleg* by 1205 and is now **Pilsley** (near Bakewell in Derbyshire). Similarly, *Burstroda*, a small settlement in Buckinghamshire became *Bolestrode* by 1195 and is now **Bulstrode.** This process of exchanging one letter for another is sometimes described as 'dissimilation'.

A few English place-names, as we have seen when considering the '*Beau-*' and '*Bel-*' group above, owe their entire existence to original Norman French words which were introduced in the century or so following the Conquest. In this section of the chapter we can look at a group of them with meanings largely related to the countryside.

The well-known Wiltshire town of **Devizes** has its origins in the French word '*devises*', indicating a division, or boundary line, which must have run close by the 12th century settlement. The interesting place-name **Guyzance** (Northumberland) originated from the Guines family, whose ancestral lands were near Calais. **Pleshey** (Essex), **Plashett** (Sussex) and **Plessey** (Northumberland) have their origins in the French place-name Le Plessis, which itself seems to derive from a word meaning a paddock enclosed by a lattice-work fence. **Boulge** (Suffolk) appears in Domesday (1086) and must be one of the earliest French names to have been introduced into England. It is a modification of '*bouge*', meaning an area of rough ground or heathland. A name evocative to novelists of the 20th century's inter-war years is **Malpas** (Cheshire, Berkshire and Cornwall), which is simply '*mal pas*', meaning a difficult or dangerous passage, perhaps between the hills or along a stretch of river. One of the the earliest references to the village of **Roche** (Cornwall) is in a land agreement of 1233, which records the village as *La Roche* and is directly from the French for 'the rock'. Indeed, an impressive rocky outcrop is still to be seen just outside the village to the south and was clearly the inspiration for the name. **Roundhay** (Yorkshire) may look unlikely to have a French connection, but its earliest known record (c. 1180) of *La Rundehaia*, reveals it to mean 'the round enclosure'. **Pallion**, a district of the city of Sunderland in the county of Durham, has its own French connection, for a 1328 mention lists it as *Le Pavylion* (perhaps with the meaning of 'the lodge'), leaving no question as to its Norman ancestry.

A rare instance of a Norman personal name which has found its way into our place-names is to be seen in the hybrid **Moresby** (Cumbria – farmstead of one, Maurice). The earliest known mention of the name is in about 1160 – *Moresceby* – which leaves us in no doubt of its Norman personal-name origin, coupled with the characteristic Danish suffix '*-by*'.

A useful benefit of the Norman influence on place-names was to provide an elegant and explanatory extension to names which might otherwise have been confused with a similarly named nearby place. There are many examples of this throughout England: the two Yorkshire **Adwicks** were eventually distinguished from each other by 'affixes' expressing their locations. The more northerly settlement of the two became **Adwick-le-Street** because of its situation against the Roman road known as Ermine Street, while the smaller village to the south-east, became **Adwick-upon-Dearne.** One is left to wonder why the French theme was not extended to this latter place to make it Adwick-sur-Dearne. **Chester-le-Street** (Durham) too, lies beside an ancient Roman way. This whole district is well served by the French definite article '*-le-*', for within a few miles of **Chester-le-Street** are **Houghton-le-Spring, Houghton-le-Side, Hetton-le-Hill** and **Hetton-le-Hole**.

Chapel-en-le-Frith (Derbyshire) is first mentioned in 1272 as *Capella de le Frith* – 'chapel of the woodland', but the name was adjusted sometime later, while still maintaining its French form, to mean 'chapel *in* the woodland'.

So, a commonly adopted pattern which employs the French definitive article ('*le*') is that which takes the form of '*le Moor(s)*', '*le Willows*', '*le Street*' and '*le Dale*', which picks out a natural feature of the landscape to enhance the original place-name – and there are many of them, as any Gazetteer of English place-names will reveal.

A few impressive Norman-English place-names, however, conceal a bitter trick: **Berwick Malviston** (Shropshire) recalls the name *Malveisin*, a 'bad neighbour', while **Boughton Malherbe** (Kent) points to the Norman family name *Malherbe*, 'evil plant'. Nevertheless, I think there can be no doubt that the mediæval Norman influence on our place-names, though comparatively modest, has enriched the genre with pleasing colour, interesting and divers alternatives to the typical English practices. How satisfying to be able to say one's home is in **Alsop-en-le-Dale** (Derbyshire), **Layer-de-la-Haye** (Essex) or **Ashby-de-la-Launde** (Lincolnshire).

Chapter 7

AFTER THE NORMANS – MODERN TIMES

IN THIS FINAL CHAPTER, I WILL BE GATHERING together some of the interesting stray threads that haven't fitted into the pattern so far: those place-names having extreme foreign origins, that is, from beyond Europe, as well as a few interesting names from within the British Isles itself and of course those place-names that have come into being after the initial Norman period of influence – the 'moderns'.

First, a couple of stray names that are too intriguing to be allowed to slip away unnoticed: **Birdoswald** and **Blennerhasset** (both Cumbria). Both are hybrids, each having a Welsh first element. The first name is made up of '*buarth*', an enclosure + *Oswald* (an English personal name, *Osweald*, meaning 'god ruler') and is first recorded about the year 1200; the second is the Welsh '*blæn*', a hill farmstead + an Old Norse ending '*heysætr*', a hay shelter and appears in written records a little earlier, in 1178.

Second, the very English-looking name of **Baldock** (Hertfordshire): this has a most unusual and surprising origin, for it seems to have been a name given, in the mid-12th century, to a village close to Letchworth, by the Knights Templar, who had returned from the Middle East after the Second Crusade. It is believed to have been originally named *Baldac*, the Old French rendering of the name

Baghdad and first appears in a pipe roll (a mediæval financial record) for the year 1168. What may have prompted the Knights to found and name an English village after a remote Middle Eastern town is unknown. Perhaps the explanation is akin to the 19th century fashion for naming places, especially suburbs and streets, after victorious battles.

And third, the village of **Semley** (Wiltshire) may have, according to Professor Ekwall[1], a curious connection with the ancient Indian language of Sanskrit. Indeed, one of the meanings of the Sanskrit word '*sōma*', to which Ekwall alludes, is water (to drink). Professor A.D.Mills[2] suggests that **Semley** is a 'woodland clearing on the **River Sem**' – a pre-English river-name, though of uncertain meaning. Ekwall's Sanskrit origin may still be applicable.

POST-NORMAN PLACE-NAMES

The Normans, as we have discovered, had introduced the French language into Britain, but it was naturally confined to the aristocracy, the court administration and of course, the newly installed landholders and their retinues. The native English would continue to use their own language. Naturally, French words and expressions soon found their way into the speech of the masses and, to a lesser extent, some English words would be adopted by the French-speaking courtiers where they were found to be appropriate. Thus, as in the days of the Roman occupation and of the Scandinavian domination of the east and the north of the country, there were two languages in parallel use in England – that of the indigenous inhabitants (the English) and that of the latest incomers. However, by the time of the Conquest in 1066 – a date and an event better remembered than any others in English history – the long period of English place-name formation was largely over. The cores of the vast majority of settlements – hamlets, villages, towns and cities – were already established in their localities. Only a small percentage of the places we see listed in the indexes of our English road maps were still to be founded.

Before considering some of the post-Norman place-names, a brief look at some of the Norman royal successions and their Plantagenet successors will help to keep us on our historical time-line.

Between the year 1066, when Duke William of Normandy took the English throne from King Harold at Hastings, thus setting in train a Norman royal line,

1. Eilert Ekwall, Concise Oxford Dictionary of English Place-names. OUP 1960 Edition

2. A.D.Mills, Dictionary of British Place Names. OUP 2003 Edition.

and 1485, when King Richard the Third, last of the Plantagenets was defeated at Bosworth by Henry Tudor (to become Henry the Seventh), there were to be eighteen English monarchs, only one of whom was a woman – Matilda, the only surviving legitimate child of Henry the First. Her reign lasted only a few months in 1141, after temporarily snatching the crown from King Stephen, who re-took the throne later that year.

The year 1485 is often felt to mark the end of the English Mediæval period and the start of the 'modern' era and it is from this date that we will again take up our place-name thread and see what developments took place over the next five hundred years. However, before we do move on, a glance at the monarchs' names of the era reveals some interesting results: there were to be William (2), Henry (6), Stephen (1), Matilda (1), Richard (3), John (1) and Edward (4) and it is interesting to notice that five out of these seven monarchs' personal names are sources of place-names. The two outsiders are Henry and Stephen. Though **Stevenage** (Hertfordshire) looks a clear candidate, its origins lie either in the Old English '*stīþan-āc*' – 'stout oak', or else in '*stīþan-hæcce*', meaning 'stout gate'. **Steventon** (Oxfordshire) is a little closer, but meant 'the farmstead of one, *Stifa*'. Here are the five monarchs' names and some place-names associated with them, together with the earliest recorded dates of each:

Monarch's name	Place-name	Location
William	**Williamscot** (1166), **Williamsthorpe** (1086)	Oxfordshire, Glos.
Matilda	**Mawdesley** (1219)	Lancashire
Richard	**Rickerby** (1247)	Cumbria
John	**Johnby** (1200)	Cumbria
Edward	**Edwardstone** (1086)	Suffolk

The place-names in the list do not in any way celebrate the monarchs themselves, but are derived from local landholders having the same names. The earliest recorded names in the table are those of William and Edward and it is not surprising that the Anglo-Saxon personal names *Wilhelm* and *Ēadweard* should feature in a place-name, for *Ēadweard* was a common name for several centuries before Domesday (1086) and *Wilhelm* was becoming better known after the days of the Conqueror. Maud is an affectionate shortening of Matilda, which itself is from the Old German female personal name *Mahthild* and has undergone a phonetic adjustment in the spelling of the English place-name.

After the mediæval period, there were the occasional newly established places that received their names from a variety of inspirations: some names would

honour a nationally important person or a local benefactor – maybe an industrialist, a distinguished local family or perhaps they would recall the memory
of a cherished deceased person, while some place-names have been adopted
directly from familiar Biblical places. Even notable military victories began
to be celebrated in some of our place-names. However, a few of our 'modern'
place-names seem to have no particular ceremonial significance, but nevertheless, some of these new places would come to form the nuclei of English towns
that would galvanise the Industrial Revolution.

INDUSTRY-RELATED PLACE-NAMES

Late established place-names often tend to speak for themselves, since they
will already be modern in form and will not have undergone the phonetic and
regional transformations that mediæval words endured before spellings began
to be more regularised in the 18th century, especially after the publication in
1755 of Dr Samuel Johnson's 'Dictionary of the English Language'.

The earliest place-name I came across in the post-Norman era that shows a
modification, or 'affix', prompted by some unusual occupational activity, was
Abinger Hammer, five miles east of Guildford in Surrey. The village of **Abinger**
('the farmstead of *Eabba's* people') was already an ancient settlement, noted in
Domesday (1086), but sometime shortly before 1600, an iron-working shop was
established, which must soon have become a noteworthy and important local
feature, for the village acquired the descriptive affix 'Hammer' in that year.

One of the indicators of a possible new industrial site is the appearance of the
prefix '*New*' in its name. **New Mills** (Derbyshire) is such an example. Again, a
mediæval hamlet became a local centre of industry, in this case cotton spinning,
in the decades after 1625. **New Ferry** (Cheshire) recalls the foundation of a
ferry across the River Mersey in about 1774. The fanciful, but rather engaging
name of **New Invention** (Staffordshire), now absorbed into the town of Walsall,
may have referred to some sort of clever 17th century mechanical device for
extracting or moving coal from the local pits.

Josiah Wedgwood, of 18th and 19th century Staffordshire china fame, can be
credited with establishing the foreign names of **Etruria** and **Dresden** as suburbs
of **Stoke-on-Trent** (Staffordshire). In 1769, Wedgwood celebrated a specific
quality of foreign porcelain, which his factory cleverly imitated, by naming
his factory estate after the **Etruria** region of north-eastern Italy. In the name
Dresden too, he recalled the famous city in Saxony where Meissen porcelain was

produced in the first half of the 18th century.

Between 1779 and 1781, Abraham Darby, a young iron-working engineer, supervised the construction of possibly the world's largest, if not the first, bridge constructed entirely of iron. The structure spanned the River Severn in **Coalbrookdale** (Shropshire – 'valley of the cold stream') and soon gathered a small settlement around itself called **Ironbridge**. Two counties away, in Derbyshire, we find **Ironville**, a village built in the mid-19th century by the Butterley Iron Works to house its workers and in neighbouring Leicestershire, the village of **Coalville** sprang up in the 1830s as a coal miners' village.

Another workers' 'model village' of the late 19th century, **Port Sunlight** (Cheshire), was named by its founder, William Lever, after the *Sunlight Soap* brand his factory was producing at the time. At much the same time, the Cadbury brothers were in the process of establishing a new village a few miles to the south of Birmingham city centre to house the workers at a newly built chocolate making factory. They called the place **Bournville** after the **Bourn Brook** which flowed through the locality, adding the now common '-*ville*' suffix which imparted an urbane Frenchness to the name.

In the early 1850s, Sir Titus Salt, a wool-spinning industrialist, built his factory and an estate of workers' houses near the River Aire outside Bradford (Yorkshire). He chose to call the new settlement **Saltaire**, a combination of his surname and the name of the river. It has now become a part of the City of Bradford.

We have now reached the 20th century in our brief glance at industrial sources of place-names and I will mention just a couple more: **Stewartby** (Bedfordshire) and **Carterton** (Oxfordshire). Each has a connection with the modern building industry and was built to house a local workforce: **Carterton**, with its Old English '-*tūn*' ending, dates from the turn of the 20th century, and was built by Mr William Carter, the owner of a nearby building company. **Stewartby**, with its Old Danish '-*by*' suffix, is more recent. It was named in 1935 after Mr Halley Stewart, chairman of a local brick-making company. It is interesting that both William Carter and Halley Stewart disdained the fashionable '-*ville*' ending in favour of two pre-Norman elements in the new village names.

People in modern place-names

The two places mentioned in the last paragraph of the section above, **Stewartby** and **Carterton**, are indeed named after their founders, but these men had local commercial interests and wished to accommodate their workers in reasonable comfort near to their places of work. The people who belong in this present section, however, were private individuals whose names were honoured by their families, were wealthy patrons and landowners, distinguished personages, or were celebrated for their philanthropic deeds.

Beginning with the earliest of the group, we have **Kingsgate** (Kent), between **Margate** and **Broadstairs**. This small settlement commemorated King Charles II's coming ashore at this point in the summer of 1683, and was probably nicknamed **Kingsgate** very soon after the event. The adjacent bay was also known as Kingsgate Bay. The suffix '-*gate*' in this context refers to a gap in the cliffs, as is the case in the names **Margate** ('*mere-geat*' – gap leading to the sea) and **Ramsgate** (*Hræfn's geat*).

Castle Howard (Yorkshire) is one of England's most impressive and beautiful stately homes. It was completed in 1712 for the Earl of Carlisle (family name Howard), but is a castle in title only, having no battlements or fortifications and being named in accordance with the fashion of the day.

Maryport, a town on the Cumbrian coast, was thus named in about 1760 by a local landowner, Humphrey Senhouse, after his wife Mary. The place had long been known as Ellenfoot, being situated at the mouth of the **River Ellen** and indeed, there is a small district of the town, **Ellenborough**, which recalls the earlier place-name.

Two well-known 18th century London names are **Pentonville** and **Camden Town**. Each owes its name to the owner of the land on which the original village was built. **Pentonville** was the result of a small community which was established by Henry Penton on his estate in about 1773, while **Camden Town** began to spring up on the land of Earl of Camden in the last decade of the 18th century. Penton adopted the long-fashionable '-*ville*' suffix for his new community.

In the years after 1785, Sir Thomas Tyrwhitt, a royal official, established a small community, together with a prison (now known as Dartmoor Prison), on a corner of the Duchy of Cornwall's estate in Devon. He named the place **Princetown**, after his master the Prince of Wales (later King George IV).

Carrington (Lincolnshire) is another small community established by a nobleman, Robert Smith (Lord Carrington) on his lands. It is recorded first in about 1812.

Jodrell Bank in Cheshire is of course, famous for its important radio telescope and observatory. The site, however, is located on land which had belonged to the Jauderell family from the mid-14th century and after whom the village is named. Professor A.D.Mills[1] mentions that the place-name is recorded from 1831.

In 1836 Sir Peter Fleetwood began the planning of a new town on the Lancashire coast, to which he gave his name, **Fleetwood**. The town plan shows an interesting regular geometric tendency.

Lastly, we move into the 20th century for a couple of very modern place-namings. **Peterlee** (Durham) is a post-Second World War town named in memory of Peter Lee, a prominent leader of local mine-workers, who died in 1935. **Telford** (Shropshire) was the name eventually given, in the 1960s, to an amalgamation and expansion of communities lying about 12 miles east of Shrewsbury. The name celebrates the memory of Thomas Telford, the late 18th and early 19th century Scottish civil engineer.

There are other places that came into existence during the 500 years after the death of King Richard the Third in 1485 and which belong in this chapter. The reader may like to research and record some of them as a pleasant diversion.

Place-names of Biblical origin

It is said that there are nearly 1200 places mentioned by name in the Bible. Some of these presumably, will not only be the names of countries, 'cities', towns and villages, but also seas, lakes and rivers. To our ancestors in the generations that followed the close of the mediæval period, the Bible was a prolific source and inspiration of names for people and new places, be they hamlets, hills, valleys or otherwise anonymous patches of ground. The reasons for adopting a Biblical name were various – reverence, gratitude, respect, remembrance, hope and even fear. Perhaps the most optimistic inspiration is that provided by the word Heaven, for there are two places listed in English Gazetteers called **Heaven's Gate** – in Shropshire and Wiltshire, while near Stroud in Gloucestershire, can be found a small community called **The Heavens.** The hamlet of **Heaven's Door** is to be encountered a few miles north-west of Sherborne in Somerset.

At the other extreme, Hell, perhaps predictably, features many more times than Heaven: **Hell Hole** appears in five counties, **Hell's Mouth** (Cornwall), a **Hell Corner** is in both Berkshire and Dorset and **Hell Gill** is in Cumbria. Doubtless each of these is frighteningly descriptive of a natural feature. **Hades Hill** near Bacup in Lancashire sounds forbidding.

Two of the most memorable cities in Biblical lore, whose importance must

---

1. A.D.Mills *Dictionary of British Place Names*. OUP 2003 Edition.

have been sharply and frequently impressed on the minds of the laity of the 16th century and onwards, were **Jerusalem** and **Jericho**. These two names have found themselves Cumbrian resting places – **Jerusalem** is a tiny hamlet close to Appleby-in-Westmorland and **Jericho**, also a hamlet, is a few miles south-west of Carlisle. In fact, **Jericho** crops up in Lancashire too – a community on the outskirts of Bury and is also a well-known small suburb of North Oxford. **Salem**, an abbreviated form of Jerusalem, can be found a few miles north-east of Redruth in Cornwall.

The list of England's Biblical place-names is extensive: **Nineveh** (Worcestershire), **Jordan** (Devon), **Babylon Hill** (Dorset), **Babel Green** (Suffolk), **Bethany** (Cornwall), **Genesis Green** (Suffolk), **Golgotha** (Kent), **Hebron** (Northumberland), **Rhodes** (Lancashire), **Tabor Hill** (Devon) and **Tyre Hill** (Worcestershire) are some of the more familiar Biblical names. Even **Egypt** and **Palestine** exist: **Egypt** can be found within five English counties and the village of **Palestine** is located a few miles south-west of Andover in Hampshire. This latter was named soon after the Great War (which ended in 1918) and recalled the recent conflict in that region.

BATTLES IN PLACE-NAMES

In the days when Britain was a truly great sea-faring nation and a supreme military force, it is probably no surprise that outstanding victories at sea and on land would be permanently commemorated by naming places after such proud triumphs. Probably the earliest example of such a memorial is the town of **Battle** in Sussex, a settlement that grew up around the Abbey which was founded on King William's instructions in the years following the Norman Conquest in 1066. Three hundred and fifty years later in 1415, a notable victory was effected by the English King Henry V over the French at Agincourt and a small gathering of dwellings near Ascot (Berkshire) is named **Agincourt**, perhaps in remembrance of the battle.

There are several small places named **Vigo** (Kent, Staffordshire, Worcestershire), a name that recalls a little-known sea battle of 1702 between the Spanish and the English in Vigo Bay off the north-west Spanish coast. **Vigo** in Kent, however, is a mid-20th century settlement.

The year 1815 is remembered for one of the most famous of all English military conflicts – that of **Waterloo**. Celebration of the Duke of Wellington's great victory quickly found its way into both the popular imagination and the

British place-name gazetteer and dozens of places soon bore the name. Lanca-shire, Northumberland, Cheshire, Shropshire, Norfolk, Derbyshire, Cumbria, Cornwall, Yorkshire, Herefordshire, London and Dorset all have a **Waterloo**, making this one of the most widely celebrated events in English history. **Water-looville** (Hampshire) too, was an early contributor to the story by reason of the name of a local inn around which, it is said, the community grew. Ten years earlier, the great sea battle of **Trafalgar** had caught the public's imagination. This too, had led to some celebratory naming, but rather of streets, buildings, farms and the like than of settlements. Cornwall, however, has its hamlet of **Trafalgar**, nestling in the valley of the River Valency a few miles inland from Boscastle.

One final modest reminder of a 19th century battle is to be found in **Balaclava Bay** in Dorset, recalling the famous battle of 1854 during the Crimean War.

A few small reminders of Great War conflicts (1914-1918) are scattered throughout the country: Vimy Ridge is recalled in a Nottinghamshire farm and Mons Hill in Dudley may be a memory of one of the first battles of the War. **Arras** (Yorkshire) is another evocative wartime name, though whether it has any connection with the 1917 battle for the French city, I have not discovered.

There are no fewer than twelve counties within whose boundaries are to be found places called **Dunkirk**. The critical success of the operation to evacuate Allied troops from the beaches of this French coastal town in June 1940 has undoubtedly been remembered in the naming or re-naming of many English places in the latter half of the 20th century.

Finally, in 1945, the ancient village of **Enham** (Hampshire) acquired the 'affix' *Alamein* to become **Enham Alamein** in reference to the treatment centre set up in the village for the servicemen wounded in the notorious 1942 battle in the West African desert.

Some miscellaneous modern place-names

The place-names in this final section span over 420 years, from the renaming of an ancient southern coastal settlement known until 1587 as *Mecinges*, when the construction of a new harbour gave rise to its new title of **Newhaven** (Sussex), to the infamous county boundary changes of 1974, when historic district names were abolished in favour of contrivances like **Cumbria, Cleveland, Merseyside** and **Tyne and Wear.** London itself had already succumbed to the amalgamated name format in 1965 when **Newham** was created out of East Ham, West Ham together with part of Woolwich.

An inn called The Duke of Normandy in Surrey gradually gathered around itself a small community of dwellings which, since 1656, is recorded as **Normandy**. This is by no means the only instance of this phenomenon, as we noted in the last section when mentioning **Waterlooville**. The 19th century textile town of **Nelson** (Lancashire) also grew up around an inn (The Lord Nelson). Queenshead, formerly a Yorkshire hamlet, named after its inn, The Queen's Head, was re-named **Queensbury** in 1863 – a reverse of the two previous procedures and happily side-stepping the fashionable impulse to become Queensville!

Two 18th century 'newtowns' worth remembering are **Brownhills** (Staffordshire) and **Stourport-on-Severn** (Worcestershire). **Brownhills** is the earlier of the two, being recorded first as such in 1749 and for a century or so before that as Brown Hill, probably because of the nearby grimy, coal and red ash-laden spoil heaps. **Stourport** is the result of the expansion of two small villages (Upper and Lower Mitton) at the confluence of the Rivers Stour and Severn.

Moving into the 19th century, three interesting place-names that come to the surface are **California** (Norfolk), **Pity Me** (Durham) and **Westward Ho!** (Devon). The first is said to have acquired its name from the discovery of a small trove of gold coins found on the beach in 1848, at a time when the American 'California Gold Rush' was a talking point. The sadly fanciful name **Pity Me** seems to have been applied in the 19th century to the rather forlorn location of a small settlement to the north of the city of Durham. There have been alternative explanations of this name, including Petty Mere and Pithead Mere. Few places in any country can have had their names lifted from a work of fiction and **Westward Ho!** is unique in England for its possession of an exclamation mark! The seaside village grew up near the Devonshire town of Bideford in the decades following the publication of Charles Kingsley's adventure novel in 1855, which was based around Bideford.

An encouraging note is easily detected in the place-name **Peacehaven** (Sussex). This is a 20th century resort on the coast a few miles east of Brighton, laid out on a fiercely geometric plan and named in about 1917 to commemorate the end of 'the war to end all wars'. Regrettably, its note of optimism was soon to be betrayed.

As a coda, I will mention the case of the curious word 'Chase'. There are several stretches of open upland in England that are called Chases: **Cannock Chase** (Staffordshire), **Enfield Chase** (Middlesex), **Waltham Chase** (Hampshire), **Fulmer Chase** (Buckinghamshire) and **Hatfield Chase** (Yorkshire) are some of them. In an Act of 1539, King Henry VIII endorsed the petition that certain tracts of unenclosed land in England be set aside for the breeding and hunting of wild animals. The Act gave these areas the name 'chases'. The word seems to have an Old French origin, 'chacier', which meant 'to hunt'.

And at this point we have reached the very end of our survey of English place-names. It has been a long journey through nearly two-thousand five-hundred years of historical activity, which has created the country we call England. I hope that the investigation of the many little place-name time capsules has proved entertaining and has stimulated the reader's interest a little.

A POSTSCRIPT

OPEN A GOOD ROAD MAP OF ENGLAND and its index will show that here are many tens of thousands of names of English places – cities, towns, villages, hamlets, rivers, hills, valleys, moors and so forth – and in this book I have touched on just over two thousand of them. Imagine the number of volumes it would require in order to examine all of them! However, I hope that I have shown that, like surnames, our place-names can be categorised simply and examined in a logical way. As I have mentioned a number of times in the text, Domesday (1086) has been a major source of information on determining the existence of early settlements and their 11th century spellings (in as much as the contemporary scribes could decode the words they were hearing spoken by the native English). Modern editions of the Domesday texts, together with their translations and commentaries, are a very worthwhile study and contain a wealth of fascinating information about many places with which most readers will be familiar. Those of us with even a small interest in history will find something engaging in tracking down the ancient details of our place of birth, or the town or village in which we are now living. The Internet is an enormous blessing in this respect, for it is now possible to access Domesday, the Anglo-Saxon Chronicle, national databases like the electoral records and much more, to help us compile detailed pictures of our localities.

Place-names are very much like both fossils and time machines. Like a fossil, an ancient place-name survives long after its parent language has either vanished or become extensively modified and will have outlived the huge changes its physical location has undergone through the centuries, leaving the name behind. It is like a time machine in that the name can transport us back through many centuries to a time long gone, marking many of the steps with a variation of spelling.

Our distant ancestors in these islands named everything they saw in the landscape, its natural features, animals and plants; they also had names for their buildings, their tools, clothes, occupations, worship rituals, ailments and much else and, because people were observant of things around them, a great many of these ancient words became crystallised in the descriptive names they gave to places. Place-names therefore give us a valuable insight into people's thinking and their use of ancient vocabulary, thus preserving many words that would otherwise have been lost.

Place-names illuminate a great deal of our varied history and culture – remember that England has been the subject of a number of occupations by foreign gate-crashers, each bringing a new culture and style of living and intro-ducing a rich new language each time.

Place-names also shine a very important light onto ancient personal names, preserving for us a fascinating insight into this most subjective of human charac-teristics. Until the appearance of the Normans in the middle of the 11th century, most personal names were rooted in Anglo-Saxon or Scandinavian traditions: *Ælle, Ealda, Creoda, Gamel, Cnūt, Hnaki and Nafni* are typical mens' names of the long pre-Norman era. Early women's names too, though not so frequently occurring as those of men, are also preserved for us in place-names: *Aldgȳþ, Bilswīþ, Ælfwynn, Gunhild* and *Kráka* for example. The Normans were instru-mental in the introduction of many more names based in the Christian tradition and so we begin to see variations of William, Simon, Stephen and Matthew for the men and Martha, Hannah, Esther and Mary for the women, with the corre-sponding decrease in the traditional Anglo-Saxon personal names.

Old texts, like Domesday and the many charters and deeds that are preserved in public archives, can also shed light on settlements that have disappeared from the map. **Quatbridge** (Shropshire), **Brunskaith** (the old Cumberland), **Eynsworth** (Essex), **Alstoe** (Rutland) and **Gainsthorpe** (Lincolnshire) are places that once existed, but are now only distant memories. A most fascinating exercise is to trace the places listed in a chosen section of Domesday – say all those settlements beginning with the letter 'P', or those in your own county – and to list all the places not now in existence according to a detailed modern roadmap; then to discover when and why these places became depopulated and vanished – was it through disease, famine, land clearance, aging inhabitants or sea encroachment? There is plenty of scope for this sort of investigation, for Domesday lists over 13,400 place-names – an astonishing achievement for the late 11th century. Another absorbing line of enquiry for those of us whose surname (or even whose first name) is a place-name, will be to research the history of that place and write it up as a family document.

Another intriguing property of many English place-names is that of 'counter-intuitive pronunciation'. While most English people will have no difficulty in saying Worcester, Bicester or Leicester correctly, even though their spellings are a little awkward and certainly puzzling to a foreign visitor seeing them for the first time, there are still many English place-names that are waiting to ambush even the well-informed English speaker. These names are either the result of centuries of regional speech mannerisms or simply the natural human tendency to shorten long-winded words into easily manageable and more convenient forms. A Londoner, especially one from the East End, is always going to pronounce **Plaistow** as '*Plarstow*' and a Gloucester dweller will surely know that **Frocester** is always '*Froster*', but only the well-informed will get **Stiffkey** and **Happisburgh** (both in Norfolk) right – 'Stewkee' and 'Haisbro'. Allow me to puzzle you with a few other little traps. Perhaps, for fun, the reader would like to try to guess the local pronunciations of the following: **Romansleigh** (Devon), **Barugh** (Yorkshire), **Cholmondeley** (Cheshire), **Alvescot** (Oxfordshire), **Frome** (Dorset) and **Puncknowle** (Devon). The answers are at the foot of the following page.

Here, after a long journey through nearly twenty-five centuries and five major foreign invasions of the country we know as England, we have to take our leave of our investigation of English place-names. I think we have done a little more than just scratch the surface of such a vast field of study, but there remains a very great deal more to explore and those with an interest in the history of their own localities will have an enjoyable time in evolving and pursuing some personal research projects. The Internet of course, now provides us with a superb research tool and there are many local history groups which can provide assistance and friendly advice.

So, apart from the wealth of absorbing information that our little place-name time capsules hold, there is a great deal of pleasure to be had in allowing them to lead us on a journey back through the ages to discover their fascinating histories and letting them surprise and delight us in the process. And who knows what else this might lead to – foreign place-names, family histories perhaps? Good hunting!

Works Consulted & Brief Bibliography

Anonymous – *The Anglo-Saxon Chronicle*.

Anonymous – *Domesday*.

Anonymous – *Oxford English Dictionary*.

Bagley, J.J. – *Life in Medieval England*. Batsford, 1971 edition.

Camden, William – *Remains Concerning Britain*. John Russell Smith, 1870 edition.

Copley, G.J. – *English Place Names and their Origins*. David and Charles, 1971 edition.

Davies, C. Stella & John Levitt – *What's In A Name?* Routledge & Keegan Paul, 1970.

Eckwall, Eilert – *The Concise Oxford Dictionary of English Place-names*. OUP, 1980 edition.

Hoskins, W.G – *The Making of the English Landscape*. Hodder & Stoughton, 1967 edition.

Lewis, William – *What's in Your Surname?* Brazen Head Publishing, 2010.

Mills, A.D. – *Dictionary of British Place Names*. OUP, 2003 edition.

Pryor, Francis – *Britain AD*. Harper Perennial, 2004.

Stenton, Frank – *Anglo-Saxon England*. OUP, 2001 edition.

Sweet, Henry – *The Student's Dictionary of Anglo-Saxon*. Clarendon Press, 1989 edition.

Thomas, Charles – *Celtic Britain*. Thames & Hudson, 1986.

Answers to the pronunciations on page 167:
Romansleigh – Rumzley
Barugh – Barf
Cholmondeley – Chumley
Alvescot – Awlscot
Frome – Froom
Puncknowle - Punel.

INDEX OF PLACE-NAMES

GENERAL INDEX

Lightning Source UK Ltd.
Milton Keynes UK
UKHW011433160420
361797UK00002B/687